Access to History
General Editor: Keith Randell

Whigs, Radicals and Liberals, 1815-1914

Duncan Watts

Hodder & Stoughton
A MEMBER OF THE HODDER

The cover illustration is a portrait of Gladstone (Courtesy of National Portrait Gallery, London).

Some other titles in the series:

Religion, Society and Reform 1800-1914 Andrina Stiles	ISBN 0 340 59704 6
Tories, Unionists and Conservatives 1815-1914 Duncan Watts	ISBN 0 340 60081 0
Labour and Reform: Working Class Movements 1815-1914 Clive Behagg	ISBN 0 340 52930 X
The British Empire 1815-1918 Frank McDonough	ISBN 0 340 59376 8
Government and Reform 1815-1918 Robert Pearce and Roger Stearn	ISBN 0 340 59814 X
The Changing Role of Women 1815-1914 Paula Bartley	ISBN 0 340 61135 9

British Library Cataloguing in Publication Data

A catalogue for this is available
from the British Library

ISBN 0-340-62703-4

First published 1995

Impression number 10 9 8 7 6 5 4 3 2
Year 1999 1998 1997 1996

Typeset by Sempringham publishing services, Bedford
Printed in Great Britain for Hodder & Stoughton Educational,
a division of Hodder Headline Plc, 338 Euston Road, London NW1 3BH
by Redwood Books, Trowbridge, Wiltshire

Contents

Preface

To the general reader

Although the *Access to History* series has been designed with the needs of students studying the subject at higher examination levels very much in mind, it also has a great deal to offer the general reader. The main body of the text (i.e. ignoring the Study Guides at the ends of chapters) forms a readable and yet stimulating survey of a coherent topic as studied by historians. However, each author's aim has not merely been to provide a clear explanation of what happened in the past (to interest and inform): it has also been assumed that most readers wish to be stimulated into thinking further about the topic and to form opinions of their own about the significance of the events that are described and discussed (to be challenged). Thus, although no prior knowledge of the topic is expected on the reader's part, she or he is treated as an intelligent and thinking person throughout. The author tends to share ideas and possibilities with the reader, rather than passing on numbers of so-called 'historical truths'.

To the student reader

There are many ways in which the series can be used by students studying History at a higher level. It will, therefore, be worthwhile thinking about your own study strategy before you start your work on this book. Obviously, your strategy will vary depending on the aim you have in mind, and the time for study that is available to you.

If, for example, you want to acquire a general overview of the topic in the shortest possible time, the following approach will probably be the most effective:

1 Read Chapter 1 and think about its contents.
2 Read the 'Making notes' section at the end of Chapter 2 and decide whether it is necessary for you to read this chapter.
3 If it is, read the chapter, stopping at each heading to note down the main points that have been made.
4 Repeat stage 2 (and stage 3 where appropriate) for all the other chapters.

If, however, your aim is to gain a thorough grasp of the topic, taking however much time is necessary to do so, you may benefit from carrying out the same procedure with each chapter, as follows:

1 Read the chapter as fast as you can, and preferably at one sitting.
2 Study the flow diagram at the end of the chapter, ensuring that you understand the general 'shape' of what you have just read.

3 Read the 'Making notes' section (and the 'Answering essay questions' section, if there is one) and decide what further work you need to do on the chapter. In particularly important sections of the book, this will involve reading the chapter a second time and stopping at each heading to think about (and to write a summary of) what you have just read.
4 Attempt the 'Source-based questions' section. It will sometimes be sufficient to think through your answers, but additional understanding will often be gained by forcing yourself to write them down.

When you have finished the main chapters of the book, study the 'Further Reading' section and decide what additional reading (if any) you will do on the topic.

This book has been designed to help make your studies both enjoyable and successful. If you can think of ways in which this could have been done more effectively, please write to tell me. In the meantime, I hope that you will gain greatly from your study of History.

Keith Randell

Acknowledgements

The Publishers would like to thank the following for permission to reproduce illustrations in this volume:

Cover - Gladstone, The National Portrait Gallery, London.

Punch Publications p. 97; Mary Evans Picture Library p. 138; Fotomas Index p. 142 and p. 150 (top); Penguin Books Ltd p. 150 (bottom).

Every effort has been made to trace and acknowledge ownership of copyright. The Publishers will be glad to make suitable arrangements with any copyright holders whom it has not been possible to contact.

CHAPTER 1

Introduction: Whigs, Radicals and Liberals

The Preamble to the Liberal Constitution clearly sets out the goal of the Liberal Party in British politics, stressing the value of people as individuals rather than as part of the class structure of society.

> 1 The Liberal Party exists to build a liberal society in which every citizen shall possess liberty, property and security, and none shall be enslaved by poverty, ignorance or conformity. Its chief care is for the rights and opportunities of the individual and in all spheres
> 5 it sets freedom first.

The word 'liberalism' derives from the Latin 'liber', meaning free or generous. From this root we gain two useful insights into the nature of the creed, for on the one hand there is the stress on individual liberty, and on the other, the emphasis on compassion and tolerance. As the doctrine developed in the seventeenth and eighteenth centuries, Liberalism placed its major emphasis on the freedom of individuals to control their own destinies.

Society is conceived as a collection of individuals. As, according to one of the foremost Liberal thinkers, John Locke, 'no government allows absolute liberty', most Liberals would settle for the pursuit of the maximum amount of liberty consistent with the idea of stability and order. The role of the state is to protect the rights of the individual from coercion by other individuals and groups.

Liberals abhor the rule of authoritarian régimes. With their strong recognition of the rights of the citizen against encroachment, Liberals are reformers, enemies of entrenched institutions, traditions and customs. As progressives, they seek to place constraints on governmental power. This means that political liberalism is associated with the idea of free parliamentary machinery, the extension of the franchise and the guarantee of civil liberties. Under such circumstances, individual freedom is maximised, and the conditions are available to promote the economic progress which can be the basis of a good life for everyone. In the economic sphere, Liberals favour the minimum of government intervention and regulation, believing in free competition at home and free trade between nations. Private initiative is seen as the basis of competition, which is itself a source of political liberty. In other words, Liberals believe that free enterprise encourages the blossoming of free institutions.

If free enterprise is thought to work to the benefit of everyone, so free trade is seen to be the means of promoting the health of mankind as a whole, because free trade encourages the elimination of conflicts and war because they get in the way of the successful pursuit of trading relationships. Liberals want a peaceful world in which their trading opportunities can be maximised for the good of all.

The Liberal creed found its fullest expression in nineteenth-century Britain. However, by the end of the century there was a growing emphasis on the idea that the state could and should be used to promote liberty. It was being increasingly understood that, although individuals were the mainspring of effort, the results of their enterprise did not provide the good life for everyone. Individualism was giving way to a developing idea of collectivism - that on occasion the state must intervene to solve problems not susceptible to individualistic solutions. It was also being realised that, once they had acquired the vote, the mass of people would expect their political masters to provide them with an improved standard of living. A failure by the Liberals to do so might lead to defeat at the polls, and the replacement of liberalism with a new creed such as socialism which emphasised the need for social provision, and which stressed the role of the state in providing solutions for social ills.

Although in 1900 political liberalism remained essentially unchanged, with its devotion to representative government, universal franchise and civil liberties, Liberals were becoming less fearful of the role of the state and more aware of what it could do for people, especially in the economic sphere. If the nineteenth century favoured individualism, in the twentieth century Liberals have increasingly favoured the use of collectivism to advance individual welfare.

1 Groupings within the Liberal Cause

There were diverse elements within the nineteenth-century Liberal Party, of which three stand out for main consideration in this book: the Whigs, the Radicals, and the Peelites. There were Radicals throughout the period, but the term 'Whig' was used widely to describe those on the progressive side of the political divide until the 1850s, although by then 'Liberal' was coming into more common usage; some politicians referred to themselves as Whig-Liberals. From the time of Gladstone's first premiership in 1868 it was more usual to speak of the Liberals, with the Whigs and the Radicals being groupings within the party fold.

a) Whigs

There were not many Whigs - a maximum of 5,000 at any one time according to Donald Southgate in his study of *The Passing of the Whigs, 1832-86.* They were a particularly privileged group among the aristocracy, great patricians who were proud of their origins and of their role in society. As was said of the Russell family, they thought that they were slightly grander than God! In the House of Lords their influence was extensive. They were proud of their tradition, and writers such as the historian and practising politician Macaulay wrote admiringly of them, putting forward a Whig interpretation of history which portrayed the past as an onward march of progress, with the Whigs on the side of increased liberty and freedom from arbitrary rule, ever striving to increase the opportunities and freedoms of all.

It was Whig groups which had dominated eighteenth-century politics, and which provided the political leadership of the Liberal cause in much of our period. Although Whigs were in a small minority among the landed classes as a whole, they counted many of the most aristocratic families among their number. With a few exceptions, they were not enthusiastic reformers, but conviction and circumstance often combined to direct them towards adopting what they thought to be necessary changes. They dominated the party until the 1860s, and it was particularly during the premierships of two of their number, Lords Grey and Melbourne (1830-41), that many important reforms were carried out.

The Whigs were instinctively rather cautious in their attitude, but they usually had a better idea of when to yield than did many Tories, for whom any change was suspect. It was in this spirit of making necessary adjustments and concessions that the Whigs introduced the first extension of the franchise in the Reform Act of 1832. Their general coolness towards reform, however, has been well-documented by John Vincent in *The Formation of the Liberal Party 1857-68*. He noted that 'there was a great deal of nominal liberalism on the Liberal benches'.

To their more progressive colleagues within the Liberal Party, the Whigs' outlook was unashamedly conservative and their attachment to the defence of property and privilege made them almost indistinguishable from the Tories.

b) The Radicals

The Radicals had more advanced opinions, and a philosophy which can be analysed. However, they were a small element, diverse in character and often in disagreement with one another. For much of the time they were a kind of parliamentary pressure group, exerting an influence for improvement and reform. In 1830, when the Whigs were forming a government, their support was needed, and most Radicals could see a possibility of achieving at least some of their aims by such co-operation.

The majority of them were representatives of the new middle classes, keen to extend opportunities in many fields by removing aristocratic privileges, to expose institutions to critical examination, and to make education more widely available so as to give people an opportunity to advance themselves. One group of them were the Utilitarians - also called Philosophical Radicals - who were followers of Jeremy Bentham. He believed in the principle of the greatest happiness of the greatest number, and that 'the end and aim of a legislator' should be to maximise the pleasure and contentment of the people. Institutions and policies were to be subjected to searching examination to see if they functioned well. If they did not meet this test of utility, then reform was necessary. Their preference was for no restrictions to be placed on people's activities by the government, but they accepted that, in the interests of efficiency and the general good, interference was justifiable in some circumstances.

Leading Radicals such as Richard Cobden, John Bright and other manufacturers in the Anti-Corn Law League campaigned successfully to bring about repeal of the Corn Laws which had been passed in 1815 to protect the interests of British agriculture. The laws were widely seen as unfair and were a cause of social unrest, for they offered protection to the landed interests but were thought to keep bread prices artificially high for the rest of the population. Their repeal in 1846 was a turning-point which represented the triumph of the industrial over the landed element in British politics. Manufacturers were concerned to dethrone what Cobden called 'the booby aristocracy' from its former pre-eminence. But they were not revolutionaries. They merely sought political and social readjustments to ensure that their importance in the community was recognised.

Cobden and Bright were representatives of the Manchester School which contained many ardent believers in *laissez-faire* and free trade. *Laissez-faire* is a belief which was widely held in the nineteenth century that there should be minimal government interference in economic affairs. Free trade was the system under which no tariffs or duties were charged on foreign goods imported into the country, in the hope that other countries would reduce or abolish their duties as well - such a mutual reduction was thought likely to promote international trade for the good of all. Supporters of these doctrines believed that if British businessmen were allowed to produce as much wealth as possible, the resulting prosperity would produce a better life for everyone, and that, on a world scale, the promotion of trade would ease international tension and lead to peaceful co-existence.

The views of businessmen like Cobden, an industrialist whose success was due to hard work, enterprise and attention to detail, and not to any assistance from the government, fused with those of other contemporaries who laid stress on limited government intervention and individualism in economic affairs. One such was Samuel Smiles (1812-1904). He was a philosopher whose book *Self Help* (1859) reflected some of the moral fervour of the age in its emphasis upon what have become known as Victorian values. He shared many Cobdenite views, and placed emphasis upon the moral virtue of providing for one's own destiny.

> 1 The spirit of self-help is the root of all genuine growth in the individual; and ... it constitutes the true source of national vigour and strength. Help from without is often enfeebling in its effects, but help from within invariably invigorates. Whatever is done for
> 5 men or classes, to a certain extent takes away the stimulus and necessity of doing for themselves; and where men are subjected to over-guidance and over-government, the inevitable tendency is to render them comparatively helpless ... it is every day becoming more clearly understood that the function of government is
> 10 negative ... being resolvable principally into protection of life, liberty and property.

That individualism, or concern for self, is one of the marks of the Victorian middle class which generally opposed attempts by government to set any limit to the freedom of a man to help himself. Many mid-century middle-class Radicals were of this disposition.

Other Radicals were members of the working classes. They tended to be suspicious of the northern capitalists whom they saw as worse than the Whigs in that they lacked their patrician sense of social obligation. Between 1830 and 1832 they had made common cause with the Whigs to bring about parliamentary reform. But when the 1832 Reform Act was implemented the working classes found that they had gained little from it and their Radical leaders felt that their involvement in the campaign had been ill-rewarded. They had been used and concluded that the Act was 'a mere trick to strengthen ... the tottering exclusiveness of our "blessed constitution"'. They wanted to see much more far-reaching reform and in particular government action to tackle social ills. In this they were distinct from Radicals of the Manchester School. Indeed, many of them turned to Chartism in the 1830s, believing that the implementation of the People's Charter offered the best hope of political and ultimately social reform.

In varying degrees and often for different reasons, Radicals wished to go further and faster than the Whigs. Early in the century, most of them were not advocating governmental regulation, and they did not believe that the government could or should do much to tackle the 'hell-holes of England'. They attacked privilege and aristocratic domination of public life, and were concerned to gain access to it for the middle classes.

c) The Peelites

A later addition to the Liberal cause was the group of Peelites, followers of Sir Robert Peel who split the Conservative Party by repealing the Corn Laws in 1846. On his death in 1850 some of these 'liberal Conservatives' returned to their original party but the more prominent did not, and they remained in the political wilderness for many years. Eventually, despite their dislike of the Whig Lord Palmerston and his foreign adventures, they came to offer support to him in preference to a Conservative grouping led by Lord Derby. This reinforcement of the more 'progressive' wing in political life was numerically small, comprising only twenty or so MPs in the mid-1850s. But the Peelites provided an infusion of talent - most notably WE Gladstone - noted for their emphasis upon administrative efficiency, the elimination of waste, and economy in government expenditure.

It was out of a combination of Whigs, Radicals and Peelites that the modern Liberal Party was formed.

2 The Formation of the Liberal Party

At a meeting on 6 June 1859 in Willis's Rooms, part of a gentlemen's club in London, the three groups agreed to act together to turn out the Conservative government. But there was little point in achieving this unless they also backed the new prime minister. This they did, and they united to support and sustain Lord Palmerston's administration in office. From this time onwards one can speak, at least in parliamentary terms, of a Liberal coalition. Yet if that was the date when the Liberals officially came into existence, there were many who called themselves by that name before 1859. Jonathan Parry, in *The Rise and Fall of Liberal Government in Britain* found that by 1847 175 MPs were calling themselves Liberal as opposed to only 52 self-identified Whigs.

However, even after 1859 it is misleading to talk of a Liberal Party if by this is meant a nationally organised party committed to a specific programme. There was no core of Liberal policy around which they could all unite, neither was there a national organisation. At that time, there was little interest in creating a Liberal machine, and the National Liberal Federation was not to be formed until 1877. What had happened in 1859 was that an agreement had been made between three groups of MPs to defeat Derby and install Palmerston.

In the Palmerston government of 1859-65, Gladstone came to prominence as a politician with a future, and from the late 1860s we can speak of the modern Liberal Party. John Bright did much to build up enthusiastic backing for Gladstone, winning him goodwill and drawing attention to his support of popular causes. His appeals to the people delivered in simple, moving oratory marked out a path which Gladstone with his superior abilities and talents was able to exploit. Such was Bright's role in uniting Nonconformist and working-class interests, that Donald Read has concluded that 'Bright, as much as Gladstone, created the Gladstonian Liberal Party'.

3 Liberal Backers in the Country

We have seen that in the country at large a Liberal Party did not exist until the third quarter of the nineteenth century. Before that time there were business and workingmen's clubs and Liberal associations, but in the middle of the century political differences in the wider community often had more to do with the religious divide of Church and Dissent than with the distinction between Conservative and Liberal.

Until late in the century the Liberals had no headquarters and no national organisation, and contact between national leaders at Westminster and Liberals in the country was very limited. However, there were several forces at work which helped to develop and sustain provincial Liberal feeling, and in the decade before Gladstone became Prime Minister in 1868 they coalesced to provide popular backing for the Liberal cause.

Foremost among these was the growing importance of religious Nonconformity or Dissent. Nonconformists are Protestants who do not conform to (and who therefore dissent from) the doctrines and customs of the Church of England. There were many Nonconformist denominations, such as Baptists, Methodists, Congregationalists, Quakers and Unitarians, each with its own distinctive form of worship, but in nearly all of them the congregation played a substantial role in the running of church affairs. Their advance in numbers in the first half of the nineteenth century was remarkable, and the 1851 religious census recorded the rapid growth since 1801. For example, the number of Baptist chapels had increased from 652 to 2789, and of Congregational places of worship from 914 to 3244.

Most Nonconformists disliked privilege as represented by the established Church of England and the existing social order. They suffered disadvantages in that they were legally disqualified from holding public offices and were unable to take degrees at Oxford and Cambridge. They were bent on removing such injustices and achieving religious equality. Many of them believed fervently in social and political causes such as temperance (no alcohol) and education, and in foreign policy were committed to the avoidance of war wherever possible. Pious in character, they emphasised the role of conscience and 'right conduct' between peoples and nations, and had become an extremely vocal force in public affairs by the middle of the century.

Many religious dissenters were drawn to the radicalism of the 1860s and 1870s. Radical Nonconformists were important in inspiring the Civic Gospel in Birmingham, where Unitarians took up the cause of practical social reform. There, George Dawson called on his mainly affluent congregation to 'clothe the naked, feed the hungry and instruct the ignorant'. His Congregational counterpart in the town, Robert William Dale, similarly saw politics as a Christian mission. Such men worked together with local Liberals to achieve social improvement. They were also stirred over events abroad such as the Bulgarian Atrocities of 1875-6 which so aroused Gladstone's righteous indignation.

They had a sense of mission, and if much of it was devoted to personal salvation ('saving souls for Christ'), they were also concerned to impart to the Liberal Party a radical strain. The two, Liberalism and Nonconformity, went hand in hand and where Dissent was strong (as for instance in Scotland and Wales), so also was the Liberal Party. In towns such as Rochdale in Lancashire, wealthy Nonconformist businessmen in effect chose the Liberal candidate, and elsewhere no Liberal MP could ignore the views of his Nonconformist constituents.

Another area of growing Liberal support was the Press. Gladstone's repeal of the tax on paper when he was Chancellor of the Exchequer (1855-8 and 1859-65) was a shrewd political move, for it was the spur to an enormous mushrooming of provincial newspapers and a massive leap in circulations. Among the London morning dailies, the pro-Liberal *Daily Telegraph* was much more widely bought than *The Times.* In the country at large, the number of provincial papers soared, rising (in England) from 135 in 1824 to 851 in 1871, with the total number of all papers in the United Kingdom increasing in the same period from 266 to 1450. Liberals controlled most local papers, such as the *Newcastle Chronicle,* the *Leeds Mercury,* and the *Manchester Examiner* which expressed the views of the Manchester School. Through this medium, Liberal views were conveyed to the middle and skilled working classes, and popularity and fame could be achieved by aspiring politicians. Gladstone's good works had a ready outlet, and via the press his reputation as the most effective Liberal at Westminster was firmly established.

A third force was the development from the early 1860s of a sense of political consciousness. Aspiring working-class men looked for the vote and for reforms which would improve their daily lives. They identified with the Liberals as the party most likely to help them. In the era after the formation of the Parliamentary Liberal Party in 1859, the development of working-class consciousness and the prominence of the Dissenting viewpoint were articulated by the popular press. This strengthened the cause of liberalism up and down the land.

4 William Ewart Gladstone (1809-98)

Over the whole Liberal movement towered William Ewart Gladstone, the person who was so closely identified with Victorian liberalism in its heyday. Deeply religious from first to last, the young reactionary Tory of the 1830s developed into the politician who most embodied the causes and principles with which Liberalism was associated - the abatement of privilege, the keeping of government expenditure to a minimum (retrenchment), and reform at home, and peace abroad. As a slogan 'Retrenchment and Reform' had been first heard in the early 1830s, but both causes were to reach their apogee in the 1870s and 1880s.

Today Gladstone is sometimes thought to have been excessively serious and high-minded. Indeed to some he appears to have been a rather a sanctimonious and pompous prig. That is how Disraeli caricatured him in his memorable description of a 'sophisticated rhetorician inebriated with the exuberance of his own verbosity'. Most Victorians did not so dismiss him, and for many of them he was a most attractive personality. He was an impressive figure, with superb mental and physical stamina even at the close of his life. He combined a powerful intellect with a gift for oratory, and this made him a devastating politician to confront. But he was more than a remarkable Westminster politician. He took his message to the people and in draughty halls throughout the land he conveyed his thoughts, holding his listeners enthralled as he did so. Many of the people idolised him, he was their 'Grand Old Man'.

5 Chamberlain, Gladstone and the Liberal Split of 1886

Gladstone's personality was awesome to those who dealt with him, and some found him charismatic and spell-binding. Others such as Joseph Chamberlain, whilst recognising his unparalleled gifts, found him frustrating and difficult to deal with. Moreover, he was a barrier to their own personal advancement and to the cause of reform. Chamberlain represented a different strand in the party. A keen exponent of municipal reform as Mayor of Birmingham in the early 1870s, he soon established himself as a committed and effective Radical reformer at Westminster. He urged the Liberal governments of the 1870s and 1880s to embrace a series of social changes ranging from graduated taxation to agrarian reform, from free education to democratic local government. He was impatient with the Whig attitude to innovation, as is shown by this diagnosis of the party and of his role within it;

> 1 In the Liberal army, there must be pioneers to clear the way and there must be men who watch the rear. Some may always be in advance; others may occasionally lag behind; but the only thing we have a right to demand is that no-one shall stand still, and that all
> 5 should be willing to follow the main line of Liberal progress to which the whole party are committed. I do not conceal from you my opinion that the pace will be a little faster in the future than it has been in the past.

For some time Gladstone held the Liberal Party, with its many diverse elements, together. Too bold for some and insufficiently radical for others, he was to the end able to maintain a personal ascendancy over them all.

Yet in his transcending mission to relieve Ireland of its injustices and grant Irishmen Home Rule, he was the man who cost the Liberal Party dearly. At various times in the nineteenth century the problems of Ireland haunted British politicians, though few of them made much effort to understand what life was like across the water. To his eternal credit, Gladstone did immerse himself in its economic and religious complexities, but he came to realise that there was more involved than particular social grievances. The two countries had been united by the Act of Union in 1800 and many Irish people wanted to repeal the Union and to govern themselves. Gladstone came to realise that nothing short of self-government (home rule) would assuage their discontents. In the pursuit of such a goal, he lost the Liberals the bulk of its Whig supporters and some of the Radicals too. Chamberlain was one of those who seceded, and as a Liberal Unionist (committed to maintaining the union of Britain and Ireland) he was to become ever more closely associated with the Conservative cause. The breakaway Whigs were to reinforce the built-in Tory majority in the House of Lords.

Gladstone's crusade, for such it was, consumed so much energy that Liberalism was diverted from adapting to the situation which the enfranchisement of the working classes had helped to create. Working men wanted social reform, and arguably the failure of the Gladstonian Liberal Party to pursue that path made the emergence of a specifically Labour Party if not inevitable, at least highly likely. For all of the efforts of Lloyd George and the 'new Liberals' who saw a more active role for the state, by 1914 Liberalism was in danger of being outflanked on the political Left.

6 The Liberal Legacy

Liberal ideas seemed less relevant to economic and social conditions in the days after the First World War, and the split which developed between Asquith and Lloyd George, the Party's two leaders, served only to weaken an already dying force. Throughout the period since 1918 the party has been in decline and its representation in Parliament has reflected its loss of support. However, the ideas of 'new Liberalism' have remained influential, and the post-1945 era, with its welfare state and managed economy, has been much influenced by Liberal thinkers, in particular Sir William Beveridge and John Maynard Keynes.

For much of the twentieth century, classical Liberalism, with its emphasis on minimal state intervention and the free market, has appeared to have gone out of fashion. It received a revival in the 1970s within the Conservative Party, in the form of the so-called neo-Liberalism, with its support for the 'enabling state' rather than the state as the provider of many services. *Laissez-faire* and a strong attachment to human freedom have been much commented upon since 1979, and the Thatcherite emphasis on Victorian values, with a vision of a society based on thrift, self-reliance, industry and perseverance, bears strong resemblance to the outlook of Samuel Smiles. The Manchester School of some 150 years earlier was suddenly back in fashion.

CHAPTER 2

The Early History of the Whigs

1 The Origins of the Whigs

The division of opinion which gave rise to political parties is usually dated from 1660, the year in which Charles II was restored to the throne after eleven years of republican government. At first, there was an upsurge of loyalty to the monarchy following the Restoration, but as opposition to the Court and government became apparent a dividing line between the opposing factions began to emerge. Some believed that the king ruled by divine right and that therefore his judgement could not be questioned. Others believed that the exercise of political power was subject to some measure of consent by the governed. People who believed in a limited monarchy (the Whigs) also believed that subjects ultimately possessed the right to resist royal authority, for example, if the king broke the promises he had made at his coronation.

The terms 'Tory' and 'Whig' were both originally terms of abuse used by the supporters of either side against each other. Tories stood for Church and king, and they labelled their opponents Whigs as a way of denigrating their reputation. The word originally alluded to outlaws (whiggamores), horse-thieves who roamed the Scottish moors, and was later applied to religious zealots who rebelled against royal authority. It was seen as an appropriate name for Englishmen who stood for a limited monarchy and jealously guarded the rights of Parliament against royal encroachments. The Whigs first came to prominence when they attempted to take action over the prospect of a Catholic king.

As Charles II had no children, his younger brother, James, Duke of York, was his heir. He was a Catholic. In 1678 a proposal was made by those alarmed at the thought of his succession that he should be excluded from the throne when Charles died. An attempt was made to pass an Act of Parliament preventing James from inheriting the crown, but it was defeated. This was a setback for the Whig politicians, who, in this 'Exclusion Crisis', had spoken of supporting Parliament against the king and claimed to speak on behalf of the liberties of the people. The Tories, as the supporters of James's right to inherit were known, were initially satisfied with the outcome. However, soon after James became king as James II in 1685 his pro-Catholic policy became unacceptable even to those who were members of the king's or 'Court' party.

In the 'Glorious Revolution' of 1688 leading Whigs and Tories invited William of Orange and his wife Mary (James's Protestant elder daughter) to assume the crown, and James went into exile. William was welcomed as the 'Great Deliverer', and the notables who met him pledged that,

> We will with our utmost endeavours assist His Highness in the obtaining of [a free parliament] ... wherein our laws, our liberties

and properties may be secured, and the Church of England in particular, with a due liberty to Protestant Dissenters.

The first Whigs, therefore, were landowning rebels who were unprepared to see their lives, liberties and estates controlled by a popish ruler. The basis of their beliefs was a refusal to accept the autocratic rule of a monarch who believed in divine right, and a desire for a form of constitutional monarchy in which there was parliamentary supremacy and some measure of popular control. Whigs supported religious toleration in Britain for all Protestant sects, but had strong reservations about Roman Catholics. Religion was a subject of clear disagreement between the early Whigs and Tories. The Tories supported the Church of England as the established Church which must be revered, and whose members alone should be allowed to play a part in the political life of the country.

2 The Revolution of 1688 and After

The Bloodless Revolution had been carried out by both Whigs and Tories, for men of all persuasions had felt driven beyond endurance by James. There had been a general revulsion against his use of arbitrary power. However, although many Tories had worked to expel the king, they were subsequently in a difficult position. Because they believed that kings ruled by hereditary succession and that this principle gave legitimacy to a monarch and was inviolable, many could not accept that the throne could ever become vacant. These Tories, known as Jacobites, soon reached the conclusion that there ought to be another Stuart restoration.

This allowed the Whigs thereafter to portray the Revolution as their own. They could claim that their ideas had triumphed in the events of 1688 and after, in measures such as the Bill of Rights and the Toleration Act of 1689 and the Act of Settlement of 1701 which laid down conditions about the way in which the country should be governed. They had demonstrated the ultimate supremacy of Parliament. They were also able to claim that they were responsible for assuring the Protestant Succession by arranging for George, the Elector of Hanover, to become King of Great Britain as George I in 1714 when Anne, the last of James II's Protestant children, died without direct heirs. After a Jacobite rebellion failed in 1715 the Whigs dominated politics until 1760.

3 John Locke (1632-1704), Political Philosopher

The seventeenth century had been a period of civil distress and revolution, and it was against this background that John Locke wrote as one of the foremost political thinkers of the day. He believed that man was basically decent, orderly, sociably-minded and quite capable of ruling himself. His political theory and the kind of government which he favoured were based on his opinion of what men were like. He saw his views as having been vindicated by the events of 1688, when the people dismissed one government for incompetence and with the minimum of disturbance selected another which they believed would perform its duties more efficiently.

Locke argued that free societies were founded on a basis of consent. They acknowledged certain fundamental human rights which belong to men because, and in so far as, they were rational beings. A society can only be called a civil society if its organisation and institutions recognise and implement these rights. In his treatise, *Of Civil Government,* he laid down the range of basic entitlements. Foremost among them was the enjoyment of property 'which is the fruit of our labours'. Religious toleration was another. 'The toleration of those that differ from others in matters of religion is so agreeable to the gospel of Jesus Christ and to the genuine reason of mankind, that it seems monstrous for men to be so blind as not to perceive the necessity and advantage of it, in so clear a light'.

There is scope for disagreement about which rights are paramount. But what is important and valuable about his theory is that he recognised that man is a moral being and that the state should therefore be a moral institution. Hence his desire for a contract between free men to form a political society for their mutual advantage and convenience. The individual man and his well-being are the end of the state, and this end is not one merely desirable but one which ought to prevail.

Locke's ideas provided a rational justification for what had been accomplished in 1688. It could be maintained that one king who had abused his position had been replaced by a ruler more willing to fulfil his obligations to those over whom he ruled. His main work was written before the Revolution took place and was a theoretical justification for resistance to royal authority. Its publication was delayed until 1690, but from then onwards his writing became an inspiration for those on the Whig side in British politics who regarded him as one of their greatest thinkers. He had a real grasp of the essentials of a modern democracy, even if the rights that he acknowledged were in his time restricted to a privileged group with wealth and status.

4 Eighteenth-Century Politics

In the eighteenth-century there was a long period of Whig hegemony, in which government was conducted by aristocratic groups and connections which regarded themselves as Whig by sentiment and tradition.

Yet any analysis of eighteenth-century politics in terms of a division between Whigs and Tories is fraught with difficulties. Many cabinets were not party ones, and many politicians wore the mantle of either party with some difficulty, for the century was marked by the politics of groups and interests, rather than of ideology and distinctive identity. Independence in the House of Commons was much valued, and often family ties (members of the same family often sat for neighbouring constituencies) and local considerations determined the vote. People continued to use the labels 'Whig' and 'Tory', but the motives of politicians were often influenced by other factors than their nominal allegiance. Men who labelled themselves similarly often quarrelled bitterly and intrigued relentlessly against each other. It would be wrong to think of them as men united by common beliefs or policies.

The long era of Whig ascendancy that opened with the accession of George I in 1714 (the Hanoverian Succession) was in large part due to the political skill of Sir Robert Walpole, the dominant figure in British politics from 1721 to 1742. He belonged to that group of politicians which was adept at placating the country gentry and wished to keep them happy. He was a Whig, though in a House of shifting loyalties it was necessary for him to gather support from wherever it could be found. He was well able to do this, much to the frustration of his Tory opponents.

During the reign of George II (1727-60), the label Whig became increasingly meaningless, and by the coming of George III in 1760 the term had lost most of its significance. He was intent on demonstrating the powers of the monarchy, and as part of the attempt to assert his paramountcy in the constitution he wished to downgrade the role of the Whig landowners who had dominated political life earlier in the century. He ruled with the help of ministers whom he favoured; they could come from either political tradition or neither. No party as such existed, and nobody had much idea what the term 'Whig' stood for, for everyone of any note claimed to be one. It was to become more meaningful at the time of the American and the French Revolutions.

5 The Foxite Whigs

The revolt of the American colonists against British rule starting in 1776 again posed the question of authority versus consent. Many men who called themselves Whigs supported the government and wished to retain the colonies for the British Crown. Others doubted the wisdom and justice of the struggle and united in opposition to the policy of coercion. The War of Independence lasted until 1783, and during that time Charles James Fox (1749-1806) bitterly attacked the conduct of hostilities and the power and influence of the Crown in a series of debating triumphs. When the war was over, he set about creating a more organised opposition to the government of William Pitt, who became Prime Minister in 1784.

Pitt was nominally a Whig and saw himself in the tradition of the Glorious Revolution but he was not really a convinced party figure at all. He believed in government by the best of the king's men, irrespective of the parliamentary grouping to which they belonged. He increasingly came to be associated with the leadership of the Tories on becoming Premier. He was seen as representing the conservative cause, and as such he secured the backing of many MPs who primarily thought of themselves as country gentlemen.

In opposition, Fox led a revived Whig Party representing the interests of religious dissenters, industrialists and all those who sought political or other reform. These were people who wished to call a halt to the growth in royal authority under George III. They were alarmed by the way in which he installed the young Pitt and sustained him in power without any recognition of the preferences of Parliament. In particular, Fox was vigorous in his denunciation of 'an Administration holding their places in defiance of the House of Commons'.

It was the outbreak of the French Revolution in 1789 which provided the basis of the modern party division. Many Whigs initially welcomed the Revolution seeing it as a chance for the French to adopt a modern constitutional monarchy along British lines. However, when the French revolutionaries were prepared to take the lives of the former king and queen and began to talk of aiding the cause of revolution everywhere, many erstwhile sympathisers in Britain drew back in alarm.

Fox himself was personally horrified by the savagery shown by some French leaders, but though lamenting the excesses he did not wish to see Britain associate itself with the reactionary Powers, Austria and Prussia, which were keen to intervene in French affairs. The more conservative Whigs led by the Duke of Portland went over to the other side, taking Edmund Burke, Fox's former friend and close associate, with them. They joined Pitt to 'maintain the constitution and save the country', and Burke became the philosopher of this new 'conservative coalition'. Fox and Charles Grey, a young whig nobleman who shared Fox's interest in parliamentary reform, were left to rally the liberal ranks, despite some misgivings about the direction of events in France.

For most of the time between 1793 and 1815, when Britain and France were at war with one another, the fortunes of the much-denuded Whig element in Parliament were at a low ebb. The party was weak and divided, and many of its MPs ceased to attend the House of Commons with any regularity. In 1798 Fox was removed from the list of Privy Councillors because of a speech he made affirming the principle of the sovereignty of the people. The climate of opinion was repressive and hostile to the expression of sentiments of this kind. The government passed a number of laws to clamp down on radical activities. The right of Habeas Corpus was suspended, which meant that in future people could be held in prison without being quickly brought to trial, and laws against trade unions, the Combination Acts of 1799-1800, were introduced.

It was left to Fox and his 'friends of liberty' to keep alive the flame of reformist Whiggism. They were in close touch with public opinion and were less easily alarmed than the Tories about the danger of radical agitation. They did not believe in tackling it by means of repression, such as the suppression of freedom of the press and the granting of powers of arbitrary arrest. Instead, they were willing to look for underlying causes of discontent and to attempt to find remedies. If pressed, they might be prepared to bring about a major change in the constitution, via a measure of parliamentary reform which would extend the limited franchise (right to vote) and make the House of Commons a more representative body.

Fox came to accept that the war against France after 1793 represented more than an attempt by reactionary powers to suppress the flame of freedom there. French conquests posed a threat to Britain and the continent, and Fox veered between criticising the governments after 1800 for failing to bring about peace and criticising them for failing to place the country in a state of adequate defence. After Pitt's death in 1806 the Whig Grenville became Prime Minister. The king lifted his earlier veto on Fox's membership of an administration, and he briefly became Foreign Secretary. However, in June 1806 he followed Pitt to the grave.

Fox was not a profound political thinker, neither was he a modern democrat. He was too sympathetic to the ownership of wealth and property to have ever wished to see decisions dictated by propertyless voters. He assumed that government by landowners was a natural state of affairs, and he would not have wished to disturb this. Yet he was 'progressive' in some respects. He despised the expression of intolerant and prejudiced views from whatever source they came, he hated oppression, and was thought of as 'a friend of liberty'. His legendary charm enabled him to overcome much hostility, and his tolerance and generosity of spirit put him firmly in a 'liberal' tradition, even though the word was yet to be coined.

Central to his outlook was a distaste for the growth in executive power whether in the hands of the king or the prime minister. This was to remain a significant feature of the Whig outlook and is an important part of his legacy. After his death he came to be seen as a saint-like figure (which he never was), and the image which lingered was of a crusader against excessive royal authority, and ministerial malpractice and corruption. The watchwords for which he was often quoted were 'Peace, Economy, Reform', and these were to be the hallmarks of nineteenth-century liberalism.

6 Whiggery, 1806-15

In opposition again, the Whigs had two prominent leaders, Grenville in the Lords and Grey in the Commons. The former was viewed by radicals as a barrier to any reform-minded schemes, and Grey who was a more sympathetic figure soon inherited a seat in the upper house. For several years (until 1817) George Ponsonby led the party in the Commons, but he received little support from the more aristocratic 'grandees' in the Lords and was unable to either keep the various factions together or to take up new initiatives. Frank O'Gorman in *The Emergence of the British Two-Party System, 1760-1832* has written critically of the Whig performance over the next few years.

> 1 So many of the weaknesses of the Whig party in the next 20 years - the apathy, the complacency, the personal recriminations, the indolence and the failure to build a solid, popular base - can be traced to failings of leadership. Charles Fox must have wept in 5 his grave.

The Whigs were to remain out of office until 1830.

7 Radicalism at the Turn of the Century

There was before 1815 a broad band of opinion to which the name Radical has been given. Deriving from the Latin word *radix* (root), a Radical was someone who wished to bring about fundamental change in political, social and economic conditions. However, other than a desire for root-and-branch reform of one sort or another, there was often little in common between those who employed the Radical label.

Rev John Wyvill, a clergyman of independent means, was the inspiration behind the Yorkshire Association, a body which campaigned for moderate parliamentary reform in the early 1780s. Radical societies of the 1790s were more ambitious. Some were aristocratic and mainly allied to parliamentary struggles for reform, but the London Corresponding Society was a national as distinct to a local body, and was made up of members of the skilled working class.

Many of these societies were really clubs which held meetings and published pamphlets, and their aims were often far-reaching for they wished to obtain universal suffrage and annual parliaments. Some of their spokesmen openly professed sympathy with the French Revolutionaries and used the French style of address, and this extremist element provided the Pitt government with an excuse to take action against all the societies and those who led them. The 1790s saw such movements largely driven underground. Yet from time to time expressions of radical belief and practice resurfaced, and the Corresponding Society was followed by the Hampden Clubs. Founded initially in London by Major John Cartwright as outlets through which wealthier and more influential radicals could press for reform, they were soon also established in the Midlands and North, where they attracted support from skilled workers and were responsible for organising much radical protest in the decade after 1815.

In 1790, Edmund Burke wrote his *Reflections on the Revolution in*

France, in which he cast doubt upon the hopes of some reformers that the fall of the Bastille would lead to the dawn of a new era of liberty; 'at the end of every vista, you can see the gallows'. Tom Paine responded with his explanation of *The Rights of Man* in 1792. He maintained that the people of a country had the right to choose or alter the form of government as they liked. This democratic view attracted many supporters, but when he issued another pamphlet in which he praised republicanism his opinions lost their earlier popularity.

There were other well-known Radicals in the early nineteenth century, such as William Cobbett (1762-1835) and Francis Place (1771-1854). Cobbett was a militant campaigner who argued that there was little to choose between Pitt and Fox; he saw both parties as being to beholden to vested interests and tainted by corruption. In the period from 1806-12, he was part of a new phase of political agitation, and was prepared to take up causes such as flogging in the army, despite the fact that it landed him in prison. He was a countryman, interested in the condition of England which he later described in his *Rural Rides* of the 1820s. He used his literary gifts to stir up the spirit of revolt against wretched living conditions in the north, and used his paper, the *National Register* (1804), to advance his claim that workers there were better off in the days of pre-industrial England. Francis Place was a London tailor whose business was so successful that he was able to hand it over to his son and concentrate on his political activity, which involved campaigning for the rights of trade unionists, the need for parliamentary reform and the then unmentionable subject of birth control. The library behind his shop became one of the main meeting-places for reformers.

One problem was that the Radicals were a motley group, lacking in cohesion and having diverse aims and beliefs. However, an influential group among them were those who did possess a distinct doctrine, that of Utilitarianism. Their creed derived from David Ricardo and Jeremy Bentham, to whose thinking we have already alluded (see pages 3-4). In his writings Bentham constantly criticised existing law and felt that many laws did not achieve what they were intended to. He wanted to see reform, and his schemes were all based on a single principle which he believed to be self-evident, namely that in any given case the solution should be chosen which would produce the greatest happiness for the greatest number of people; 'The end and aim of a legislator should be the happiness of the people. In matters of legislation, general utility should be his guiding principle.'

His principle of utility was, of course, a subjective one, and his natural caution predisposed him to favour the maintenance of the status quo unless the grounds for reform were clearly apparent. But he was also a practical reformer, and in his interest in change and in his concern for the physical well-being of the greatest number of the people his approach was to be influential in the Whig-Liberal politics of the nineteenth century.

8 The Whigs, 1815-30

After the French Wars the Tories were in undisputed control of Parliament and had substantial support among the limited electorate. The Whigs, in opposition to them, were for much of the time weak and divided, though after 1815 some new figures emerged and the party gained wider backing among influential sections of the community. Following the 1812 election they had the support of approximately 150 MPs. In the election of 1818 they added about 30 seats, and achieved further gains two years later. Despite this steady improvement in their parliamentary position, such was the weakness of party ties that these supporters could not be viewed as a homogeneous group. The strength of family connections still mattered and allegiances could be switched.

Within the House of Commons the Whigs were for much of the time very disorganised, lacking in recognised leadership. There was no-one strong enough to weld the diverse individuals and groups into an effective and harmonious team. The two most influential Whigs after 1815 were Lords, Grenville (until his defection to the Liverpool camp in 1822), a former prime minister, and Grey. Grey was the more widely viewed by his associates as the natural heir to the Foxite tradition, and from 1817 he led the party from the Second Chamber. However, he imparted little sense of direction. His interest in politics was spasmodic and he spent much of his time on his estates and was politically inactive for long periods, having more concern to stifle than to promote any internal debate.

More enterprising politicians were needed in the Lower House to mount an effective challenge to government policy. None were available, or rather, those who were able and vigorous, were unable to achieve any real ascendancy over their colleagues. Tierney followed Ponsonby as the Whig leader in the Commons in 1817, but he was just as ineffectual as his predecessor, although he made a more promising start. He seemed to lose heart when it proved difficult to reconcile conflicting personalities and interests within the party. After 1821, when he retired, there was no official leader in the Commons for nine years. Eventually Althorpe, who had earlier declined the vacancy, took up the leadership following a petition by the whips and he attempted to end the period of prolonged drift. He was more effective than his predecessors but his leadership was hardly decisive, for again he preferred the leisured life of supervising his estates and saw political involvement as 'an entire sacrifice'. He was once described as 'the tortoise on whose back the world reposes'.

An altogether more impressive and striking figure was Lord Brougham (pronounced Broom), for he was clever, quick-witted, eloquent and forceful. His gifts as a political operator and resourceful debater were widely recognised. However, he was widely distrusted as being 'too clever by half' and had often been out of touch with his colleagues who suspected him of being unduly ambitious and deceitful. More seriously, according to Grey, he lacked 'ballast'; he was seen by some as a lightweight, lacking stability or *gravitas*.

Lord John Russell appeared to be a politician with a future, even if he was as yet too young (23 in 1815) to make much of a mark. He and other representatives of a wealthy and privileged background often met together at Holland House, the home of Lord Holland, a nephew of Charles Fox. There, they socialised with others who shared a growing interest in the Whig cause. There were lawyers like Romilly and wits and writers like the Rev Sidney Smith and the young Thomas Babington Macaulay, a noted essayist and historian. In the pages of the *Edinburgh Review* these men and others exchanged their political ideas, revealing not so much a distinctive doctrine, but a probing approach to the problems of the day.

There was much dissension among the Whigs over issues of policy. The distress around the country in the years immediately following the return of peace in 1815 led to widespread discontent and popular agitation. The Tories believed that Radical leaders were inflaming the passions of a 'deluded' people, and many Whigs had similar fears. They were no friends of such 'troublemakers' and it was Grey who remarked that mob leaders wanted 'not Reform, but Revolution'. He was alarmed by the excesses of some rioting, and several of his colleagues agreed that those involved must be dealt with harshly.

However, Brougham and others wished to keep open some lines of communication to the more moderate Radicals. So there was a compromise over parliamentary tactics. When the government curbed civil liberties, the opposition recognised that there was a target for them to attack and exploited it. For instance, ministers suspended Habeas Corpus in 1817. This enabled them to hold people in prison without bringing them to trial. Grey agreed to condemn such an infringement of basic freedoms. But the attack on the government was by no means whole-hearted, and the Whigs were prepared to acquiesce in some other restrictions, such as those in the Seditious Meetings Act of the same year which curbed the holding of mass demonstrations.

Although the Whigs were prepared to defend freedoms, they had little understanding of the causes of the discontent or idea how to remove them. One common theme in the protest around the country between 1815 and 1820 was the lack of parliamentary reform. If ever there was a tailor-made cause for an opposition to exploit, it was the state of the unreformed Parliament. Here was an issue which should have rallied aspiring politicians and gained them much public sympathy. However, within Whig ranks the issue tended to produce disagreement rather than unity. Many landed magnates controlled pocket boroughs, which they were reluctant to give up, and the aristocratic Lord Holland spoke for many of them when he declared that 'the nearer I am to parliamentary reform, the less I own I like it'. Tierney was able to detect 'a thousand different shades of opinion' on the Whig benches, remarking that such reform could 'never be a bond of party'.

If parliamentary reform failed to unite the Whigs, one area of broad agreement was support for Catholic Emancipation. Before 1829 Roman Catholics were not allowed to become Members of Parliament, and most Whigs believed that this was unjust. But, other than on this issue, their views were broadly similar to those of many of the more moderate Tories. They backed the changes introduced by the government in what is often known as the more 'liberal' era of the 1820s. There was widespread agreement between moderates on either side in favour of an extension of free trade, modification of the criminal law and the establishment of a police force - though some Whigs feared that in the hands of a Tory government the police could be a tool of reaction, opposing civil liberties.

In fact a few Whigs served in the 'moderate' administrations of George Canning and his successor in 1827 and 1828, but when the Duke of Wellington became prime minister in 1828 they felt unable to continue in office. It was soon apparent that there was less room in this Tory government for reformers, and some 'liberal Tories' moved over to the Whig side. Among these were Huskisson, Palmerston and Lamb (later Lord Melbourne). Wellington's ministers did introduce legislation to repeal the Test and Corporations Acts which had kept Protestant Nonconformists out of Parliament, and of course this was an issue on which Whigs could give enthusiastic backing. Indeed, running through the era 1815-30 there is a broad Whig commitment in favour of political liberty, whether it be in opposition to the suspension of Habeas Corpus or in support of the rights of those excluded from the House of Commons, be they Dissenters or Catholics.

There had been earlier attempts to introduce Catholic Emancipation, though they had narrowly failed, defeated in 1819 in the Commons and in the Lords two years later. The Whigs were generally strongly in favour, and the passing of the Act in 1829 helped to give them a new unity and at the same time served to undermine the cohesion of the Cabinet. The Whigs were now almost ready to assume governmental responsibilities and tackle the other major issue which divided the Tories. This was parliamentary reform, for which by 1830 all Whigs could see the need. Wellington's unwillingness to contemplate such a change was to prove his undoing.

Making notes on *'The Early History of the Whigs'*

As we are not primarily concerned to study the origins of Liberal thought and of the Liberal Party before 1815, there will be no need to make notes on this chapter. However, by carefully considering about what you have read you should come to understand the development of the Liberals as a political force in the nineteenth century more clearly. Notice in particular the contribution of thinkers and writers such as John Locke and Jeremy Bentham, for their attitudes were significant to this development.

CHAPTER 3

The Whig Reformers, 1830-41

1 Introduction

There was much disillusion with the Wellington ministry in 1830 and in the elections of that year the Whigs made some 30 gains. Soon afterwards, Tory extremists (Ultras), moderate Tories, Whigs, and independent country members brought about the Tory government's defeat in the House of Commons. Not since 1804 had a government been brought down by a hostile vote in the lower house, and the defeat resulted in the first complete change of parliamentary control since 1807. In 1830 the Whigs formed the first of their administrations of the years 1830-41. They had at last again become a 'party of government'.

It is on the strength of their performance, especially between 1830 and 1835, that the reputation of the 'Whig reformers' rests. In these years not only did they produce the first instalment of parliamentary reform but they also introduced far-reaching changes affecting many important areas of British life. Their efforts mark the beginnings of the Age of Reform.

The ministry which took over in late 1830 was a coalition of Whigs, Radicals and Canningites, and with such a motley composition, was unlikely to have a coherent reforming outlook. Over it presided Lord Grey, thought of as a firebrand in his Foxite youth but now an ageing figure whose ardour for change had largely disappeared. The events of recent years - especially the discontent after 1815 and the turbulence in 1830 over parliamentary reform - troubled him, for as a member of the old aristocracy he was alarmed at the new industrial world, and viewed with distaste both some of the leaders who had emerged and their clamour for radical change. At the height of the troubles over parliamentary reform, he was to say, 'Damn reform, I wish I had never touched it'.

The Cabinet he chose illustrates the importance of 'connections' among the Whig aristocracy. Many of its members were related and it has been well described by Donald Southgate in *The Passing of the Whigs 1832-86* as a 'mannequin parade of rank and property', for amongst its members there were only 2 out of 13 who could be described as commoners. On the threshold were rising talents of the younger generation, such as Edward Stanley (later Lord Derby, Tory Prime Minister) and Lord John Russell. As we have seen, the government was not wholly Whig and it even included one ultra Tory, the Duke of Richmond.

Such men gathered in the great country houses of the land or met in Brooks Club. They were an exclusive circle of the privileged aristocracy, closed to most outside the group. Yet despite their social exclusiveness, they were able to reach out beyond their narrow bounds to other sections in the community. In the City they had the support of many financiers and merchants, and in the provinces many of the factory owners were sympathetic, as were some prominent newspaper proprietors such as the editor of the *Leeds Mercury* who roused the Yorkshire manufacturers with his indignant observations on the conditions of those who worked for them. The voice of religious Dissent was also sympathetic to the Whigs.

Such groups did not agree with everything the Whigs did or said. Indeed, they were often frustrated by the inactivity of ministers, but they and other groups found the Whigs to be a useful vehicle through which they could seek to achieve their particular goals. Those who favoured progress in whatever degree found it better to co-operate with the government than to shun it, for it offered the prospect of change in a way that Wellington had never done. But the reason the Radicals were willing to work with the Whigs was not because they expected that major changes would come about: it was because, as Bentham had put it in 1818, 'the Tories are the people's avowed enemies'. He was favourably disposed to the Whigs and after his death in 1832 his Utilitarian followers saw some prospect that the Whigs as a party of progress would succumb to pressure for far-reaching reforms. The Philosophical Radicals, as the followers of Bentham were collectively known, had strong support outside Parliament among the professional and manufacturing classes. Inside the Chamber their spokesman was Joseph Hume. Working-class leaders such as Burdett, Cobbett and Hunt echoed their demands for sweeping change.

These groups and interests were seeking 'improvement' of some sort, and the Whigs varied in their response to the tide of opinion. Some were cautious and restrained and found the process largely distasteful. Typical of this group was Grey who would accept innovation only because of his fear that resistance was 'certain destruction', but the attitude of his son-in-law, Lord Durham, popularly known as Radical Jack, was very different. He claimed to observe 'with regret every hour which passes over the existence of acknowledged but unreformed abuse'. There were other more liberal members, among them the Leader of the House of Commons, Lord Althorpe. He was personally in favour of the secret ballot and wanted to see ministers adopt a reformist approach. Moreover, his ability to keep the divergent elements of the Administration together was widely recognised, for all could respect his integrity, fairness and willingness to compromise. Not clever or eloquent, he nonetheless proved to be an able member of the Cabinet.

Among the convinced reformers, and much more zealous than the plodding Althorpe, was Henry Brougham who could accept the changed condition of the country since industrialisation, and was prepared to implement policies which reflected the transformation. Formerly a distinguished advocate at the Bar, he was now Lord Chancellor. His obvious abilities might have taken him to the premiership, but he was regarded as too ambitious and lacking in gentlemanly connections to be acceptable to the narrow-minded Whig oligarches of whom he had often been a critic. He was a strong supporter of parliamentary reform which he saw as necessary to provide recognition to the middle classes whom his fellow Peers were, in his view, 'wont to despise'.

The predominantly Whig ministry held together until the mid-1830s, and during those years important work was done. But it was, as has been suggested, 'a regiment that marched in echelon with one section in advance of another'.

2 The Situation in 1830

Expectations were high when the Whigs took over, but the times were tense and any failure to tackle the situation could have had catastrophic results. It mattered immensely whether the Grey administration succeeded or failed, for on its shoulders were carried the hopes of all who all who wanted to see an improvement in the state of public affairs.

One of the first tasks was to restore order. Riots were widespread in the south, provoked by levels of unemployment and near-starvation which recalled the bad days after Waterloo. Rebellious farm labourers were treated harshly by the new Home Secretary, Lord Melbourne. His response was repressive: nine men were hanged and 450 men and boys were transported to Australia. Although there was little danger of co-ordinated conspiracy in these outbreaks, there was a potentially more serious protest developing in the towns.

Middle-class Political Unions had been set up in Birmingham and elsewhere. Thomas Attwood, a banker and currency reformer, established the Birmingham Political Union to agitate for parliamentary reform, and his example was followed by sympathisers in several other large industrial centres. Place and Burdett co-ordinated the local societies into a vast National Political Union which sought to unify the working and middle classes in various parts of the country behind the movement. The Political Unions began to adopt parliamentary candidates; one supporter, 'Orator' Hunt of Peterloo fame, had been MP for Preston since 1829. Outside the House, Place and Attwood pressed for non-payment of taxation until Parliament showed itself to be more sensitive to their demands. This really alarmed the Whig government, and with the spectre of revolt seeming close at hand, Grey was persuaded that parliamentary reform was the only safeguard against chaos and disintegration.

3 Parliamentary Reform

The existing parliamentary system had evolved between the fourteenth and seventeenth centuries, and it was out of date. It was no longer adequate either in the system of election or in the composition of the House of Commons. It reflected life in pre-industrial England, and the growth of manufacturing and commerce had produced a new class of well-to-do people who had little connection with the land and who were poorly represented in the House of Commons. In particular, the rapid growth of population, especially in the new urban areas, meant that there were large towns and cities which lacked any representation. Leeds, Manchester and Birmingham had no MPs, yet small and insignificant boroughs often had two.

In essence there were three anomalies of the old system:

1. The allocation of seats still reflected the distribution of wealth and population of bygone days. Cornwall returned 42 members and Dorset 18, whereas in each of Cambridgeshire and Cheshire there were only two county and two borough members. Several dozen 'rotten' (ie, decayed almost to the point of non-existence) and 'pocket' (so-called because they were 'in the pocket' of a single landowner who could in effect nominate their MPs) boroughs still returned two members each. For example, Dunwich in Suffolk, as a result of coastal erosion, had almost fallen into the sea, Old Sarum in Wiltshire was a mound of earth, Gatton in Surrey had only six houses and one elector, and Rattery, a hamlet in Devon where the tenants regularly voted as instructed by the local landowner, Sir Walter Carew. Such boroughs were regularly advertised for sale. Overall, the effect was greatly to over-represent the south of England at the expense of the Midlands and the North.

2. Widespread corruption affected the conduct and outcome of elections. Bribery could have a significant effect on the outcome in constituencies such as Totnes which had 78 voters in 1820 or Winchelsea with only seven. Much money often changed hands, sometimes on the purchase of 'septennial ale' or other forms of inducement. In 1811 the election for the County of York was reputed to be the most expensive ever, with £200,000 being spent by those involved. But there were other malpractices, such as personation, (impersonating a voter), and in the worst boroughs various forms of intimidation such as kidnapping and beatings up did sometimes occur. The underlying problem was the absence of a secret ballot, for with voting being conducted at the open hustings everyone knew how everyone else had voted. It was worthwhile, therefore, to spend money 'influencing' electors, for the corruptor was able to check that his bribe or other form of influence had worked.

3. The electorate was small in number, with only an estimated 478,000 entitled to vote out of a population in 1830 of over 24 million. In the counties, the franchise was limited but at least was relatively clearly defined, forty shilling freeholders possessing the right to vote. The main complication was disagreement over what constituted a freehold. In the boroughs, the pattern was hideously confused, and whereas usually the bulk of people were excluded, in some

constituencies such as Preston a person could vote even if he only lodged in the town overnight. In most borough constituencies a large majority of the population, including many men (no women could vote) belonging to the middle classes, did not meet these tests of eligibility.

It is clear, therefore, that an unrepresentative group of voters determined the composition of the House of Commons, and events such as the passing of the Corn Laws in 1815 and the abolition of Income Tax the following year convinced many Radicals that a parliament so constituted tended to act in the interests of those who were represented there. Radicals regularly claimed that the reform of Parliament was the key to effecting further changes, but as long as there was popular agitation and unrest most merchants and factory owners recoiled from joining the Radical campaign. By the 1820s pressure for change was gaining momentum, and sections of the middle class allied themselves with Radical leaders to campaign for reform and break the stranglehold of the landlord class over the main legislative body.

4 The Attitude of the Whigs towards Parliamentary Reform

In his youth, Grey, like Fox, had been committed to constitutional reform, but the widespread discontent after 1815 had cooled his enthusiasm, for it had shown the danger presented by irresponsible Radical agitators. By 1817, in the midst of public disorder, his position had become noticeably more cautious.

> 1 I am still a reformer, but with some modification of my former opinions; with more fear of the effect of sudden and inconsiderate changes, with a most complete conviction that to be successful reform must be gradual, and must be carefully limited to the
> 5 necessity which has proved it to be wanting ... Of the House of Commons, as it at present exists, I am not unwilling to say that I think it is, with all its imperfections on its head, one of the best securities the people of this country ever had for the preservation of their freedom.

Thereafter he asserted his 'predilection for old institutions'. Like that of many of his colleagues, his approach was a conservative one. However, he possessed the shrewd facility that has come to be associated with the English governing classes of knowing when to give way. By 1830 it was clear to him that it would be prudent to yield to popular demands. He certainly did not favour anything resembling popular control, and he had a horror of mob rule. Democratic notions were unpalatable to him as he believed in the preservation of the essential elements of the existing distribution of political power and influence. Rank and property were in his eyes the natural determinants of power, but he thought that the only way to maintain the current political system was for the landed magnates to make a timely concession to the middle classes by bringing those who had acquired considerable wealth from industry or commerce more clearly within its scope.

He did not much care for such people, and would almost certainly have shared the disdainful view of Melbourne that the middle classes were 'all affectation and conceit, and pretence and concealment'. Yet he appreciated that new forms of property had come into prominence, and that its commercial and industrial forms had to receive recognition. He believed that only by giving their possessors a modicum of political power could the demand for sweeping change be averted. His view was that it was necessary to concede enough influence to this new grouping to placate those who were dissatisfied. If this was done, then the middle classes, having been 'bought off', would cease to ally themselves with the Radicals, and would be a barrier against further change. Failure to give way might create a very dangerous situation, and to do insufficient to satisfy reasonable expectations would probably be worse than doing nothing at all.

Thus property was at the heart of the debate in 1830-2. But whereas the Tories thought that reform would undermine the existing society, the Whigs considered that the recognition of new forms of property would safeguard the traditional landed interest. Grey had a strong case in arguing for 'ordered change' whilst it was still possible. He did not accept that the almost inevitable consequence of passing one reform would be to fuel the demand for further change at a later date, or if he did have such thoughts he kept them to himself. He saw the urgent need for a practical remedy, which was both sufficient to satisfy popular clamour and prudent enough to ensure that Parliament would pass it.

Therefore it is clear that the primary aim of the government was an essentially conservative one, even if those who worked with and through the administration had other aspirations. The opinion of ministers was that the existing system had clear weaknesses and that repair work was necessary to correct its shortcomings. The changes proposed were sold to fellow-Whigs as moderate ones to meet the needs of the immediate situation. However, Melbourne recognised that there was a need to listen to the public voice; 'All experience proves, when the wishes of the people are founded on reason and justice and when they are consistent with the fundamental principles of the Constitution, that there must come a time when both the legislative and executive powers must yield to the popular voice or be annihilated.'

He pointed to the danger that angry and discontented feelings would be revived and renewed in every time of public distress. In 1831 Macaulay similarly caught the spirit of the Whig approach of making reasonable concessions to avert catastrophe in a speech to fellow MPs.

1 Every argument which would induce me to oppose universal
suffrage induces me to support the plan which is now before us. I

am opposed to universal suffrage, because ... it would produce a destructive revolution. I support this plan; I am sure it is our best
5 security against a revolution.

That we may exclude those whom it is necessary to exclude, we must admit those whom it may be safe to admit ... We say that it is not by mere numbers, but by property and intelligence, that the nation ought to be governed. Yet, saying this, we exclude great
10 masses of property and intelligence ... We do more. We drive over to the side of revolution those whom we shut out from power. History is full of revolutions, produced by causes similar to those which are now operating in England. A portion of the community which had been of no account expands, and becomes strong. It
15 demands a place in the system, suited to its present power. If this is granted, all is well. If this is refused, then comes the struggle between the young energy of one class and the ancient privileges of another. Such is the struggle which the middle classes in England are maintaining against an aristocracy.

Some of Grey's colleagues were prepared to go further than he was, and thought less in terms of gentlemanly repair to the patchwork of the constitution. Brougham recognised the changes which had overtaken the country and its representative system, and suggested that 'We don't live in the days of barons - we live in the days of Leeds, of Bradford, of Halifax and Huddersfield. We live in the days when men are industrious and desire to be free'. Lord Russell and Lord Durham similarly favoured a bolder approach to the issue, and their view was endorsed by what has been referred to as 'a heterogeneous mass of Liberal and Radical enthusiasts', many of whom were prepared to go considerably further than they were themselves.

5 The Passage of the First Reform Bill

Piecemeal reform, such as the disenfranchisement of Grampound in 1821 and of East Retford and Penryn in 1828, had taken place in the 1820s, but such tinkering was no longer an answer. The country wanted something more drastic. Grey implicitly accepted the need for a radical revision by appointing Durham as the chairman of a special committee of four to draw up a bill. Brougham and Ponsonby served as well, but it was the fourth member, Lord John Russell, who was given the task of introducing the measure in the Commons. As Russell read out the list of boroughs to be disenfranchised there were some startled gasps from the packed House, for the bill went further than many MPs had expected.

In the debate which followed Palmerston put the case for practical reform to remedy existing deficiencies very clearly; 'Any man who looked at the workings of the present system must see that there are great and peculiar blemishes [in the constitution] which it is necessary to remove, in order to fit it for the intelligence and feelings of the times in which we live.' He claimed that the plan then before the House applied to all these defects, and that 'if calmly and dispassionately examined', there was 'not an evil they generated' for which it did not provide 'a sure and effectual remedy'.

The details of the passage of the bill are to be found in another volume in the series. Here it is sufficient to say that when the Lords rejected it in October 1831 there was popular fury. Some of those who voted against were attacked and their homes damaged. In the north there was drilling and arming, and in the south general disorder, including rick-burning and rioting. The signs were alarming, but the Whigs were able to use the imminent danger of revolutionary upheaval as a means of inducing MPs to offer their support. Attwood, Cobbett, Hunt and other Radicals whipped up a campaign in the country against the Second Chamber and any there who opposed reform. The peers backed down when faced with the prospect of 50 new peerages being created by the king to enable the government to pass the bill, and it was placed on the statute book in June 1832.

By the act the borough franchise was given to all who possessed or occupied a house of £10 annual rental, and in the countryside new categories of voters were introduced. Fifty-six boroughs with less than 2000 inhabitants lost both MPs, and constituencies such as Old Sarum therefore ceased to exist. Small boroughs with between 2,000 and 4,000 inhabitants lost one member. Of the 143 seats thereby made available for redistribution, 65 went to the counties and 78 were granted to large towns and cities such as Birmingham, Manchester and Sheffield, which gained separate representation for the first time. Similar changes were made for Ireland and Scotland, which between them gained 13 additional seats via the passage of separate legislation.

6 The Merits and Demerits of the 1832 Act

News of the passing of reform was greeted with processions and celebrations up and down the country, but even while the ringing of bells and the staging of banquets was taking place, the Radicals were complaining that the act seemed like a betrayal. They had worked hard to bring about the reform but they had gained few of their objectives. Among their reforming goals was the secret ballot and a system of annual elections, both of which would have helped to remove corruption and make parliament more representative; neither was introduced. By contrast, the changes which were made were modest in extent. In their disappointment and bitterness the Radicals were reflecting the views of many reformers, for in several ways the Reform Act fell far short of their expectations. Its limitations were most evident in four areas.

1. Corruption had not been tackled, and indeed electoral malpractice was to survive until late in the century. In some respects the situation

was worse than before, for the enfranchisement of the tenants-at-will, a group especially beholden to their landlords, meant that the control of landowners over those on their estates had been strengthened. In Rattery, the voting pattern of the new voters was to continue to follow the example of Sir Walter Carew, and whilst in some cases the reason for this was the tendency of many country people to follow their local gentry, in other cases the threat of eviction, so potent under open voting, was another.

2. The redistribution of seats had been cautious, and although most pocket and rotten boroughs had disappeared, the larger towns were still seriously underrepresented, for there was no equation between population and representation. It was difficult to justify a situation in which 371 MPs continued to come from south of the line linking the Wash to the Severn, whilst only 120 came from the area to the north, for the centre of gravity of the population had moved towards the new industrial districts of the Midlands and the North.

3. The number of voters was still small, for the electorate had only been increased by an estimated 217,000 in England, and in the whole UK from 478,000 to 810,000 (less than 4% of the population). The middle classes had generally gained, although some of those who owned their own homes in places such as Leeds failed to acquire the vote because property values there were too low for many houses to qualify. Artisans (skilled workers) were still left unsatisfied, and some working-class people who had been able to vote under the previous system found that they had lost their former privilege. In Preston, the old rights disappeared at once (and with them the MP Orator Hunt); in other places, it expired with the death of the current voter. The working classes, which had done so much to agitate for the franchise, found themselves no better off than before.

4. The social composition of the House remained largely unchanged. It still represented the landed interest, and was largely composed of men of title with a private income. Although the representation of middle-class businessmen in Parliament increased, they were still in a minority. In 1865 there were 180 sons and relations of peers in the lower chamber and, in total, some 400 representatives of the aristocracy.

Yet, despite the act's deficiencies, the changes did make parliament somewhat more representative than before, and showed that it was open to pressure from outside. Although Russell could speak in 1837 of the act as a 'final settlement' - hence his nickname of 'Finality Jack' - this was unlikely to be the case indefinitely. Pressure for further change would follow, for in this respect at least the Tory case in 1831-2 was correct. Many of their spokesmen had foreseen that, once the door marked 'reform' had been opened, it would not easily be closed again.

Disappointment was inevitable when the results of the Great Reform Act became apparent, and some feared that there would be rioting when new elections were held. But this did not happen, and in the election that followed in December 1832 Grey was rewarded with a huge majority. In the new House of Commons more than 500 out of 658 members had been supporters of reform. These included a small Radical element which would be pressing for advances in other areas now that their central goal had been achieved. They were eager to see an annual instalment of change, for the 1832 measure was seen as the precursor of wholesale action.

As an essentially Benthamite measure, the Reform Act had satisfied the middle classes, Brougham's 'genuine depositories of sober, rational, intelligent and honest English feeling'. The House of Commons had been subjected to the test of utility and found wanting. Practical reform had ensured a revitalised House which had more authority to govern. Power was in the hands of those more likely to use their influence to promote 'the greatest happiness of the greatest number'.

The reform says much about the attitude of the Whigs, their strengths and their limitations. It went far enough to win the approval of the majority of the middle classes, for as Althorpe had recognised 'if the middling classes in this or any other country were hostile to the form of government under which they lived, the government would never be safe'. In the words of the pro-Whig *Edinburgh Review,* the Reform Act removed the danger of an 'estrangement between themselves and the community at large', and in so doing it had done much to secure the survival and reputation of the traditional ruling class. It was, in Southgate's words, 'a rescue operation on behalf of rank and property'. The Whigs, not for the first time, had performed a mediatory role of taking the heat out of a situation which seemed in danger of getting out of control. They had shown that, whilst they were not democrats, neither were they obscurantists.

In the new partnership between the aristocracy and the middle classes, the Whigs felt that they had secured the best possible outcome. Their measure had averted a national catastrophe, and, they believed, it had brought the Constitution somewhere near to perfection. However, by itself it was not enough to placate those committed to reform, for there was a spirit of anticipation in the air. Shortly after the 1832 election, Durham advised his father-in-law that 'the Reform will lead to Revolution', unless there were accompanying measures. He recognised that public opinion was full of expectation, and that once one aristocratic bastion had been tackled public attention would turn to the many other issues urgently awaiting governmental action.

In the measures which followed, the Whigs were to show their commitment to the idea of 'progress'. Some members of the Cabinet were more enthusiastic than others, and Althorpe, Stanley and especially Brougham were keen to see further changes. They recognised that there were institutions in need of reform and grievances which awaited legislative remedy. In tackling their tasks, ministers were to be influenced by the Benthamite ideal of utility, by their traditional concern for economy and dislike of waste, and by the broad humanitarian feelings which from time to time urged the need for governmental action. However, by 1836 the reforming zeal had cooled. This was a reflection both of the wide range of issues they had already dealt with and of the limited expectations of any government at this time. Governments were generally thought of as having a restricted role, and in the 1830s the Whigs went as far as could reasonably have been expected from any body of men with their social background and lifestyle.

7 Slavery

The slave trade had been outlawed in the British Empire in 1807 and many other countries had also made it illegal. But the suppression only related to the trade and not to the institution, so that in the West Indies and other parts of the Empire the public auctioning of slaves was a regular feature and the smuggling of slaves across the Atlantic from Africa was conducted in conditions of much brutality. Humanitarians such as William Wilberforce and others in the Anti-Slavery Society had done much to inform MPs and the population at large of the horrors associated with slavery, though it was not easy to rouse the conscience of some people about practices of which they had no real understanding or experience. Reformers also met with considerable opposition from those who represented the interests of the slave-owners.

In 1833 the Whig Colonial Secretary, Lord Stanley, introduced a bill to abolish slavery in the British Empire. Under the terms of the Emancipation Act freedom was granted immediately to slaves under six, while those who were older gained their liberty over a transitional period of seven years, during which time they would work part of the time for the masters, and the rest as free wage-labourers. It was an unsatisfactory compromise, designed to soften the impact of change on the plantation owners, and it offered no immediate satisfaction to the slaves. In the event, all slaves became fully free within five years. Owners were paid a total of £20m in compensation, an amount they considered insufficient to cover the market value of their slaves.

The abolition was a popular non-party reform, inspired by genuinely benevolent impulses. It united all Whig backers, be they middle-class Radicals, Dissenters or other humanitarians, and it fitted especially well into Whig thinking, for Fox had been much involved in the original abolition of the slave trade. It was just the sort of change that Althorp was urging on his colleagues. They wanted to avoid demands for 'dangerous' innovations such as annual elections and the secret ballot, and so by pursuing a 'liberal' policy on issues such as slavery they could still command respect for 'taking a lead in Popular Measures'. Differing interpretations of this issue are discussed in Frank McDonough's volume, *The British Empire, 1815-1914,* in the series.

8 Factories

Also in 1833, Parliament enacted another significant reform, the Factory Act. There had been earlier legislation on conditions in the factories, mainly in the cotton industry, but there had been no means of enforcing its provisions. The government had relied on magistrates, themselves often manufacturers, to inspect factories and bring anyone transgressing the law to justice, and not surprisingly almost nothing had been done. In 1830 Parliament established a Select Committee to investigate conditions and it found some horrific examples of children who in the busy periods began work at 3 am and ended their labour at 10 pm. There were some relatively enlightened employers who had a paternalistic concern for their employees but these were rare.

The cause was taken up by the philanthropist Lord Ashley (later Lord Shaftesbury), who with fellow Evangelicals was appalled at the conditions the Committee unearthed. He introduced a far-reaching bill which the manufacturers disliked. To forestall his efforts, the government acted quickly and a Royal Commission under Edwin Chadwick, a convinced Benthamite, toured the north to gather information. It was derided by wealthy humanitarians and the working classes as a stooge of the manufacturers, and its recommendations were more modest than those proposed by Ashley.

It limited the hours which children could work in textile factories. No child under nine could be employed, those between nine and thirteen were allowed to work only between 5.30 am and 8.30 pm (a maximum of 9 hours a day, 48 hours a week) and those 13-18 were limited to 12 hours a day, 69 hours a week. Time was set aside for meals, and two hours was allowed for schooling. The bill was skilfully framed in such a way that adult work would not be limited, for by operating a relay system of children throughout the day the machines could be kept going for a long period.

However, the bill did lay down that there were to be four factory inspectors and, because they were to be civil servants, it was unlikely that they would be susceptible to local influences in making their judgements about the prosecution of those who infringed the new regulations. This was therefore the first effective factory reform, with its cautious move to central authority. It was a break with the doctrine of *laissez-faire,* for the principle that Parliament could interfere in the running of private industry was clearly established. Here was an example of Benthamite procedures being followed in the dealing with a problem, in that the pattern of investigation, legislation, and some centralised control was adopted.

The campaign of humanitarians such as Ashley ran up against the prevailing view of the political economists who stressed an individual's right to work as many hours as he wished. Here was an example of the conflict which could arise between supporters of the Whig ministry, for some Radical businessmen were unhappy with the limitations on their freedom and the departure from *laissez-faire.* Even a person sympathetic to the plight of the working classes, such as Francis Place, could reject the appeal to humanitarianism and claim that 'all legislative interference must be pernicious. Men must be left to make their own bargains'. By contrast, humanitarians saw this as an overwhelming case for government action to remove a widely acknowledged evil. It was Oastler, a Tory radical, who in a letter to the *Leeds Mercury* in 1830 had drawn a comparison with the campaign to end slavery in the West Indies, and pointed out that, 'thousands of our fellow creatures ... are at this very moment existing in a state of slavery more horrid than are the victims of that hellish system, colonial slavery'. Like other Tory Evangelicals, he was happy to score a point off the middle-class industrialists, and announced that he hated 'Whig politics with a most perfect hatred'.

9 Education

1833 was also the year in which the government for the first time interfered with the arrangements for providing education in Britain. Most elementary education was in the hands of two rival societies, the Anglican 'National Society' and the smaller, Nonconformist 'British and Foreign Society'. Ministers believed that the societies were doing a satisfactory job, but recognised the need to build more schools, for in many areas there were none at all. £20,000 was set aside for the two societies to share, as a supplement to the funds donated by their wealthy backers, and this grant, small though it was, marked the beginning of state involvement in the provision of education. However, despite this state assistance, elementary education in Britain remained woefully backward compared to that provided in countries such as Prussia and Austria. The situation was not significantly changed in 1839 when the amount of the annual grant was increased to £30,000 provided that a Committee of the Privy Council was established to supervise the spending of the money. State inspection soon followed.

Jeremy Bentham had favoured a separate state system of elementary education, free of religious involvement, for he and his supporters regarded the rivalry of the Anglicans and Nonconformists as a barrier to progress. However, it was not until 1870 that these views were largely put into practice. In the meantime, religious rivalries stopped effective action from being taken. This issue is fully discussed in Andrina Stiles' volume, *Religion, Society and Reform,* in the series.

10 The New Poor Law

The people collectively labelled as very poor (paupers) included a variety of different groups ranging from the old to the sick, the mentally defective, the disabled, the one-parent families where the main bread-winner had died, the orphans and the unemployed. Amongst them were some who may have been idle and feckless, but the vast majority were poor through circumstances beyond their control. The unemployed for instance would include the unemployable such as the disabled, those whose skill had been displaced by inventions of the Industrial Revolution and those who were the victims of cyclical fluctuations of the economy.

The extent of pauperism in the early nineteenth century is difficult to gauge and is bound up with a wider academic debate about living standards. The evidence is very partial, highly contentious, and open to propagandising by writers of differing political persuasions. However, despite the uncertainty about the statistics, there is broad agreement that poverty and hunger were widespread. In the bad years, a downturn in the business cycle could prove catastrophic and significantly increase the number of people needing help.

Relief was given to paupers under the 1601 Elizabethan Poor Law according to which each parish had responsibility for its own poor. The quality of provision varied enormously, and the scale of assistance was dependent on the particular conditions in each parish and on the way in which officials known as overseers allocated the proceeds of the local poor rate. Measures had been subsequently introduced to extend the forms of relief available, and under the 1782 Gilbert's Act parishes could unite to build workhouses, institutions to which the aged and infirm poor could be sent for basic shelter and care. Then, in 1795, the magistrates at Speenhamland in Berkshire had decided that the wages of low-paid workers could be supplemented out of the poor rates, with the amount of relief varying according to the size of the family and the cost of bread. The system (known as the Speenhamland system) was widely copied especially in the south.

The Speenhamland system was believed by the political economists of the day to be a cause of rural pauperism, in that the easy availability of assistance provided no incentive for workers to improve their own position and employers were encouraged to pay inadequate wages in the knowledge that they could be 'topped-up' by such relief. Economists argued that the natural workings of supply and demand would regulate the conditions under which men laboured and that such intervention as the Speenham system was undesirable and unnecessary. It was also expensive and nationally the costs of the scheme increased significantly from £2 million in 1795 to just under £7 million in 1831, much to the alarm of the property-owning classes who paid the bulk of the poor rate.

Grey's government set up a Royal Commission to report on the state of the Poor Law, and on it sat a number of Utilitarians as well as Whigs and Tories. They subjected the system to a searching enquiry and found it wanting. Clearly, it was due for an overhaul and drastic surgery was diagnosed as being needed.

The Commission produced seven bulky volumes of evidence which detailed numerous examples of incompetence and corruption in the running of the law. The Commission's conclusions used to be taken pretty much at face value but recent research has been critical of them. They have been seen as slanted and, according to Professor Mark Blaug ('The Poor Law Report Re-examined', *Journal of Economic History*, June 1964), 'wildly unstatistical' and unrelated to the mass of evidence collected. He has questioned whether wages were in fact driven down by the Speenhamland system (they were already very low before it got underway) and has pointed out that, far from increasing in scale as the Commission claimed, outdoor allowances were gradually dying out in many areas by the early 'thirties. However, whatever the accuracy of the picture painted in the Report, it was certainly influential and was to become 'one of the pillars of the social policy of the nineteenth century'.

In the light of the many abuses it uncovered, the Commission made far-reaching proposals for reform. It recommended the abolition of all outdoor relief (i.e., outside the workhouse) for the able-bodied. Such relief was to be confined to the sick, aged and infirm. For the able-bodied labourer seeking assistance, the workhouse was to be the answer. The principle of the workhouse test was to be applied. This was that no labourer was to receive assistance unless he and his dependants were willing to become inmates of the workhouse. Another Utilitarian principle was that of 'less eligibility', under which conditions in the workhouse were to be made sufficiently unattractive to discourage applications and to encourage every possible effort by the labourer to find work; 'Nothing is necessary to arrest the progress of pauperism except that all who receive relief from the parish should work for the parish exclusively, as hard and for less wages than independent labourers work for individual employers.'

These proposals were embodied in the Poor Law Amendment Act of 1834 (the New Poor Law), and for the purposes of its administration parishes were grouped into unions. A Board of Guardians, elected by those paying the poor rate, was given the task of supervising the administration of each poor law union. The Guardians, in turn, appointed workhouse masters to run the new workhouses.

At the centre, superintending and enforcing the new law throughout the country, were three commissioners, 'the three Bashaws of Somerset House'. Their secretary and the driving force behind the Poor Law Commission's work was the devoted Benthamite, Edwin Chadwick. The Act and its operation owed much to his intervention, and he believed it to be 'the first great piece of legislation based upon scientific or economical principles'. He proceeded to issue numerous edicts to ensure uniformity of provision.

A major problem was caused by the fact that, by the time most of the new workhouses were ready to go into operation in 1836-7, the country was just entering an economic depression and there was mounting unemployment. When the working classes realised the fate that awaited them if they fell on hard times there was outrage and indignation, and in the north where economic distress was more acute there was intense opposition to the Act. The Old Poor Law had been effective in Lancashire, and workhouses there had been generally well-run and carefully regulated. After 1834, the treatment meted out was often more harsh and in the institutions built especially for the new statute conditions were much more spartan and oppressive.

Hatred of the 'Bastilles' was intense, and those forced to seek refuge in them as a desperate last resort felt humiliated. They suffered a loss of self-respect as well as all the other hardships. The degradation led to such bitterness that many workers, already disappointed with the results of the 1832 Reform Act, turned to Chartism as an outlet for their grievances. In their campaign for political reform based on the People's Charter, Chartist leaders were easily able to arouse popular feeling by denunciations of the accursed New Poor Law.

Opposition was led by popular Radicals of the non-Benthamite kind, and a number of humanitarian Tories who disagreed with official party policy on the issue. Officially the Tories had backed the measure, but as the decade progressed many realised the scope which the 1834 Act offered them for criticising the government and blaming the often pro-Whig manufacturers who favoured it.

Whatever its limitations, the old system had provided most paupers with a basic level of social welfare, in some cases a not ungenerous one. Historians have generally been extremely critical of the arrangements which replaced it. Many of them would claim that the Poor Law Amendment Act was based on false information, in that the criticisms made by the Commission were unfair and unproven. It has been argued that the system adopted in Speenhamland was already dying out, that wages were not widely driven down by the supplements paid, and that there is no evidence that the poor had been encouraged to have large families to secure extra relief. Moreover, although it has been agreed that to encourage labourers to look for work and keep themselves out of the workhouse was all very well if work was available, it has been pointed out that in the late 1830s there was often heavy, if localised, unemployment.

Four particular criticisms have often been made.

1. The Act made no attempt to deal with the fundamental causes of destitution, but only tackled symptoms, such as the cost of relief. No attempt was made to analyse why poverty occurred.

2. Little distinction was made between different categories of pauper, such as the idle and those temporarily out of work. In implementing the

scheme of workhouses, the original plan of separate institutions for separate categories was abandoned, and all types of pauper were treated the same way.

3. The law was no answer to the sort of situation which arose in the industrial areas of the north of England. There was a great deal of short-term unemployment amongst factory workers and these people simply needed some sort of outdoor relief to tide them over while their places of work had temporarily closed down. Entry into the workhouse seemed inappropriate to their situation, so there was enormous resistance to these places when they were constructed.

4. Even if the law itself had been a reasonable solution, the way in which it was administered was monstrously inhumane. While it is true that opponents of the Act fabricated stories about events in workhouses or distorted events, there were many examples of cruelty which were substantiated, such as the events in Andover where fights broke out between hungry inmates over the possession of bone marrow when bones were crushed. Regulations were very strict in accordance with the principle of less eligibility, and there were appalling examples of sadism, petty-mindedness and greed. Husbands and wives were separated to prevent the further begetting of children, and children were isolated from parents. The institutions were run in such a way as to make life miserable, there being in most workhouses a mean regime with little scope for exercise, few visitors, a very restricted diet, and overcrowding. Too often the spirit pervading their operation was harsh and unjust. In 1836 it was Chadwick himself who issued a circular to all overseers to stop the bells from being tolled at paupers' funerals because the cost was unwarranted.

Of course, it is possible to make a case for the Act's success. It was intended to replace the diverse and inefficient practices of the old system with more uniform arrangements. This was largely achieved, with the creation of central machinery of surveillance at the national level, and by promoting unions of parishes locally. Six hundred unions provided more viable administrative machinery than 15,000 parishes. Moreover, the solution that the Act introduced - relief in the workhouse - at least offered regular food and shelter for those inside, whereas outside the institution the poor were more vulnerable to fluctuations in their ability to provide for their necessities. Above all, in that the principle of 'less eligibility' discouraged many people from seeking assistance, the burden of poor relief fell dramatically, from an average of nine shillings per person per year in 1834 to six shillings twenty years later. Certainly, the immediate results of the Act were striking in some areas. For instance, in Thingoe (Suffolk) expenditure fell from an average of £13,538 in the three years before the Act to £9,026 six years after its passing.

However, in considering the reasons for the drop in spending on poor law provision, allowance has to be made for a number of factors. There was a decline in prices over the generation after 1834 which would have lowered costs in any case. Also, the drop in expenditure was actually already happening in many areas before the Act was passed. Above all, however, is the fact that the reduction was primarily a response to better economic circumstances. When depression struck again, relief expenditure rose accordingly. For example, in Thingoe it was more than £17,500 in 1853.

The New Poor Law never did bring about the abolition of outdoor relief, and for several years many of the able-bodied still depended on it. Figures show that of more than one million paupers a decade after its introduction, the overwhelming majority received assistance outside the workhouses, and less than 200,000 within them. Overall, the 1834 Act offered an answer to the deficiencies of the Old Poor Law, but not a very satisfactory one, and its failure to tackle the problems of mass urban poverty in years of trade depression was perhaps the most serious defect. In an age of self-help, few politicians or political economists understood such issues, and it was unlikely that any government would have arrived at a solution which did not reflect the prevalent thinking of the day.

11 Grey's Resignation: Melbourne In and Out of Office

Events in Ireland were to prove the undoing of the Grey government. As early as 1832 the Prime Minister confessed that his Cabinet had been on the point of breaking up over its handling of Irish issues. There was still much discontent on the island, and in 1832 alone there were said to have been 9,000 acts of violence. In 1833 Lord Stanley, on behalf of the government, piloted through Parliament a Coercion Act aimed at stamping out disorder, but whereas he and the Prime Minister favoured a very firm approach to lawlessness, others such as Brougham, Durham and Russell wished to see a policy of moderate reform to deal with legitimate grievances.

A particular cause of discontent concerned the payment of the tithe to the established Anglican Church. Most Irishmen were Catholics and they profoundly disliked their enforced contribution to an institution of which they so disapproved. The government advanced £1 million to tithe-owners as a settlement of unpaid arrears but the tithe itself was not abolished. Instead, an Irish Church Act was passed which removed ten bishoprics (sees) and did away with a number of parishes which had no Protestant congregation. The £69,000 per annum saved from these closures was to be used to enable the government to abolish another unpopular tax, the church rate.

In 1834 there were plans to replace the tithe with a land tax which would be paid by landowners rather than by tenants. The income from this would be handed over to the clergy for ecclesiastical use, but Russell wanted to see some of it used for secular (non-religious) purposes. 'Johnny Russell has upset the coach' remarked Stanley, and he and three others in the Cabinet resigned. After further dissension on Irish matters, Grey himself resigned, for he had wearied of a situation in which ministers were unprepared to pull in the same direction. He returned to his Northumbrian estates.

Melbourne took over, but from the outset he ran into difficulties over the composition of his ministry. Althorpe, who had been an effective and much-respected leader of the House of Commons, inherited his father's seat in the Lords. The Prime Minister wanted to replace him with Russell, a choice most unpalatable to the king, William IV. The sovereign had already become disillusioned with Whig ministers and this was the last straw. Melbourne was indecisive, and when he half-proffered his resignation it was quickly accepted and the premiership was offered to Peel who took office. This effectively amounted to a dismissal, a move which many Whig sympathisers thought was unconstitutional as it seemed to go against the spirit of the Reform Act, which implied that it was the popular will in the form of the House of Commons which should decide such questions.

In February 1835 Melbourne and the Whigs made an agreement, known as the Lichfield House Compact, with the Irish in the House of Commons. The two groups were to work together to bring down the Peel government as soon as possible, and in return for Irish support in the voting lobbies a new Whig administration was to produce measures to tackle Irish grievances. Armed with such a deal, Whigs and Irishmen joined with the Radicals in relentlessly attacking the Tories, and after a series of defeats Peel resigned. Melbourne was back in office in April 1835.

a) Melbourne as Prime Minister, 1835-41

Melbourne failed to provide any reforming drive, for he did not much care for improvement. In his cynical way, he had an amused contempt for many of those who clamoured for change, and found the middle classes rather distasteful. For example, although he respected the Tory leader as a statesman, he was disdainful of his background and observed that, 'One cannot be in the same room with Peel without hearing the grinding of mill-wheels'.

In 1835 he announced that 'I am for holding the ground already taken, but not for occupying new ground rashly'. He was indifferent to the growing social demands of the late 1830s, and was largely unmoved by the coming of economic recession, the development of Chartism, and the movement to repeal the Corn Laws. He also disliked the sort of measures which some Radicals were proposing, whether it was the secret ballot or state education. This was not the time for the sort of tranquillity for which he craved, but without the talents of Brougham and Durham, who were omitted from the cabinet, there was no-one in the ministry to press for a stronger lead. Meanwhile, Melbourne was content to be 'the companion rather than the guide' of his ministers. He devoted himself not to the economic and political difficulties of the country but to the political education of the young Queen Victoria, who ascended the throne in 1837 at the age of 18, and found in Melbourne a source of fatherly guidance.

Benthamites were seeking further reform, for they wished to see efficient administration in all fields of activity, but their denunciations of waste and incompetence generally fell on deaf ears. However, their influence was to be felt in one measure which particularly stood to the credit of the Melbourne administration of 1835-41, the reform of urban local government.

b) The Municipal Corporations Act, 1835

Following logically on from the reform of government at Westminster, Grey had set up another Royal Commission in 1833 to enquire into the ramshackle state of English local government. It enquired into 285 towns with corporations established by royal charter. These varied in size from small hamlets to large centres such as Birmingham and Manchester, which had grown so rapidly during the Industrial Revolution. The commission's report was very condemnatory, and disclosed a state of inefficiency, corruption and chaos. Some towns had no council. Few councils were well-run and the overwhelming majority were administered by self-appointed oligarchs who often milked the resources of the corporation for their own personal gain. They often plundered endowments and misused the funds to hold lavish social events or to line their own pockets. Often, seats on the corporation passed from father to son. It was rare to find any evidence of an elective system, and there was a confusion of bodies with responsibility for administering particular tasks. Various authorities had been established over the years for running different services, and the boundaries of their responsibilities were often unclear.

The Municipal Corporations Act which followed publication of the report was a major measure. New borough councils were to be elected for a three-year period by all male ratepayers, a wider franchise than that which applied to parliamentary elections. The councils were to choose a mayor and aldermen, the latter forming one quarter of the council and sitting for six years. Accounts were to be made available for audit, and the new councils were allowed to assume responsibility for many areas of activity such as paving and lighting previously run by local boards.

The significance of this reform was enormous, for of the many changes which occurred in nineteenth-century England, the transformation of the English towns and cities was one of the most remarkable. This Act laid down the basis for such changes over much of the country, and inaugurated the system of municipal administration which prevailed into the late twentieth century. To the Radical Parkes it was a 'smasher', and other Benthamites were pleased to see a further instalment of uniformity and efficiency in public life. Dissenters and other representatives of middle-class opinion shared in the pleasure that a parallel transfer of power was to occur in local government as had been brought about nationally. The Act was the logical outcome of reform in 1832, and echoed its spirit and provisions by creating a more uniform pattern of electoral qualifications and systems, and by removing ancient abuses and traditions. But, of course, it did not apply to rural areas, where the major landowners continued to hold sway.

c) Other Melbourne Reforms

After 1835 the Whigs ran out of steam, and the scale and pace of reform slackened. However, there were some measures worthy of brief consideration, notably the Registration of Births, Marriages and Deaths Act of 1836. This enabled factory inspectors to enforce the 1833 legislation more effectively, as in future the age of young workers would be known, and the accurate statistics concerning the population were to be helpful in formulating other legislation. The Marriage Act of the same year allowed people to be married in church or chapel, or before a Registrar. This pleased the Dissenters who were thereby free to marry other than in an Anglican Church. The reduction by ministers of the stamp duty on newspapers and periodicals from fourpence to one penny was another welcome reform. The original increase had been imposed by the Tory government to counter Radical propaganda in the years after 1815.

Still in 1836, the Companies Act for the first time allowed the formation of limited liability companies, in which shareholders would not be responsible for all the losses if a business enterprise failed. Many railway companies did fail in the 'railway mania' which quickly followed, but the limitation of liability meant that there was more incentive for those who were prepared to invest in new projects.

The 1830s saw a great interest in the subject of Church reform. The United Committee of Dissenters was looking for concessions. Dissenters felt that they suffered from the privileged position of the Anglicans, and had backed the establishment of a Royal Commission into the financing of the Church. As a result of this and other enquiries the Established Church Act was passed in 1836. It defined the territorial responsibilities of the bishops, and laid down new regulations concerning financial administration - in particular, it did something to supplement the stipend (salary) of poorer parish priests. Ecclesiastical Commissioners were appointed to supervise the implementation of the changes.

A number of Radicals were unhappy with what had been done, for they wanted to see the disestablishment of the Church of England; they saw it as privileged, affluent and corrupt. Many Dissenters were less concerned about these failings than about achieving parity of esteem.

They wanted to see their religious disabilities removed, and welcomed the measures above, as they did the replacement of the tithe by a money payment and the opening of London University as a non-sectarian body, both in 1836. It is difficult for us to appreciate the amount of time spent on discussing Church issues in the 1830s, but this was a reflection of the interest that Church matters aroused in the towns and cities up and down the country. Nonconformists had an obvious interest in keeping the issue alive, and as we have seen there was a strong connection between religious Dissent and political radicalism.

In 1840 the Penny Post was established, thanks largely to the efforts of Rowland Hill, who had advocated the use of an adhesive stamp in his publication, *Post Office Reform; its Importance and Practice.* As a result of the new system, the Post Office experienced a great increase in its business, and trade and commerce, as well as social letter writing, received a notable boost. Also in 1840, a Railway Act introduced a greater degree of regulation over the development of railway companies, an illusration of the greater willingness of the Whigs to use powers of central control as events made it desirable.

There was also a series of useful legal changes, several associated with the Lord Chancellor, Brougham. Following on from Peel's earlier reform of the criminal code, the Whigs had in 1832 further reduced the number of capital offences, and since 1838 no-one in Britain has been hanged except for treason, murder or (to 1861) attempted murder. As a result of a government enquiry into the operation of prisons in 1835, some improvements were made by the Home Secretary, Russell, to allow more productive work, better conditions and more effective inspection. Finally, in 1839, the findings of a Royal Commission led to the adoption of a police system over the whole country, a recognition of the value of the Metropolitan Police created in London ten years before.

12 A Loss of Reforming Zeal?

With the exception of the Municipal Corporations Act, the reforming measures of the Melbourne era were generally less spectacular and lacked the significance of those of Lord Grey's premiership. Yet as Disraeli later observed, 'the measures of the Melbourne Government were generally moderate, well-matured and statesmanlike schemes', and Gladstone found that whereas Peel was not noted for 'general legislation' the period from 1835-41 'had witnessed the enactment of many important laws, useful in their general character and well-suited to the condition of the public mind'. The reforms compare favourably with the work of other administrations of the reformed Parliament, 1832-67, other than Peel's Second Ministry of 1841-6. However, compared to the triumphant period of 1832-5, there is no doubt that the changes appear to be mainly small-scale and useful, rather than wide-ranging and fundamental. Why had the reforming impetus been so much weaker during the Melbourne years?

The amount of reform was not much more than the basic minimum which many Whig supporters expected, for their hopes had been aroused by the earlier wave of innovation. But it was about what the majority in the House of Commons thought prudent, for Peelite Tories and conservative Whig ministers were broadly agreed on what needed to be done, and they carried between them more votes than did the remnants of the Whig coalition of earlier years. In addition, ministers were handicapped by their lack of parliamentary strength after the 1835 election, so even if they had been disposed to produce more far-reaching measures, they might have found insufficient backing for them.

However, it is very doubtful whether Lord Melbourne wanted to do much more, for at heart he was a dilettante and was not committed to active political leadership. Disraeli caught something of his outlook in describing him as 'sauntering over the destinies of a nation and lounging away the glories of an Empire'. Like Peel, he believed in maintaining the Conservative Cause, for before the term became isolated to be associated with one party, he was a statesman who believed in the maintenance of the social and political order, with the propertied classes making enough 'timely concessions to assuage discontent' (Southgate).

Even if he had wanted to do more and had possessed the requisite support in the House of Commons, the House of Lords would have been a barrier to innovation. Although the peers had suffered a setback in 1832, their resistance was not weakened by defeat. They mutilated or blocked a number of Irish bills and caused major difficulties over the reform of local government. Although Russell was attracted to the idea of teaching the Second Chamber a lesson, most other Whigs preferred a quieter life. With parliamentary reform out of the way, it was their opinion that there was no major issue worthy of another daunting constitutional struggle, and most ministers wished to avoid creating one.

In this they differed from the Radicals, their former allies, who wished to continue with the earlier pace of reform and to prod ministers into more active government. They saw Melbourne as a man out of place in a more democratic age. Whereas he wanted a quiet life, they wanted to keep politics alive. The Radicals and Whigs became increasingly antagonistic to each other as the decade progressed, but the Radical voice was often an ineffective one. Lacking in unity and recognised leadership, they fought desultory and unco-ordinated skirmishes, and in Southgate's words, 'their trumpets sounded, but the walls stood firm; they rarely sounded in perfect harmony'.

The Whig coalition had never been a cohesive one. The mixture of aristocratic Whigs and middle-class Radicals was an unlikely blend, made even more so when it received an infusion of Irish support. It was difficult for ministers to hold it together, and they were unable or unwilling to act firmly to do so. Often, they were unwilling to subordinate their own preferences in favour of a team approach, and

Melbourne was disinclined to lay down a firm line. As for the Radicals, he refused to take them seriously; he denied advancement to Lord Durham, who was a frustrated would-be leader of the radical cause.

The obstacles to reform were considerable - a slim majority in the House of Commons, dependence on the Irish for votes, obstruction by a hostile Lords, internal party schism - these were daunting problems for any government. Given the lack of energetic leadership, the wonder is not their failure to achieve more; it is that they managed to accomplish so many useful, if modest, changes.

13 The Whigs and Working-Class Discontent

We have seen that the Whigs were fearful of popular unrest and had dealt with the situation in 1830 in a firm, even repressive, manner. Then they had become embroiled in the passing of the Reform Act which placed them on the side of those who were working for reform, during which time they had been able to imply that it was the Tory enemy which blocked progress on parliamentary change. However, when the results of the 1832 Act became apparent, working-class Radical leaders felt that they had been betrayed and denounced the measure as a fraud against the people.

The years that followed were ones of recurrent economic difficulty and, particularly in 1836-7, there was widespread unemployment. This was just at the time when the New Poor Law was becoming operative, and intense dislike of the workhouses and frustration over 1832 combined to interest the workers in Chartism as a way forward to remedy their grievances. The six points of the People's Charter were the focal point of a radical campaign for parliamentary reform which was seen as the prerequisite for further social and economic improvement. The Charter was published in 1838, and the fortunes of the movement based around it fluctuated considerably over the following decade. For a fuller discussion of the subject, Clive Behagg's volume in this series (*Labour and Reform*) is an invaluable guide.

Another contributory cause of Chartism was the failure of attempts at organised trade unionism. In the early 1830s, there were several large unions but the one which caused particular anxiety was that formed by the enlightened factory owner, Robert Owen, known as the Grand National Consolidated Trade Union (GNCTU). It quickly gained widespread support, and ministers took fright. Some would have liked to ban union activity, but instead the Home Secretary dealt severely with those who were easy victims, by way of making an example. Six farm labourers in Tolpuddle, Dorset, were arrested for the technical offence of swearing an illegal oath, and sentenced by the magistrates to seven years' transportation. There was much sympathy for the six martyrs, sober and God-fearing Methodists, and eventually after a campaign of protest they were pardoned and brought back from Australia.

Their fate well illustrates the attitude of the Whigs to the position of trade unions; they were alarmed by their activities, fearing any popular movement which they could not control. The Tolpuddle Martyrs were perhaps the most famous victims of governmental repression, but around the country there were other members of the GNCTU who were charged with 'molestation' or 'illegal conspiracy'. Melbourne was viewed with distrust by working people, for he was uncharacteristically active in the bid to clamp down on the trade union challenge.

14 The Decline of the Whigs

After the spate of reform in the early 1830s, the Whigs had by the end of the decade lost momentum. Most of their reforming mission had been accomplished, though they continued to provide useful measures whilst in office until 1841. The country's trading position deteriorated, and the 1837 election, in which the Whigs lost their majority in England and Wales, showed that ministers were losing support, increasingly reliant on the backing of Scottish and Irish MPs and Peel's responsible approach to opposition. By 1841, they were described as,

> 1 absolutely without a chief, hating, distrusting, despising one another, having no principles and on plans, living from hand to mouth, able to do nothing, and indifferent whether they did anything or not, proposing measures without the hope or the
> 5 expectation of carrying them, and clinging to their places for no other reason than that they felt themselves bound to the Queen.

As the deficit in the national finances increased, Peel derided the Chancellor as 'seated on an empty chest ... fishing for a budget'.

Melbourne had tried to resign in 1839, but when Peel tried to insist that the queen should appoint some Tories as 'Ladies of the Bedchamber', her refusal led to his unwillingness to take over. Melbourne continued for two years more, and then dissolved the House in 1841. Despite the offer of a radical change to modernise the Corn Laws, the Whigs lost the election.

15 Reflections on the Whigs and their Reforms

a) The Whig Approach, and the Influences upon Ministers

When the Whigs assumed power the time was ripe for a major period of social and administrative reform. There had been important constitutional measures before 1830, but often they had been pressed on the Tory Government and passed with some reluctance, as in the case of Repeal of the Test and Corporation Acts and Catholic Emancipation. Of the social improvements of the 'Liberal Tory' era in the twenties, a few were passed against the wishes of ministers, and some were a response to the findings of all-party committees. In other words, though useful changes were made, they were in most cases piecemeal and not part of a wide-ranging policy of innovation.

The Whigs were generally more sympathetic to reform, though not strongly committed to individual measures. They prided themselves on their attachment to civil and religious liberty, but did not come to power armed with a ready programme of legislative action to translate such a belief into practice. However, they could recognise that something had to be done, especially over parliamentary reform, and realised that expectations were high among the populace that this would be but the forerunner to other developments.

Some ministers were motivated by fear as much as by broad sympathy for 'improvement', for the situation in the country was tense and uneasy, but whatever their own doubts about embarking on a programme of sweeping change they were open to persuasion. In the years up to 1834 particularly, individuals and groups found that they could work with Whig ministers to attain their objectives, and any allocation of credit for what was achieved must recognise the influence of various 'interests' at this time - the middle-class manufacturers, the humanitarians, the religious Nonconformists and the Philosophical Radicals.

The Radicals were a small but important group, broadly on the Left of the Whig coalition. They tended to be forward-looking and fairly well in touch with the wishes of the people. Later in the decade they took up popular causes, such as Chartism or the Anti-Corn Law League. Often these Radicals were industrialists or men of commerce, and the more enlightened manufacturers were convinced that philanthropy and the pursuit of profit could coincide. Robert Owen, a factory owner himself, was certain that factories could be well-run and successful, on the basis of providing good working conditions for those who were employed in them; he similarly favoured provision for popular education. Many other manufacturers who thought of themselves as Radicals were unenthusiastic about legislation to curb long working hours, and their attitude to factory reform in 1833 illustrates their anxieties.

The humanitarian influence on many Whig reforms is evident in a number of cases, particularly over the abolition of slavery, factory reform and the first tentative moves towards state involvement in education. 'Humanitarians' were sometimes Tory Radicals who had the satisfaction of being able to attack Whig ministers for their attitude to social conditions. Often, they were religious evangelicals, who had a burning social conscience; men such as the Tory Lord Ashley felt that, born to privilege himself, he had a moral duty to work to mitigate the plight of those less fortunately placed in society. Wilberforce was another who shared the view that society could be improved by the action of individuals who had an obligation to work for the betterment of its citizens. Many Methodists and other Dissenters, coming from the lower-middle and respectable working classes, helped to fire the consciences of reformers and themselves fought against obvious social injustices.

Philosophical Radicals or Utilitarians were a distinctive grouping. Though their initial preference was for *laissez-faire,* they came to recognise that when their test of utility was applied in many areas of public life there was a need for government action and regulation, and as time went on they became more associated with the idea of uniformity, efficiency and central control. Their distinctive contribution was evident in the areas of factory reform, the new poor law and municipal reform, and over the coming years they were to become associated with other interventionist legislation.

Chadwick and some of his colleagues saw value in co-operating with the Whigs, for even though they anticipated no dynamic leadership from ministers, at least they were able to conduct their own detailed research which could be used to persuade the government of the merits of legislation. They were an influential voice in the Royal Commissions of which the Whigs made extensive use to analyse a problem and make recommendations. These disciples of Bentham argued their case forcefully on such Commissions, and often had a very influential effect on the subsequent report, as over the Poor Law and the overhaul of municipal government. In establishing this pattern of investigation, the Whigs were setting the trend for a procedure which was to be employed regularly by mid-Victorian parliaments. They realised, at an early stage, that if they packed the enquiry with persons sympathetic to their own outlook, they would get the findings they wanted to hear. For example, the commission which examined the state of local corporations was peopled by men already committed to a particular type of reform.

b) The Reforms Themselves

The reforms were often limited in scope, and it is easy to identify their inadequacies. The Great Reform Act provided no solution to the corruption endemic in the voting system, and after its passage still only one in five adult men could vote. On social issues, from the beginning ministers were intent on suppressing signs of discontent, and it was Melbourne who, as Home Secretary, transported the Tolpuddle Martyrs. The Tory paternalism of Lord Ashley and others offered more prospect of action to help the working classes than did the Whigs, with their preference for *laissez-faire.* Their factory reform left adults working excessively long hours, and working conditions were still often highly unpleasant and in many cases unsafe. They offered no solution to meet the Chartist challenge of the late 1830s, by which time Whig reform had all but died away.

If some things had been left untouched, many would find that one area of activity would have been better left undone. The Poor Law

Amendment Act is widely seen as obnoxious in its original form, and contemporary critics found it brutal and inhumane. Many working-class Radicals had become very disillusioned with the ministry by the end of the decade, and had become convinced that the government was not really receptive to their 'advanced' opinions.

Yet against this view there are other considerations. Working-class leaders might have become dispirited and attacked the reforms from the progressive side. On the Right of British politics, there were others, especially some Tory Peers, who found most of them unpalatable, and the 1832 Act had been particularly offensive to them. It was a middle-of-the-road, safe and cautious approach rather than a boldly experimental one which Ministers put forward. If it was criticised by people at either end of the political spectrum, it nonetheless enabled the country to move steadily forward along an evolutionary path of political and social progress.

Moreover, the reforms have to be seen in the light of what had previously been done. The Whig changes were more wide-ranging and fundamental than those which had gone before, and in sheer volume alone were an impressive package. Rather than just disenfranchising particular boroughs, the whole system of representation had been tackled. Rather than abolishing the slave trade, important though that was, the whole system of slavery in British possessions had been eradicated. In many other areas, useful measures had been accomplished, and if they only marked the first step on the road to reform they provided foundations upon which other developments could follow; factory reform, reform in national and local government, and the growth of state intervention in education were all inevitably going to be taken further now that the flood-gates of reform had been opened.

Macaulay portrayed the nineteenth century as 'the history of physical, moral and intellectual improvement'. The period was indeed an 'Age of Reform', in which civil and political rights were extended, government became more democratic and the worst abuses of those who worked in factories and mines were removed. It is fair to say that it was the Whig ministers and their allies of the 1830s who can be viewed as the effective instigators of that period of transformation.

Making notes on *'The Whigs Reformers, 1830-41'*

Your aims in making notes on this chapter should be to equip yourself with enough basic information to understand the motives of the Whigs as reformers and to familiarise yourself with several key reforms. You would be wise to check back to the previous chapter to acquaint yourself with the leading Whig politicians and their outlook. You could make a list of them and summarise their approach. From this chapter especially, ensure that you have sections on Grey and

Melbourne, their strengths and limitations.

Parliamentary reform is an important area of study in itself and needs to be fully covered; useful headings might be:

Why reform was needed
The Whig and Tory approach to reform
Details of the changes made
The results of the changes

You should be familiar with the other main Whig reforms which in this case are best approached chronologically; your notes should cover the reforms of 1833-5, with a section perhaps on other changes such as those affecting the Church and the legal system. In each case, be clear about why the act was necessary, and how effective it was in dealing with the problem it attempted to solve. Try to identify what the approach to the handling of the individual reform tells you about the attitude to reform of the Whigs in general. For each measure, try also to identify what influences were at work in its passing - humanitarian impulses, a desire for economy, the influence of the Benthamites etc.

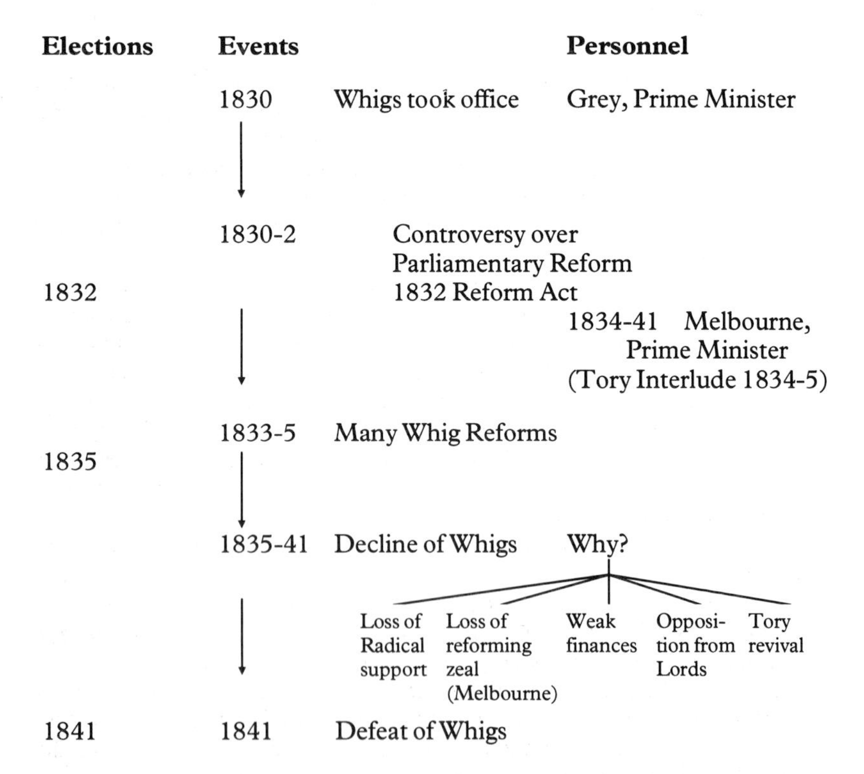

Summary - The Whig Reformers, 1830-41

Answering essay questions on *'The Whigs Reformers, 1830-41'*

Frequently questions are set on the single issue of parliamentary reform. The question may invite you to assess the extent to which the 1832 Act righted the anomalies of the unreformed system, but a more probing one would be, 'In what ways was the 1832 Reform Act an essentially conservative measure?'. The danger is that the candidate sees the words 'Reform Act' and immediately writes at length on the problems before 1832, and the details of the Act and of its passing, before coming to realise that much time has been wasted - for the question has not been tackled. The key task is to discuss the word 'conservative' in relation to the Act. Decide what it means in this context. Perhaps the Act was conservative in two senses;

1. It was not very radical or far-reaching; i.e., modest in scope
2. Its purpose was a conservative one, namely to preserve the existing form of society which emphasised the importance of rank and property in safeguarding the country against revolutionary change.

Quotations can be useful and add weight to your case. But be sure that the point of the remark is evident; you achieve this by keeping it brief and to the point. Quotes can be especially useful in the introduction and conclusion, perhaps being used to compare the approaches of historians to the subject under discussion - showing that you appreciate that history is a matter of interpretation of evidence, and that different experts have different viewpoints.

More general questions on the Whig reforms are common. You might be asked to comment on the view that the Whigs were 'reluctant reformers'. Here, you would need to dwell on the Whig motives for reform. Were they concessions, born of a desire to maintain society in its existing form, or changes born of genuine conviction? Did all Whigs have the same approach? You would need to think about other groups who worked through the Whig ministries and pressed changes upon them. Does a study of individual measures suggest that they were limited in extent, reflecting a cautious attitude to affairs?

You might be invited to decide whether 'the reforming impetus of the Whigs was exhausted by 1835'. You will have seen that most major reforms were carried out by then. Why was this? Was it because of such factors as a declining parliamentary majority as the 1830s progressed, a gradual loss of Radical backing, fear of resistance in the House of Lords, and a lack of money because of the state of Whig finances, or was it because they had already carried out so wide-ranging a programme that further reform was unnecessary or undesirable? Do not forget the prevailing view of minimal governmental intervention.

Finally, a question might refer to the motives for reform. 'Were the Whig reforms of 1833-41 the result of enlightened humanitarianism or a reflection of the needs of a middle-class electorate? (or indeed of some other consideration, such as a zeal for economy or administrative efficiency)'. If you have done as suggested in making notes, you should have a clear idea of the influences behind particular reforms. Remember that sometimes the backers of the Whig ministries wanted different things. For example, Radical industrialists were often less than enthusiastic about the demands of philanthropists for restrictions on employment in the mines and factories. Neither did they like the Benthamite emphasis on the merits of central inspection.

Source-based questions on *'The Whigs Reformers, 1830-41'*

1 Parliamentary Reform

Read again the extracts on pages 26, 27, 27-8, 28-9 and the section on the details of the 1832 Reform Act. Answer the following questions.

a) Compare the case made out by Palmerston for reform in the debate on the Reform Bill with that expressed by Grey. (4 marks)
b) What differences do you detect in the attitudes of Grey, Melbourne and Macaulay to the middle classes? (4 marks)
c) In what way was 'property' the key to the Whig approach to the question of reform? (4 marks)
d) What was the significance of Brougham's observation? Why could they be viewed as being more radical than the approach of Grey? (4 marks)
e) From the evidence presented, how accurate would it be to claim that fear was an important Whig motive for reform? (4 marks)
f) To what extent was the 1832 Act in line with Grey's preference (as expressed in 1817) for 'gradual reform ... limited to the necessity which has proved it to be wanting? (5 marks)

2 Benthamism and the Whig Reforms

Study the extracts on pages 18, 26 and 27-8 and the coverage given to the relevant reforms. Answer the following questions.

a) What did Bentham mean by the principle of 'utility'? (3 marks)
b) How could the 'utility' principle be used to justify the growth of intervention by the central government? (4 marks)
c) Compare the sentiments in Grey's speech of 1817 with the views expressed by Bentham. How might their approaches to the system of representation have differed? (5 marks)
d) What were the differences between Macaulay and Bentham in their general thinking about the issue of reform? (4 marks)
e) Why might the Benthamites have been expected to favour i) The spread of popular education and ii) the reform of municipal corporations? (4 marks) f) In what ways was the new poor law of 1834 a typical Benthamite measure? (5 marks)

CHAPTER 4

From Whigs to Liberals, 1841-68

1 Introduction

For two decades after the repeal of the Corn Laws in 1846, politics was in a confused state. The Whig coalition which had seemed strong in the early 1830s had by the mid-1840s lost much of its cohesion, and the Conservatives, in office after 1841, had been seriously divided by the events of 1846. After the crisis surrounding repeal it was difficult to identify distinctive differences between the parties, for events were determined more by the fortunes of individuals - Peel and Disraeli on the Conservative side, and Palmerston, Russell and Gladstone on the other - than by policies.

There were no great issues around which politicians could unite, ones which divided the forces of progress from the forces of reaction. On parliamentary reform, the Crimean War of 1854-6 and the American Civil War of 1861-5, the key personalities took up positions which had little to do with party allegiances. In such a situation, where boundaries were so blurred, governments could not count on the support of the backbenchers who were nominally on their side. As a result, there was much cross-voting and ministries were more often brought down by defeat in the House of Commons than by the electorate in a general election.

In this era of 'twenty years' delay', the Whigs, or rather Whig personalities, particularly Palmerston and Russell, dominated the administrations which were created. Predominantly aristocratic in temperament as well as in social status, they were keen to preserve their privileged position in society and were unlikely to embark on major changes. Landowning magnates continued to monopolise Cabinet positions throughout the period of Palmerston, Aberdeen and Russell, much to the dismay of some radical backbenchers and middle-class industrialists who resented their own exclusion from real influence. However, the public appeared to be willing to accept aristocratic control. Walter Bagehot, the contemporary political commentator, put it in this way in *The English Constitution:* 'The English constitution in its palpable form is this - the mass of the people yield obedience to a select few'.

The Radicals, many of whom had become increasingly alienated from Whig leaders, remained divided. They were a diverse bunch. One of their great thinkers, John Stuart Mill, the Benthamite intellectual, warned about the dangers of democracy if the franchise was widened too much. John Bright was a committed reformer who wanted to see the vote greatly extended. He wished to end the predominance of the landed interest, and was willing to work with any party or politician who might provide reform. Others hesitated over the pace of further change, and divisions were also apparent on matters of foreign policy. Some were anti-Russian and supported Palmerston's vigorous championing of British interests by whatever means were necessary. Others followed Cobden and Bright in their opposition to war and their pursuit of the goal of international peace.

The grouping which was particularly important was the Peelite one. Its members were in a quandary after Peel's death in 1850. They found Disraeli's conversion to free trade (made official in 1852) unconvincing, and were acutely aware of his lack of principle and political opportunism - points which the Whigs were happy to reinforce. Gladstone, in particular, could not forgive Disraeli his attacks on Peel, but neither was he (in common with his Peelite colleagues) much attracted to the Whigs. As a High Churchman, he disliked the anti-clericalism of some Whig leaders and the latitudinarian (free-thinking) approach of others. He especially disliked the way in which Palmerston and Russell handled questions of foreign policy. He found their conduct almost as opportunistic and unprincipled as Disraeli's. As a result, Gladstone agonised over the choice of party and remained in the political wilderness for many years. Ultimately, however, in the late 1850s, he and the remaining Peelites threw in their lot with the Whigs, so that by the beginning of the next decade the scene was almost set for a more clear-cut divide between the Liberal forces of progress and the Conservatives - between Gladstone and Disraeli.

The most important factor which delayed the full *rapprochement* between the Whigs and the Peelites was the continued predominance of Palmerston. Palmerston was doubtful of the wisdom of further domestic change. Therefore, while he presided over national affairs, British domestic politics were generally uneventful for he wished to avoid any contentious measures. That slumber was broken by his death in 1865, when a new phase in British politics began. The era of Whigs, Peelites and Protectionists was over and the age of Gladstone and Disraeli was about to dawn.

2 General Developments, 1846-67

The Whigs combined with the Radicals and Protectionists to defeat Peel after the Repeal of the Corn Laws in 1846, and it was Russell who succeeded him as Prime Minister. He formed a free-trade ministry, with an input from the Radicals on the Left and the Peelites on the Right. The government was re-elected in 1847 against a divided Conservative opposition, and the ministry lasted until 1852. It was able to pass useful measures on public health in 1848, and factory reform in 1847 and 1850.

The government's fall was brought about by Palmerston in a famous tit-for-tat with Russell, after Russell had dismissed him a year earlier. A brief Conservative interlude - a minority ministry which stood no realistic chance of surviving for long - was followed by a Whig-Peelite coalition headed by Lord Aberdeen. This was a talented ministry, with Palmerston at the Home Office, Russell (initially) at the Foreign Office, Gladstone at the Treasury, and with prominent positions given to other Peelites such as Graham and Herbert. However, the disappointing conduct of the Crimean War, which it had stumbled into in 1854, destroyed the government. Reports of maladministration and dissatisfaction with the leadership culminated in a successful parliamentary motion of censure in 1855.

Palmerston was seen by many as the only person capable of heading the war effort. 'I am, for the moment, *l'inevitable'*, he gleefully observed. Disraeli was unconvinced and caught something of the spirit of the man with his description of him as 'voluble ... pert ... at best only ginger beer and not champagne'. The Peelites also doubted his quality and quickly deserted the new prime minister. However, Palmerston speedily brought hostilities to a successful conclusion. He then won the 1857 general election handsomely and continued in office until his ministry was brought down in early 1858. By that time his high-handed manner in the Commons had aroused much resentment.

Governments of the Period 1841-67

Date	**Prime Minister**	**Predominant Party**
1841-6	Sir Robert Peel	Conservative
1846-52	Lord Russell	Whig
1852	Lord Derby	Conservative
1852-5	Lord Aberdeen	Whig-Peelite
1855-8	Lord Palmerston	Whig
1858-9	Lord Derby	Conservative
1859-65	Lord Palmerston	Whig-Liberal
1865-6	Lord Russell	Whig-Liberal
1866-8	Lord Derby	Conservative

Following a brief Derby-Disraeli administration in 1858-9, Palmerston was back again as Prime Minister. This was something of a watershed in British politics, for by now divisions had become more polarised. The Liberal Party is often said to have come into being as a result of the meeting at Willis' Room in June 1859, when the Whigs were joined by the Radicals and remaining Peelites such as Gladstone over the Italian Question. They faced the Conservatives of Lord Derby who in the main comprised the former Protectionist element of Peel's party.

The Liberal coalition was not always an easy one to lead. Palmerston was mainly interested in foreign affairs and lacked an interest in innovation at home, while Gladstone, who was growing in influence, was becoming markedly more liberal, and many Radicals such as Bright were full of plans for reform. However, the ministry lasted until Palmerston's death in 1865. He was the last prime minister to expire in office and did so memorably, supposedly remarking at the last, 'Die, my dear fellow, that's the last thing I will do'. The Whig-Liberal leadership passed to Russell, by then a sick man, until the government fell over parliamentary reform in 1866.

It was obvious that Gladstone was now the most suitable man to lead the Liberal forces. The Whigs, a surprisingly resilient element, were soon to find their new leader too bold and daring, but Gladstone's attraction for some of the younger Radicals was enormous. He was a politician of undoubted genius. Palmerston had warned; 'Wait till I'm dead. If Gladstone gets my place, you'll see some strange things'. Gladstone had taken his place, and was now, in his own word, 'unmuzzled'.

In any study of mid-Victorian Liberalism three politicians stand out - Palmerston, Russell and the emerging Gladstone. But before we turn to each in turn it is necessary to say a word about the Radicals, that diverse grouping whose members frequently featured in the politics of the era.

3 Mid-Victorian Radicalism

Many working-class Radicals had despaired of the parliamentary approach after the disappointment of the 1832 Reform Act and had devoted their energies to the Chartist or trade union movements. As a result, although there was a small group of Philosophical Radicals, typical of whom were intellectuals such as John Stuart Mill, the Radical tradition was mainly represented in Parliament by middle-class industrialists who were often Dissenters. Throughout the mid-Victorian period business and religion provided the main impulse of Radicalism, which was still primarily an individualistic creed, favouring *laissez-faire* economics and the removal of governmental restrictions on all aspects of life.

Richard Cobden (1804-65) and John Bright (1811-89) were foremost among the Radical industrialists of northern England. They and others from the new manufacturing classes made up the so-called 'Manchester School' which flourished from the 1840s onwards and was committed to free trade, *laissez-faire* and international collaboration rather than conflict. Both men had been active in the Anti-Corn Law League, Cobden as the mastermind behind its strategy, and Bright as its great campaigner. Cobden employed his reason to persuade people, Bright relied more on his emotion. They co-operated together in Parliament for 24 years, from 1841 until Cobden's death.

Coming from a Quaker background, Bright had an abhorrence of bloodshed and though he ceased to be identified with Quakerism and accepted the necessity of war in certain circumstances, he had a strongly internationalist belief in the importance of free trade as a means of promoting goodwill between nations. Like Cobden he lost the support of many of his fellow-manufacturers over his opposition to the Crimean conflict, and he was denounced by Palmerston for his 'peace at any price' approach. However, after a period of quiescence his career blossomed again as a leader of responsible working-class opinion, and in the 1860s he was a key figure on the left of the Liberal Party.

Bright was a spokesman for 'popular' Radicalism, and his speeches adopted a notably anti-aristocratic tone. He wished to end the supremacy of the landed interest, and disliked Conservatism 'be it Tory or be it Whig ... the true national peril ... we have to face'. His antipathy to the upper classes was evident from his frequent criticism of the short-sightedness and folly of those who sought to 'dam the stream', and he asserted that the time would come when 'the waters will burst their banks, and these men, who fancy they are stemming this imaginary apparition of democracy, will be swept away by the resolute will of a united and determined people'.

He disapproved of trade unions and the idea of mob rule, but he saw in the working people a source of national strength. His rhetoric, simple, moralistic and moving, won him widespread support and struck some fear into the minds of the Whigs, one of whom said that he felt 'an almost unconquerable desire to give him a good thrashing'. Yet Bright was never likely to become a popular leader himself, for he was disliked and distrusted even by some fellow Radicals, who found him too ambitious, too full of his self-importance, and in one case, a 'silver-tongued old hypocrite'.

Bright's most significant political contribution in the 1860s was in preparing the way for Gladstone's leadership, hence John Vincent's portrayal of him as the 'John the Baptist of Gladstonian Liberalism'. He and Cobden regarded Gladstone as the most reform-minded member of the Cabinet, and Bright believed that Palmerston and Russell were 'full of the traditions of the last century ... a wiser and a higher morality are sighed for by the best of our people, and there is a prevalent feeling that you [Gladstone] are destined to guide that wise policy and to teach that higher morality'. He saw Gladstone as the key link between Westminster and the people, and was prepared to stump the country in the 1860s to popularise his achievements and to help establish his reputation.

4 Lord Palmerston (1784-1865)

Born Henry John Temple, Viscount Palmerston succeeded to his title in 1802, but as an Irish Peer he was eligible to remain in the Commons. There he sat as an MP for five different constituencies in his long career from 1807 to 1865, his time in the House spanning the age from Fox to Gladstone. He was a member of every administration between 1809 and his death, with the exception of those of Peel and Derby. He began his political career as a Tory. At the War Office (1809-28) he was noted for his immense energy, his power of sustained industry and his ability to master complex problems. But, although he was diligent and efficient, his was not an outstanding or original talent so that, in Canning's judgement, he only reached 'the summit of mediocrity'. He had an undoubted gift for negotiation, but was intellectually shallow, and in the early years he was seen by many contemporaries as more of a social figure than a politician with a future.

In 1828 he left the Tory Party along with Huskisson, for he was a Canningite of enlightened sympathies and found Wellingtonian Toryism unpalatable. Indeed, he saw the Tories as the 'stupid party', in that they did not know when it was time to yield on topics such as Catholic emancipation and parliamentary reform. He joined the Whigs, although he was never to be a strong party man. Despite this, he was to become a remarkably popular figure in the country, and at Westminster he had an impressive record of ministerial office.

He was always young at heart, and even into old age could still be taken for someone considerably younger than he was, not least because he always dyed his whiskers rather than look aged. He acquired the nickname 'Lord Cupid', which referred not only his good looks but also to the fact that he maintained a lively interest in women. This he did until extreme old age, even bed-hopping in Buckingham Palace to the horror of Queen Victoria. 'Lord Pumicestone' - his other popular nickname - referred to a different side of his personality - the way in which he treated others, especially foreign diplomats, to the rough edge of his tongue. He was not aware of any need to conciliate those with whom he dealt. He could be brusque and aggressive, and he was jaunty in manner. He bristled with the arrogance and self-assurance of the aristocracy.

Yet for all his truculence there was a redeemingly generous side. For example, in 1818 he paid counsel to conduct the defence of a mad lieutenant who tried to kill him when he was at the War Office! His energy was proverbial. He rarely slept for more than four hours a night, he wrote his despatches by hand, and he was in the habit of jumping over the railings of his London home even when he had reached his early eighties. In 1864 he was still capable of making a speech of nearly four hours in length into the early hours of the morning, and then, when he had finished and won the vote, of running up the steps of the Ladies Gallery to receive the plaudits of Lady Palmerston. Not only was he never much of a party figure but neither was he a good House of Commons man - he attended only under pressure. Although he was capable of performing effectively in debate, he was often a poor speaker.

a) Palmerston and Foreign Policy

It is as Foreign Secretary (1830-41 and 1846-51), and Prime Minister dealing with overseas issues (1855-8 and 1859-65) that Palmerston is best remembered. Foreign policy is dealt with in detail in another volume of in the series. It will be sufficient here to make a few general observations about Palmerston's policy which explain not only his broad outlook but the reasons for his popularity in the country.

Convinced that he was better informed than any of his fellow ministers, he wanted to exert personal control over foreign policy; he had no doubt of the direction he intended to follow. He was determined to secure British interests and cheerfully used any means to promote this end. Like Canning, he was a nationalist, keen to avoid European entanglements, for Britain was 'a power sufficiently strong to steer her own course and not tie herself as an unnecessary appendage to the policy of any other government'. He suggested the basis of his policy in 1848 when he spoke of his wish 'to maintain peace and friendly understanding with all nations, as long as it is possible to do so consistently with a due regard to the interests, honour and dignity of this country'. He was keen to quote Canning's maxim that 'with every British minister the interests of England ought to be the shibboleth of his policy'.

He was a stout defender of liberal regimes abroad, and sought to promote constitutional and free government; he generally backed liberal rebellions against tyrannous regimes and believed it was prudent for rulers to avert revolution by timely concessions. Britain was to be the 'champion of justice and right, pursuing that course with moderation and prudence'.

The views were not particularly exceptional in themselves, and many people in Victorian England would have shared his vigorous defence of British interests and his broad sympathy for the new spirit of nationalism abroad. That he was alive to those national movements and their significance was to his credit, but what was more doubtful was the way in which he implemented his approach. It was not the theory but the practice which landed him in difficulty, and according to his critics was a blot on England's good name.

In his study of *Britain in Europe,* Professor Seton-Watson noted 'that he [Palmerston] was not merely provocative, but provocative with a veneer of flippancy and raciness such as foreigners could neither understand nor appreciate, and despite his very considerable acquaintance with the Continent, he was yet lacking in the sympathies which created a diplomatic atmosphere'. Hence Metternich, the Austrian statesman, could find him *'un tres mauvais coucheur'* (an awkward bedfellow) who 'gave free rein to his personal hates'. He went on to suggest that 'he has a kink in the mind which always prevents him from being entirely right in any affair. Where his mind goes straight in principle, he forgets to scrutinise the means of execution, whereas where his attitude is wrong in fundamentals, he is fertile in expedients'.

Harold Nicolson, himself an experienced diplomat in the early part of the twentieth century, discerned three periods in the development of Palmerston's character;

1. The period of passive diffidence to 1830 - the shy, studious boy at Cambridge, determined but dull; at 25 he refused the offer of the Exchequer because he distrusted his own powers.

2. The period of dynamic caution, 1830-41 - when his policies were generally consistent and reputable, if at moments eccentric. He seemed quite happy to provoke and embarrass the French, and constantly humiliated King Louis Philippe and his ministers by a high-handed approach.

3. The period of arrogant recklessness and blustering adventure from 1841 onwards - in this later era, his policies were increasingly coloured by personal animosities, and his actions became increasingly arrogant. Policy ceased to be 'intelligent or consistent, but became sensational as Palmerston whipped up popular feeling and prejudices in the country'. In Nicolson's judgement, he showed some of his worst defects in diplomacy in his later years. When British power and authority in Europe was unrivalled, his 'reckless and antagonistic' methods were less serious. By the 1860s, a policy of bluff could be disastrous for there were more astute statesman in Europe such as Bismarck, who was by then becoming a key figure on the European scene. After 1859, when British power was beginning to be questioned, his forthright expression, combined with Foreign Secretary Russell's didactic and meddlesome tones were calculated to offend foreigners because they were expressed so insolently.

b) The Don Pacifico Episode, 1850

Palmerston's attitude was clearly expressed in the Don Pacific episode which is a useful example not only of his approach but of the differing one posed by Gladstone, his long-term successor as Liberal leader. Pacifico was a Portuguese Jew who claimed British citizenship as a former resident of Gibraltar. As a result of his dubious monetary transactions, he had his Athens' house pillaged by a mob. He demanded an extortionate sum in compensation from the Greek government, and Palmerston endorsed every demand in its most exaggerated form. When the Greek government prevaricated, he ordered a British squadron to Greek waters. His peremptory style was a strong response and his language to King Otto was thoroughly unreasonable.

In a four-day debate in the House of Commons, there were moments of great drama as a group of distinguished political enemies joined in the onslaught against him. He defended himself in a remarkable speech, described by Gladstone as a 'gigantic intellectual and physical effort'. It was one of the few supreme set-piece performances he ever gave. In it he reviewed the principles and practice of British foreign policy since Canning, having used over 2,000 volumes of Foreign Office papers to write his script. His triumphant peroration was an unashamedly chauvinistic appeal to the patriotic instincts of the British people. In a challenge to those present, 'as representing a political, a commercial, a constitutional country', he asked

> 1 whether the principles on which the foreign policy of Her Majesty's Government has been conducted, and the sense of duty which has led us to think ourselves bound to afford protection to our fellow subjects abroad, are proper and fitting guides for those who are
> 5 charged with the Government of England; and whether, as the Roman, in days of old, held himself free from indignity, when he could say Civis Romanus Sum; so also a British subject, in whatever land he may be shall feel confident that the watchful eye and the strong arm of England will protect him against injustice
> 10 and wrong.

Gladstone led the counter-attack, and his speech gives a valuable insight into his thinking on the relationship between the behaviour of states and morality. Its tone was one which he would often strike again;

> 1 And now I will grapple with the noble Lord on the ground which he selected for himself, in the most triumphant portion of his speech, by his reference to those emphatic words, 'Civis Romanus sum'. He vaunted, amidst the cheers of his supporters, that under
> 5 his administration an Englishman should be, throughout the world, what the citizen of Rome had been. What then, Sir, was a Roman citizen? He was the member of a privileged caste; he belonged to a conquering race, to a nation that held all others bound down by the strong arm of power. ... Does he make the
> 10 claim for us, that we are to be uplifted upon a platform high above the standing-ground of all other nations?
>
> What, Sir, ought a Foreign Secretary to be? ... I understand it to be is duty to conciliate peace with dignity. I think it to be the very first of all his duties studiously to observe, and to exalt in honour
> 15 among mankind, that great code of principles which is termed the law of nations ... let us recognise, and recognise with frankness, the equality of the weak with the strong; the principles of brotherhood among nations, and of sacred independence. When we are asking for the maintenance of rights which belong to our
> 20 fellow-subjects resident in Greece, let us do as we would be done by ... Let us refrain from all gratuitous and arbitrary meddling in the internal concerns of other States, even as we should resent the same interference if it were attempted to be practised towards ourselves ...

c) Palmerston and Domestic Policy

While Palmerston was alive Whiggery could feel secure. One historian has described how he 'found himself in that enlightened section of Tories which the Whigs invited to join them in order that their own position might be secured', and thereafter he drifted with them, using his influence to moderate domestic reform. In his youth he was a supporter of the abolition of the slave trade, and in 1832 he had favoured parliamentary reform. But he believed that the 1832 Act represented the ultimate in perfection, and opposed further change in the electoral system. Although he favoured free trade and commercial treaties, he was unenthusiastic about the repeal of the corn laws which he felt showed scant concern for the interests of landowners. He was uneasy about any policy which would shift the balance of power from the aristocracy to the manufacturing, commercial and working classes.

In office, as Prime Minister after 1859, he used his influence to check his destined successors, Russell and Gladstone, and to block any significant reform. Other than the work of Gladstone, who followed an independent line at the Treasury, the ministry had no obvious domestic policy at all. Although there were able men in the administration, including several former Peelites, and although the government was not overtly Whig in nature, it was concerned to maintain the interests of the landed class whose security Palmerston believed to be essential for the stability of the country. He wished to maintain the existing ordered society and believed that; 'We cannot go on legislating for ever. Oh! There is nothing really to be done. We cannot go on adding to the statute book *ad infinitum*'. His loyalty to the 'conservative cause' was shown when he attacked Gladstone's proposals for legacy duties (on the passing on of property at death) in 1853 as 'confiscatory, a great individual oppression'.

His attitude was smug and complacent, for he was typical of those Whigs who had no wish to take up reform which might be the 'thin end of the wedge' and open the door to further change; 'We have shown the example of a nation in which every class of society accepts with cheerfulness the lot which Providence has assigned to it; while at the same time, every individual of each class is constantly striving to raise himself in the social scheme, not by injustice and wrong, not by violence'.

This ministry was, as Donald Southgate has suggested, 'the Indian summer of Whiggery ... when everyone was waiting for Palmerston to die'. Tories were reluctant to seek to dislodge him in the House of Commons for they knew that if there was an election he would triumph in the country. But anyway they felt no need to rid the country of his rule for his views were entirely inoffensive to those of conservative disposition.

d) Palmerston's Popularity in Mid-Victorian England

Without the benefit of modern means of communication Palmerston succeeded in creating a favourable image of himself in the eyes of the nation at large, among whom he was affectionately known as 'Pam'. In the 1850s he seemed to be the most representative public figure, symbolising the optimistic, self-confident nation of the Great Exhibition. Appropriately, in his biography Donald Southgate calls him 'The Most English Minister'. He was representative in his liberal conservatism at home and in his sometimes high-handed insistence on a due regard for the interests of British subjects in foreign lands. He said and wrote what he felt, whereas other statesmen would not have felt as he did or, if they had, would not have written it. English people found him intelligible, and the majority found him likeable as well and were proud of him. His breezy gaiety and his ostentatious disdain for foreigners promoted his popularity among those who admired a jaunty if rather bellicose patriotism. As a result, he was idolised by large sections of the British public and he in turn rarely miscalculated their feelings.

Queen Victoria did not share this widespread admiration. She found him a difficult politician with whom to work and was in constant disagreement with him. In 1848, during Russell's premiership, she protested against the 'intemperate tone' of the Foreign Secretary and told the Prime Minister that Palmerston 'often endangered the honour of England by taking a very prejudiced and one-sided view of a question'. She wanted him removed but gave way, and for three years she merely continued to protest.

Their differences were often over issues of policy where she felt that his approach was damaging to relations with other countries and their rulers. But at a personal level she also deeply resented his manner. Her only consolation was that she found him less objectionable than Russell, although she thought that they were both 'dreadful old men'. On Palmerston's death, she wrote to King Leopold of Belgium that her late-prime minister had many qualities 'though many bad ones, and we had, God knows, terrible trouble with him about foreign affairs ... he was very vindictive, and personal feelings influenced his political acts very much'. She had a chance to observe him from close quarters, but her judgements cannot be accepted uncritically, for she could be notoriously partisan.

5 Lord John Russell (1792-1872)

Lord John Russell was the son of the Duke of Bedford, and heir to his family title. He had become a Whig MP in 1813, and was from 1819 a supporter of parliamentary reform. He had piloted the Reform Bill through the House of Commons in 1832 and as Home Secretary under Melbourne after 1835 was responsible for the complementary Act which reformed local government and for the further reduction in the number of offences which carried the death penalty.

He saw himself and his family as representatives of Whiggery at its best. The Whig tradition was rooted in support for increased liberty and dislike of despotism and arbitrary rule, and he located the Russells in this line of descent, stressing that, 'In all times of popular movement the Russells have been on the "forward" side'. His support for reform echoed such feelings, and he understood that for the self-preservation of his class it must not allow itself to be excessively defensive of its privileges. In 1822, he argued that,

> It is my persuasion that the liberties of Englishmen, being founded upon the general consent of all, must remain upon that basis, or must altogether cease ... We cannot confine liberty in this country to one class of men.

As Whig Prime Minister from 1846-52 he was the irresolute head of a cabinet lacking in cohesion. Professor Smellie, in *A Hundred Years of English Government,* has noted that whereas Peel's government was 'a real unity', the administrations of Grey, Melbourne and Russell were 'republican', in the sense that there was 'no overruling authority'. Peel was the dominant and overriding figure, whereas the Whig prime ministers did not assert such leadership. Of Russell's premiership Southgate remarks, 'government was by departments and policy-making by conclave, by a sort of select committee of Brooks' Club'. Such an attitude was typical of some of the great Whig families, who thought in terms of shared power rather than individual monopoly of it.

Russell was not particularly interested in dotting the 'i's and crossing the 't's of policy. He was more concerned about its broad sweep. Moreover, in temperament, he lacked the urgency and reserves of strength to press for measures he believed in, such as land reform in Ireland. He was physically not up to the job of detailed management of his party and his cabinet. However, for some while his parliamentary position was secure, for the Whigs won a small victory in the 1847 election and the opposing Conservatives were divided between the Protectionists and the Peelites. As a result, some useful reforms were introduced such as the Factory Acts which brought in the maximum ten hour day for all women and young persons (1847) and defined the hours of factory opening (1850), and the Public Health Act of 1848 which was a truly Benthamite measure which attempted to impose some central control over conditions in the urban areas to bring about improved standards of sanitation.

Russell's interests were evident in the abortive attempts to pass a Jewish Disabilities Bill and a bill outlawing electoral bribery in 1847. He also took up the theme of free trade, and the repeal of the Navigation Acts in 1849, for which the Peelites were keen to take credit, opened the ports to shipping of all nations, and the remaining restrictions on colonial trade were removed.

One controversy of the administration was the Prime Minister's opposition to the decision of the Papacy to establish Roman Catholic diocese in England. This came at a time when anti-Catholicism was at a peak. The passing of Catholic Emancipation had generated hostility and the secession of some prominent Anglicans to the Church of Rome in the 1840s and 1850s added to a mood of intolerance. Russell's Ecclesiastical Titles Act (1851) banned Catholic clergy from employing titles used in the Church of England. In the event, the measure was to prove to be unimportant, for Catholic diocese did not adopt Anglican nomenclatures, and no-one ever having been fined for so doing, the legislation was repealed by Gladstone in 1871. However, the move is of interest, for it appeared to be a deviation from the principle of religious liberty. In deciding to legislate, Russell had the support of several Protectionists - although, not surprisingly, the Irish, backed by the Peelites, opposed the measure.

Internal dissension over tax and electoral reform had prompted the Prime Minister to attempt resignation in 1851, but in the absence of any willing takers he resumed office and in the extra year his anti-Catholic legislation was placed on the statute book, after some delay in gaining assent over its details. Otherwise, the years of the premiership were dominated by the foreign secretaryship of Palmerston. Russell found it difficult to control his wayward minister, and as we have seen the queen became resentful of Palmerston's behaviour and in particular of his 'intemperate language'. Russell feared 'making Palmerston an enemy by displacing him'. In the end he did dismiss him in December 1851, but Palmerston subsequently achieved his 'tit-for-tat' by bringing about the ministry's downfall.

Russell served under Palmerston as foreign secretary from 1859-65, during which time he succeeded to his family seat in 1861. He followed Palmerston as Prime Minister for the second time, but was by then in ailing health and had even less vigour than before. On the failure of Gladstone's attempts to bring about reform of the electoral system in 1866, he resigned and it was Gladstone who succeeded to the Liberal leadership.

6 Gladstone's Early Political Career

Born the son of a very wealthy merchant in Liverpool, William Ewart Gladstone belonged to that growing number of middle-class people whose fortunes derived from the worlds of commerce and industry. His father was a religious evangelical, but one with a deeply acquisitive instinct. He had made much of his money from his ownership of slaves and sugar plantations in the West Indies. His mother was intensely religious, and it was from her that the young William learned many of the ideals which were to influence his conduct later in life - in particular, a set of attitudes which stressed sin, suffering and submission to God's will. The Gladstone household was a strictly Tory one, although the father was a Canningite and had supported Catholic Emancipation.

At Oxford University the influences were High Tory, and during his time there Gladstone met people who were sceptical of reform - especially parliamentary reform, which he also opposed. He revered the aristocracy and believed in its right to rule. He saw the attempt to reform Parliament as a 'threat to the very foundations of society' and took up other extreme positions. His last speech in the Oxford Union was in defence of slavery, although it was a cause he adopted out of filial respect rather than from natural inclination.

At this time Gladstone was a convinced Anglican and was much influenced by the sermons and writings of well-known clergymen. He was attracted to the ritual of the High Church, although he had no desire to join the Church of Rome as some prominent High Churchmen were to do. He contemplated a career in the Church but turned instead to politics, and in 1833 began a long parliamentary career as an MP for the rotten borough of Newark in Nottinghamshire. He was then in the mainstream of the Tory Party. He soon made a favourable impression on other MPs and was appointed to junior office in Peel's first ministry of 1834-5.

Although he was hostile to the 'dangerous radicalism' of the Whigs, he was not opposed to all reform. He adopted a Peelite approach and claimed that the 'reform of abuses' was 'a sacred duty ... not inimical to true and determined principles'. However, his willingness to tackle acknowledged evils did not yet extend to slavery. He sat on the Select Committee which examined the workings of the 1833 Act, and used his influence to defend the plantation owners against accusations made against them. In 1838 he defended them for the last time and thereafter began to develop a concern for the position of the ex-slaves. His attitudes at this time were - beneath the exterior - more those of a Canningite Tory than those of a die-hard, but the expression of distinctly High Church views gave a different impression.

In 1838 he published *The Church and its Relations with the State,* one of his many literary outpourings, and he received a warm tribute from Macaulay, the Whig writer and MP, who in reviewing the book wrote,

> 1 The author of this volume is a young man of unblemished character, and of distinguished parliamentary talents, the rising hope of those stern and unbending Tories ... We are much pleased to see a grave treatise on an important part of the philosophy of
> 5 Government proceed from the pen of a young man who is rising to eminence in the House of Commons.

'Grave' he often was and unblemished also. He was a young man of great passions, but they were repressed. Highly intelligent and other-worldly, he was at first unsuccessful in love. He was more successful in politics and was appointed as Vice-President of the Board of Trade under Peel, and by the time he was elevated to the Presidency of that department in 1843 he was showing distinct political promise. By then very sympathetic to Peel, he only differed with him on Church matters and on the problems of the West Indian planters.

He did much of the detailed work on the preparation of Peel's 'free trade' budgets of the 1840s, and was keen to see the sliding-scale on the corn laws made less rigid. He had always seen the prosperity of the landed interest as basic to the national interest, and at this stage accepted the case for retaining the laws in some form. He wanted to see a bold solution which would have effectively ended protection once the price of wheat reached 61 shillings a quarter. As time passed, he came to doubt the value of the laws in any form and in 1845-6 he supported Peel over the need to repeal them. This brought him into conflict with Disraeli who so bitterly attacked Peel for his betrayal of the Conservative Party. Gladstone was indignant at the attacks and could never forgive the savagery of Disraeli's assault.

In 1846, after the breakup of the Conservative Party, he was for a while without office or even a seat in the House. He won the nomination for Oxford University in 1847 and re-entered the Commons where he showed a developing liberal approach on two matters - he voted for the admission of Jews to the House of Commons in 1847 and for the repeal of the navigation laws in 1849. He was a dedicated follower of Peel but found the time frustrating for, although Peel commanded national respect, he exercised no decisive leadership over his band of followers. On the ex-Prime Minister's death in 1850, Gladstone and the Peelites were left in the wilderness, an orchestra which had lost its conductor.

They were, after all, Conservatives by background and training, but they were deeply suspicious of the Protectionist element which they blamed for Peel's downfall. They doubted the sincerity of Disraeli's belated conversion to free trade. They remained, in Gladstone's words, with 'no organisation, no whipper-in ... a public nuisance'. He idolised the memory of his former leader, and believed him to have been 'taken all round, the greatest man I have ever known'. Peel was his guide and mentor. Perhaps he identified so strongly with Peel because they shared similar backgrounds: they both came from very affluent families which depended on the wealth their fathers had made in commerce and industry. In addition, neither was completely at home with members of the aristocracy, for both men retained the manifestations of their middle-class upbringing. They were serious, highly-controlled people whose calm exteriors masked the intense feelings that lay beneath.

In the year of Peel's death (1850), Gladstone delivered one of his most effective parliamentary performances when he tackled Lord Palmerston in the Don Pacifico debate (see page 60-1). Repelled by the bluster and cock-sure arrogance of the noble lord, he laid down the basis of his ideas on the need for moral conduct in international relations. A year later foreign affairs were again to impact significantly upon his career, for it was his visit to Italy which stirred his conscience and confirmed his attitude as being increasingly on the side of Liberal causes. Appalled by what he had seen of oppressive Austrian rule in the peninsula, he returned to denounce the atrocities in his *Letters to Lord Aberdeen*. The effect was sensational, more so perhaps than Gladstone intended. He was to develop a habit of unleashing public forces by making explosive utterances, a product of what his biographer, Philip Magnus, called the 'volcanic eruptions' of his mind.

His attitude shocked many English Conservatives, for he had appeared to align himself with nationalists and even revolutionaries. As the decade progressed there was growing hostility to him on the Tory benches both for his views on foreign and economic policy and for the whole tenor of his outlook which seemed to suggest that his home was on the other side of the political fence to their own.

In 1852 he was appointed chancellor of the exchequer under Lord Aberdeen in what was a Whig-Peelite administration. He was now a liberal Conservative on most issues of policy. He told Sir James Graham that he felt happier to be 'on the Liberal side of the Conservative Party rather than on the Conservative side of the Liberal Party'. Yet on all issues other than parliamentary reform he was in growing sympathy with the Liberals, and on the electoral system his attitude was to bend as the decade advanced. He viewed society as a conservative and still had a strong preference for aristocratic rule. However, his political attitudes were becoming distinctly more progressive.

a) Gladstone at the Exchequer (1852-5 and 1859-65)

As a convinced Peelite, Gladstone was determined to continue the broad sweep of his master's policy, and soon earned himself a similar reputation for sound financial management, or what one biographer has called his 'thrifty husbandry'. He said of Peel that, 'he was a rigid economist [somebody who spent money very carefully]. Oh! he was a most rigid economist', and his own thinking echoed the importance of being watchful over both personal and national financial affairs. As he later said, 'economy is the first and great article ... in my financial creed'.

Gladstone shared Peel's concern to improve the condition of the people by fiscal measures. In his first budget he abolished or reduced some 200 import duties, so that many articles such as foodstuffs and partly-manufactured goods were now freed from customs duties all together. He also introduced new scales of death duties on inherited land and wealth, a policy to be developed by the Liberals in forthcoming decades. However, his aim of abolishing income tax received a setback with the outbreak of the Crimean

War, and the Indian Mutiny actually forced him to double the rate.

What was remarkable about his performance as chancellor was his ability to arouse interest in government finance, the details of which were often arid and complex. Particularly in the House of Commons he was able to deliver clear and comprehensive expositions on financial matters which held members spellbound. In the office again in 1859, he once more demonstrated his ability as a financier and parliamentarian by his mastery of complex points. He was sure that there was still considerable work to be done in the financial field and was inspired by the prospect of carrying on with the task. In particular, he wished to reduce income tax and further reduce restrictions on trade.

His aim to destroy the remaining relics of protectionism and abolish income tax left him out of sympathy with Palmerston's desire to spend money on building shore defences against a possible French invasion, at a time of another war-scare with France. By contrast, his own approach was to seek reconciliation across the Channel by building financial bridges, and the Cobden-Chevalier Treaty of 1860 marks the high watermark of the policy of free trade. Cobden strongly believed that free trade was the key to permanent peace between great nations, and with Gladstone's active backing he went to Paris to negotiate with the government of Napoleon III. By the treaty's terms, France was to lower duties on the import of British coal and manufactured goods and in return Britain abolished nearly all duties on French manufactures and reduced duties on wines. Domestic prosperity and international peace were, in Gladstone's view, the outcome of the agreement, and he was pleased to have helped 'knit together in amity these two great nations, whose conflicts have so often shaken the world'.

In his four hour Budget speech in 1860, Gladstone surveyed the national finances and set out his proposals. He was unwell at the time but, as was said by one observer, a 'heroic will ... mastered even a rebellious uvula (mouth ailment) in the cause of duty'. The performance was a parliamentary triumph, noted for its review of Britain's growing prosperity which he attributed to the development of free-trade policies. His aim was to remove all remaining duties on food, raw materials and manufactures which would lower prices to consumers and costs to manufactures. All in the community would benefit and trade and industry would be promoted. Only on some 48 goods did duty remain: in total Peel and his successor had done away with tariffs on more than 1,000 items. To cover the cost of the immediate loss of revenue in 1860 the rate of income tax rose by a penny in the pound, although he was to more than halve that rate over the years to 1865.

Despite its initial reception, discussion of the Budget was soon overtaken by controversy. Gladstone tried to repeal the excise duty on paper which had been portrayed by many critics as a 'tax on knowledge'. This had been a Radical aspiration for many years, and Gladstone was well aware that repeal would have the effect of creating a cheap - and probably sympathetic - press as well as cheaper books. The House of Lords threw out the measure and in the ensuing crisis Derby began negotiations with Palmerston in the hope of forming a coalition government. Relations between Palmerston and his chancellor were never easy, but the Prime Minister's overt sympathy with the peers made Gladstone's dilemma all the greater. He found a way out of the difficulty by compressing all money bills for the next 1861 session into the budget. Custom dictated that the Lords would either reject a budget in its entirety or leave it alone. To reject would cause a constitutional crisis, and the Peers backed down and in a major victory over the Second Chamber the paper duty was repealed.

The issue was important in many ways other than its intrinsic desirability. It won Gladstone the sympathy of the Radicals, a number of whom were beginning to identify him as the most reform-minded member of the Cabinet. In the same way, it earned him the distrust of a number of Whigs as well as of the Tories, his former allies. Above all, it made him more popular in the country with the masses who as yet had little say in deciding the fate of political issues but whose political consciousness was beginning to develop. With the growing support of a provincial press, Gladstone was able to present himself as a strong supporter of basic rights - ones which were being denied by those who monopolised the bastions of power in the land.

This second period at the Exchequer was a busy and fruitful one, and several other innovations were introduced. Gladstone encouraged personal saving by establishing a Post Office Savings Bank. He was convinced of the merits of thrift in private as well as public life, and his idea was a spur to saving by the working classes, much in line with his wish to see them help themselves by their own efforts. Another landmark was his creation of the Public Accounts Committee, a powerful body which kept a watchful eye on public expenditure. He was looking for a new spirit of probity in public affairs and tight control over all aspects of expenditure was part of this outlook. He reduced spending from £72 million in 1861 to £62 million four years later. The emphasis was upon economy and efficiency rather than mere parsimony. He wanted value for money, for he had a loathing of waste.

b) Assessment of Gladstone's Work at the Exchequer

Gladstone's period at the Exchequer has been widely praised. His policies were in line with the trend towards free trade, and his desire to free manufacturers from restraints helped Britain compete on advantageous terms in world trade, exchanging manufactured goods for food and raw materials. Such policies contributed to an enormous increase in industry and trade over the coming years, which was good for manufacturers but also for the working classes who might expect to profit from the increased prosperity of the nation - particularly by gaining higher wages. However, his policies offered them little direct help with social problems, for retrenchment in public spending meant that money was not spent on projects that would have done this. But this was a period when *laissez-faire* doctrines held sway, and Gladstone was in this respect, as in many others, a man of his times, sharing its prevailing philosophy.

Gladstone pursued his goals with passion and conviction, and his desire for economy and good administration was basic to his outlook. The desire to save even on insignificant issues invited some ridicule, as when he insisted that the address on the labels on his government dispatch bag should be obliterated so that the bags could be re-used. But he believed that economy by governments and saving by individuals offered the prospect of an improved way of life for all. Aware as he was of social evils, he did not see it as the role of government to correct them, even if it could do so; he was keen that the state should enable the individual to be the mainspring of his own betterment. Of course, it would be misleading to ascribe to him all the successes of British prosperity in the 1860s and early-1870s, for he was carrying on a programme which others had pioneered and which commanded wide approval. Nevertheless his reputation remains as one of the great and most innovative Chancellors of all time.

Beyond his financial achievements, Gladstone had used his chancellorship to demonstrate his considerable talents and expertise to fellow-parliamentarians. Even more important perhaps, he had won the enthusiastic admiration of many consumers and potential voters. Lower prices, reduced taxation, and an attack on the Lords were promising ingredients in a recipe designed to enhance the stature of a rising politician.

c) Gladstone and the Road to Liberalism; His Choice of Party in 1859

Gladstone had refused Lord Derby's invitation to join his minority administration in 1858, and in so doing had won the backing of John Bright who recognised the potential of Gladstone as a reinforcement on the Liberal side. Warning him of the likely failure of the Derby government, he wrote, 'If you remain on our side of the House ... I know nothing that can prevent your being PM ... I think I am not mistaken in the opinion I have formed of the direction in which your views have for some years been tending'. Gladstone was impressed by the eloquence of Bright and the logic of Cobden's mind, and felt that these were people with whom he could share some attitudes, whatever his continuing reservations about Palmerston's manner and policies.

In 1859, conscious of being in his own words, 'the one remaining Ishmael in the House of Commons' (a Biblical allusion to Abraham's son who was made an outcast), Gladstone felt it was time to join the mainstream again. Because of his immense standing in Parliament he was an asset whom the Liberals were keen to recruit, and Palmerston offered him the Exchequer for the second time (see page 70). His decision, after much soul-searching and agonising, to accept was the crucial one in his career, and it was followed in March of the following year by his resignation from the Carlton Club, the social centre of Tory politics.

Gladstone's acceptance of office in 1859 was a turning point not only in his own life but in British politics as well. He had moved slowly from the Toryism of his upbringing to this later position, a journey accomplished as a result of both his experience and his convictions. His explanation was a clear one: 'My Toryism was accepted by me on authority and in good faith. But on every subject as I came to deal with it practically, I had to deal with it as a Liberal'. Or again, 'I was brought up to distrust and dislike liberty, I learned to believe in it. That is the key to all my changes'. Thus Gladstone's explanation was that he came to be a passionate believer in liberty and justice, and that over the question of Italy in particular he came to see a fundamental issue of principle, of justice against oppression, as he later was to do over Ireland as well.

'Never had I an easier question to determine than when I was asked to join the government. I can hardly now think how I could have looked any one in the face, had I refused my aid (such as it is) at such a time and under such circumstances'. So he claimed, and he elaborated on his motives more fully in a letter he wrote to his friend Sir John (later Lord) Acton in 1864.

> 1 When I took my present office in 1859, I had several negative and several positive reasons for accepting it. Of the first, there were these ... I felt myself to be mischievous in an isolated position, outside the regular party organisation of parliament. And I was
> 5 aware of no differences of opinion or tendency likely to disturb the new government. Then on the positive side. I felt sure that there was in finance much useful work to be done. I was desirous to co-operate in settling the question of the franchise, and failed to anticipate the disaster that it was to undergo. My friends were
> 10 enlisted, or I knew would enlist; Sir James Graham indeed declining office, but taking his position in the party. And the overwhelming interest and weight of the Italian question, and of our foreign policy in connection with it, joined to my entire mistrust of the former government in relation to it, led me to
> 15 decide without one moment's hesitation.

d) The Italian Question and Other Considerations

Gladstone was much attracted to Italy, and particularly to its language and culture. But only slowly did he develop the interest in the problems of the peninsula which were to awaken his conscience. In his first visit to the country he was not greatly stirred by its problems. However, in 1848 he went to Sicily where the conditions forced themselves on him. He saw the terrible suffering of cholera victims and witnessed the severity of the King of Naples' régime. Yet he was still not stirred by Italian nationalist sentiment.

His return there in 1850 was a very different matter. In the aftermath of the 1848 revolutions he witnessed horrors which made a profound impression on him. For shouting 'Long live the constitutional king', and thus emphasising that the king was subject to a constitution, one man was given 100 lashes. At a trial of 40 well-known patriots Gladstone saw the obvious fabrication of evidence, and on visiting the gaols he learned of some 20,000 political prisoners being held in confinement. Conditions were an outrage against civilised standards. Hence his description of them as 'the negation of God erected into a system of government'.

As a Conservative he knew the party was a staunch ally of all established European governments, including those that ruled Italy so repressively. He published two pamphlets and tried to convince the Tories of the evils of the Italian régimes. His whole heart was in the struggle for the liberty of an oppressed people, and Palmerston and Russell could share his views. Hence his claim in 1892 that he had been 'enlisted in the army of liberty almost without knowing it'.

It is reasonable to assume that the question of Italy was an important factor in Gladstone's journey into the Liberal Party, for he and the Prime Minister were united in their belief in self-determination for small nations. John Morley, writing in 1903, stressed how Gladstone was drawn 'by the native ardour of his humanity, unconsciously and involuntarily ... into that great European stream of liberalism which was destined to carry him so far'. More recent historians have recognised the importance of the Italian question, and E.J. Feuchtwanger has argued that 'the dictates of justice and morality outweighted every other consideration with him and he was prepared to go against all his preconceived conservative notions on the politics of Europe and the dangers of revolution on the continent ... He let moral conviction prevail'. D.M. Shreuder, in an article in the English Historical Review ('Gladstone and Italian unification; the making of a Liberal?', 1970) has similarly suggested that unless we understand Gladstone's attitude to the Italian question we cannot understand why he was able to become a Liberal. For Peter Clarke (*A Question of Leadership; Gladstone to Thatcher*), this was also the source of his inspiration - 'Not for Gladstone a Liberalism derived from cool libertarian logic'. This then was a creed which had become something 'felt in his bones', deriving from his experience and sense of compassion rather than from a study of the great Liberal philosophers. It is a flattering picture of highmindedness.

However, there were also other factors which persuaded Gladstone to join the Palmerston government, some of which he alluded to in the letter to Acton, already quoted. Political ambition was one, and his intense personal dislike and distrust of Disraeli was another. Since the death of Peel, Gladstone had been in the political wilderness. If he was to again hold office and wield political influence, he realised he must not continue to stand aside from party life. An independent position offered no prospect of advancement. For years he had stood outside the main parties; now in his fiftieth year, the sands were running out and for a man of his ability his career seemed near to failure. As the views of Palmerston and his own coincided on at least some issues, it seemed better to work within the Liberal Party rather than remain 'mischievous in an isolated position'. Moreover, as a financial disciple of Peel, the Exchequer offered him a great chance to further the work of free trade. A sceptic might add that in the year in question Palmerston was 75 and Russell 67. The highest place in the Liberal Party would almost certainly fall vacant soon. As Forster, a future Liberal minister, observed, there were 'no new Whigs', and Radicals such as Cobden and Bright could never have commanded widespread allegiance.

There was also the matter of the relationship between Disraeli and Gladstone. In 1855 Gladstone had been offered a place in Derby's government, in spite of the disdain which many Conservatives exhibited towards him. Gladstone seriously contemplated joining, for he was then antagonistic to Palmerston and Russell, but he was held back by loyalty to his old Peelite friends. In 1858, acutely aware of the lack of talent and the need for intellectual reinforcement in the Conservative Party, Derby renewed the offer. Disraeli literally implored him to join ('I almost went down on my knees to him') and wrote admiringly of his 'shining qualities'. But Gladstone, who could recognise Disraeli's considerable talents, profoundly disliked him. For all of his uncommon ability and brilliant style, he was not to be trusted. To Gladstone, ethics were an essential ingredient in politics; Disraeli lacked scruple and principle, and in addition was ostentatious and vulgar. Moreover, the Peelites had an even greater antipathy to him than did Gladstone himself. If Gladstone joined the Conservatives, he could not expect to take his erstwhile colleagues with him.

It had been a reluctant conversion to Liberalism. It had proved easier to break with the Conservatives than to link up with the Liberals. Now the dye was cast and whatever the paramount considerations in his thinking, the moment was a decisive one. Effectively it marked the end of the Peelite phase in British politics, for most who had not already rejoined the Conservative Party went with him. In any case, within four years Aberdeen, Graham, Herbert and Newcastle were dead.

e) Gladstone's Political Outlook

Even in 1859, when he was officially a Liberal, Gladstone still defended anomalies - for example, he referred to rotten boroughs as 'nurseries of statesmen'. Indeed, in some ways, he was still a fundamentally conservative politician, respecting antiquity as Peel had done. But he would certainly accept and initiate change if it was necessitated by some existing injustice. He had a passion for improvement where something clearly needed to be done, and as a member of the new mercantile class, like Peel, he took his politics seriously and was prepared to tackle any abuse in need of legislative attention.

Between 1859 and 1865 he was building up goodwill among the Radicals and an increasing number of the public. Whiggery already viewed him with anxiety and distrust. Clarendon grasped that he was both a progressive politician and a popular leader, calling him 'an audacious innovator with an insatiable desire for change'. To many a traditional Whig Gladstone's outlook became increasingly incomprehensible. By 1868 Clarendon could see 'no germ of approximation' between them, especially when Gladstone brought moral passion to politics - as he did over Italy, and later was to do over Ireland and Bulgaria. Gladstone increasingly flourished on popular acclaim and found himself 'on the side of the masses against the classes'. He became 'the People's William'.

Recent research has stressed the role of John Bright in building up Gladstone's reputation with the working classes around the country in the years just before he became Prime Minister. Gladstone was able to exploit this popular backing, and gathered the support of working-class leaders, middle-class Nonconformists and parliamentary Liberals. At the same time, given his immense talent, he was able to retain the grudging support of the Whigs. Out of this coalition the Gladstonian Liberal Party was formed.

Yet despite his growing political radicalism and popular appeal, in his personal attitudes Gladstone admired people with a certain social or educational stamp upon them. Shortly before he died in 1898 Balfour was to say of him, 'He is and always was, in everything except essentials, a tremendous old Tory, and is particularly sensitive in the matter of dignities'.

f) Gladstone and Parliamentary Reform

It was over the matter of parliamentary reform that Gladstone was able to develop his popular reputation as a reformer. In spite of his previous misgivings, he made a speech in 1864 which transformed discussion of the subject. He told the House of Commons that 'I venture to say that every man who is not presumably incapacitated by some consideration of personal unfitness or of political danger, is morally entitled to come within the pale of the constitution'. His listeners were surprised and, in some cases, appalled. Disraeli claimed to detect the dangerous influence of Tom Paine at work. Palmerston strenuously resisted the notion of a 'moral right to vote' and remarked that 'the function of a government is to calm rather than to excite agitation'.

Gladstone would never have seen himself as an agitator and alleged that he was amazed at the response to his remarks. He suggested that he was proposing nothing more than Russell had proposed in a Bill in 1860. In fact, his remarks were general and left an escape-route for people who worried about the prospect of a mass franchise. Far from being an enthusiastic affirmation of democratic principle, his utterance was heavily qualified by the phrase 'not presumably incapacitated'. Yet he had discussed the subject in different terms to those used by many others. He had placed the emphasis upon the right to vote, unless there were good reasons for denying it, whereas others often portrayed voting as a 'trust' to be earned.

In Gladstone's opinion many of his fellow-citizens had earned the right to vote by virtue of their 'self-command, self-confidence, respect for order, patience under suffering, confidence in the law and respect for superiors'. He still had no sympathy for 'sudden or violent or excessive or intoxicating change', but had come to see the industrious working classes as being a worthy and necessary influence to balance the power of the aristocracy. He still believed in aristocratic rule, but believed that by their example, their earnestness, thrift and sobriety, the skilled artisans had much to contribute.

If his observations repelled the 'classes', they attracted the 'masses', and working people up and down the country saw him as foremost among the reformers. Whereas Palmerston was received by the workingmen of Bradford in stony silence in 1864, Gladstone was greeted with acclaim. He clearly enjoyed this popular enthusiasm, and observed, 'It is impossible not to love the people from whom such manifestations come, as meet me in every quarter'. As Philip Magnus observed, he 'used the masses to find the respect which his nature craved, but which he had ceased to find in the social world in which he moved'. Again, as over Italy, Gladstone's behaviour elicited a response far greater than he claimed to imagine possible.

However, recent research has suggested that Gladstone, for all his emphasis on morality, was a more calculating politician than was often appreciated by his early biographers, and that in his devious way he was deliberately wooing working-class support by proclaiming ideas which would appeal to them. His speeches enabled him to strengthen his links with Bright, and John Vincent has suggested that he consciously used both the cause and Bright to widen his radical appeal and prepare his bid for the leadership.

g) The Fate of the Reform Bills 1866-7

When Palmerston died Russell's administration was free to press ahead with parliamentary reform. However, it did not rush to do so, and the

House elected in July 1865 only debated Gladstone's Bill in the following March. It was a modest measure, giving the vote to £7 householders in the towns and £14 tenants in the counties; it also included some fancy franchises, such as the one which would reward with an additional vote those who had saved £50 in Gladstone's Post Office savings scheme. Altogether it would have added only some 400,000 voters to the Register.

This moderate Bill ran into immediate problems because a group of dissident Whigs were unhappy at its terms. Foremost among these objectors was Robert Lowe who feared that power would pass to 'impulsive, unreflecting and violent people', known for their 'venality, ignorance and drunkenness'. He sat for the pocket borough of Calne, controlled by Lord Lansdowne, but his arguments were not based primarily on fear of losing his own seat. He feared the extension of the franchise, the more so as it had not been preceded by educational reform. He believed that, because they were poorly educated, the working classes might use their vote unwisely, and in their ignorance become the dupes of any unscrupulous rabble-rouser who promised the moon in order to win their support.

However, most Liberals did not share Lowe's view that Parliament as reformed in 1832 was the ultimate in perfection, and Gladstone was appalled at his denunciation of the working classes, 'our fellow-subjects, our fellow-Christians, our own flesh and blood'. Bright suggested that Lowe and his supporters were 'Adullamites', for they had retired to the Biblical cave of Adullam where David took refuge from Saul and brought together other discontented elements. It has been claimed that the group numbered no more than 12, but the revolt of the Adullamites was not easily contained. They were able to attract the backing of other malcontents such as the Whigs, rural Liberals and some Radical industrialists, and Russell resigned after a parliamentary defeat was inflicted by this combination on the Liberal Bill.

In the Derby government of 1866-8, it was Disraeli who successfully piloted a Reform Bill through the Commons. It was more radical than Gladstone had sought to achieve. Liberal biographers such as Morley were wont to suggest that the Conservative measure owed more to their good work than to the efforts of Derby and Disraeli, but many recent historians have been sceptical of such a viewpoint. For one thing, the final Act bore little resemblance to the one Gladstone was seeking to pass. Indeed, most of the amendments accepted by Disraeli did not derive from Gladstone. He was rather ineffective for a while, for though he remained a central figure in the discussion of the Bill and had a good grasp of its complexities, his interventions seemed to bore a House weary of these technicalities.

h) The Events of 1868

During Disraeli's brief premiership in 1868, Gladstone took up the cause of Disestablishment of the Irish Church. We have seen (page 39) that the mainly-Catholic Irish people objected to the presence of an established Protestant Church which they did not recognise. By offering to remove their grievance, Gladstone was responsible for a brilliant party stroke which exploited one of the Prime Minister's major weaknesses. Conservatives were defenders of the Protestant Church, and Disraeli felt he had to rally to the cause, though its endowments and preponderance were not easily defensible in a Church which ministered to only one-eighth of the Irish population. In shifting the political battleground, Gladstone was attacking from conviction and exploiting a chink in the Conservative armoury. He was also unifying his own party, and would be able to use the issue effectively in the forthcoming general election.

In the 1868 campaign Disraeli's appeal fell flat. In Ireland the Liberal majority increased from 5 in 1865 to 25 in 1868 as a result of Gladstone's espousal of the Irish cause. The other Liberal gains were also in the Celtic fringe, for in Wales, Liberal MPs increased in number from 18 to 22, in Scotland from 41 to 52, while in England they remained about the same. The Liberals did particularly well in the big cities where there was a large Irish population, but conversely did less well in Lancashire and Cheshire where there was a Protestant anti-Irish backlash, and in the south, among middle-class opinion. There were already the early signs that business and suburban villadom were beginning to desert the Liberal Party, a movement which was to contribute so much to the Conservative ascendancy of the end of the century.

However, in 1868 what was more apparent was that a new political age had dawned. After years of political instability and party confusion, the time was ripe for one of the great parliamentary duels, that between Gladstone and Disraeli. As the Conservative leader remarked; 'The truce of parties is over. I foresee tempestuous times, and great vicissitudes in public life'.

Making notes on *'From Whigs to Liberals, 1841-68'*

In compiling your notes on this chapter different approaches need to be adopted towards the two main topics that it covers - the predominance of Palmerston in party politics and the developing career of Gladstone. You do not need to record detailed information about Palmerston's approach to international relations. All you need are brief notes under the headings: 1 Palmerston and Gladstone: their views on Britain's position and aims in the world; 2 Don Pacifico Affair: differing attitudes; 3 Popularity of Palmerston in mid-Victorian England.

On Gladstone your notes should be devised to help you track the main stages in his progress from Conservatism to Liberalism up to 1868. The following headings will help you to identify these key aspects: 1 First Reform Act; 2 Slavery; 3 Peel's Budgets and the Repeal of the Corn Laws; 4 Admission of Jews; 5 Don Pacifico Affair; 6 Italian Question.

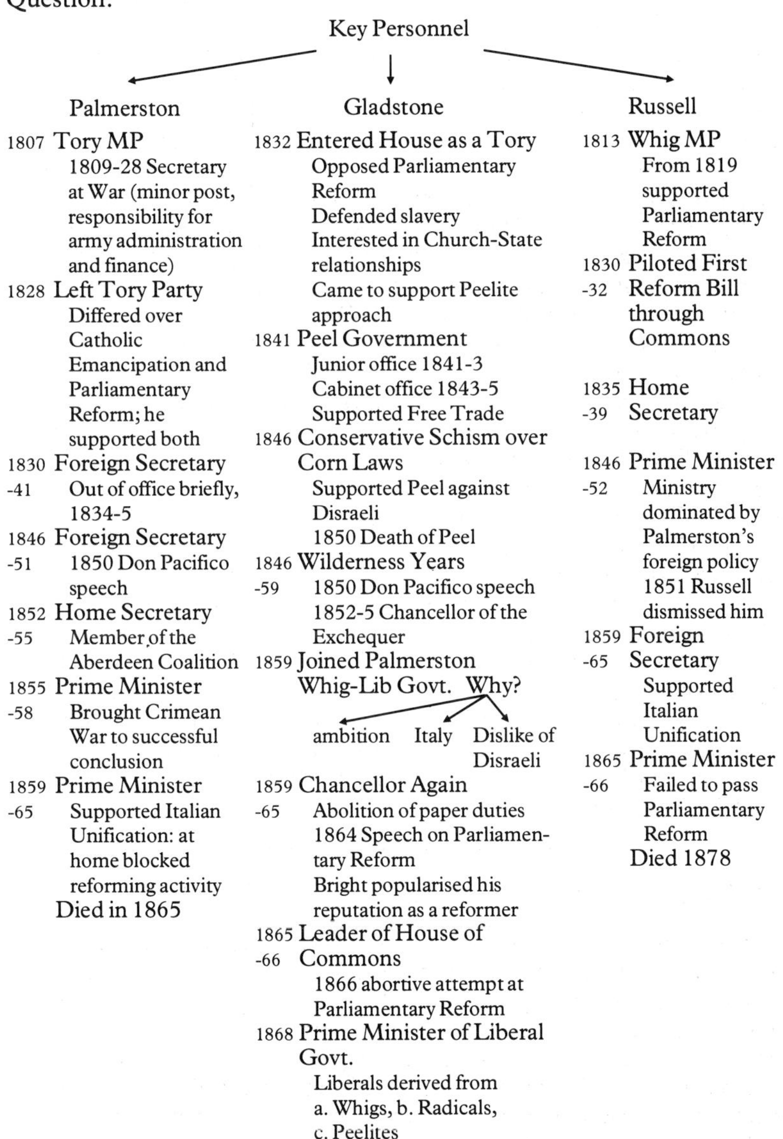

Summary - From Whigs to Liberals, 1841-68

Answering essay questions on *'From Whigs to Liberals,* 1841-68'

Gladstone's early political career appears to be an increasingly popular topic among examiners. Because the topic is a narrow one, questions on it tend to be phrased in a straightforward manner, for example inviting you to 'Analyse Gladstone's political progress to 1868 and explain his change of party'. Although an answer to such a question will probably take the form of a chronological narrative, it is important that an understanding of how each episode marks a stage in his political journey - i.e., how he came to unlearn his early attitudes - is displayed. Note the word 'Analyse'. Questions frequently use terms such as this. At the level at which you are studying you will not be asked to 'write an account'. Instead you will be required to do things such as to 'analyse', 'explain', 'assess' or 'examine'. To analyse is to break down complex issues and ideas into their component parts and to recognise how they are related to each other.

Consider the following question which adopts the technique which examiners use of including a quotation.

> To what extent and for what reasons had Gladstone changed by 1868 from being 'the rising hope of the stern unbending Tories' to the 'People's William'?

Your essay needs to take the form of a clear and reasoned argument. Only then will you be able to demonstrate your understanding of the subject. You need to start with an introduction, made up of an initial statement of the standpoint to be adopted and a description of the sort of information which is pertinent to the answer. It is worthwhile doing this in order to demonstrate the direction in which you are intending to head. This is preferable to launching straight into your argument.

Your introduction might point out that when Gladstone entered the House of Commons he was a convinced Tory who took up a highly conservative stance on such issues as parliamentary reform, slavery and the rights of the established Church - that he was, as Macaulay noted in his observation, an 'unbending Tory'. You could contrast this with the statement that by the 1860s he was a popular politician, flourishing on popular acclaim - after his image had been carefully nurtured by Gladstone himself and by Bright, the 'John the Baptist' of Gladstonian Liberalism. However, you could state that there has been controversy over how much his views and outlook really changed, and that Balfour was later to note that in many ways the 'People's William' remained a Tory 'in all but essentials' to the end of his life.

Thereafter, your essay will chart Gladstone's political progress, showing how he moved to the liberal side of the Conservative Party (becoming a Peelite), and eventually to the Liberal Party. An examination of the importance of the Italian Question in his political pilgrimage is highly relevant, but you need to consider also the fact that

Gladstone's career was a relative disappointment in the 1850s, given his evident talent. What was the role of ambition and of his antipathy to Disraeli in the transition? By the end of your essay you will have assessed how far his thinking had moved on key issues, and what the reasons had been for the changes. You could pull these ideas together in a conclusion. It would be good practice for you to attempt to write a concluding paragraph for this essay.

***Source-based questions on** 'From Whigs to Liberals, 1841-68'*

1 Gladstone, Palmerston and Don Pacifico

Study the extracts on page 61 and the section on Palmerston and foreign policy. Answer the following questions.

a) How did Palmerston and Gladstone differ in their approach to the protection of British citizens throughout the world? (4 marks)
b) What was Gladstone's view of the role of a British Foreign Secretary, and how far did Palmerston's behaviour in the 1850 episode live up to this? (5 marks)
c) Comment on the tone of the extracts from the two speeches. (5 marks)
d) Compare Palmerston and Gladstone's views about the way in which foreigners should be treated. (4 marks)
e) 'In foreign policy, Palmerston was more concerned with patriotism and power, Gladstone with what was just and right'. To what extent do the extracts and the coverage of Palmerston's handling of foreign policy issues confirm this judgement? (7 marks)

2 Gladstone's Movement to Liberalism

Study the extracts on pages 71-2, 72 and 73 and the section on Gladstone's early career in general. Answer the following questions.

a) Why and with what justice did Gladstone consider himself the 'one remaining Ishmael' in the House of Commons? (4 marks)
b) What did Gladstone consider to be the main positive and negative reasons influencing his decision to join the Palmerston government in 1859? (5 marks)
c) What evidence is there to doubt his view that 'the overwhelming interest and weight of the Italian Question' was the main reason for his joining that administration? (5 marks)
d) 'I was brought up to distrust and dislike liberty, I learned to believe in it. That is the key to all my changes'. To what extent does a study of the course of Gladstone's career to 1868 suggest that this was true? (7 marks)
e) What evidence is there in the events of his career to 1868 to support Morley's view that Gladstone was driven by the 'native ardour of his humanity ... into that ... stream of liberalism'? (4 marks)

CHAPTER 5

The Age of Gladstone, 1868-95

Part A: Liberalism, 1868-85

1 Introduction

Gladstone's accession followed a prolonged period of fluid party ties, and in 1868 when he took over the premiership it was not certain that the majority would hold or that the administration would remain cohesive. It did and the period from 1868 marks the beginning of the modern party system. Gladstone and Disraeli, as leaders of the Liberals and the Conservatives respectively, became the essential link between the parties in the country and their parliamentary combinations in the House.

Writing of the 1868 election, Walter Bagehot claimed that 'Mr Gladstone's personal popularity was such as has not been seen since the time of Mr Pitt, and such as may never be seen again. A bad speaker is said to have been asked how he got on as a candidate. 'Oh,' he answered, 'when I don't know what to say, I say "Gladstone", and then they are sure to cheer, and I have time to think'.

2 Domestic Policy in Gladstone's First Ministry, 1868-74

The situation which Gladstone faced in 1868 was in some ways comparable to that which confronted the Whigs in the 1830s - the government had a very large majority and there were numerous topics awaiting reform. A few stood out as needing swift action. Events in the Crimean War had pointed to the need for army reform, and the extension of the vote had strengthened the case for an overhaul of the educational system. The state of British industry also suggested that there was a need for a better trained workforce, as there were ominous signs at the Paris Exhibition of 1867 that Britain's lead in manufacturing was ebbing away. The widening of the franchise led to new demands by the working classes for improved conditions, notably in trade union law. However, it was to be the middle class which particularly benefited from the reforming impulse.

Gladstone felt that it was time to break the stranglehold of the aristocracy over many British institutions - the army, the civil service and the universities - and to enable the growing middle classes to take up the role in society for which he thought they were well fitted. The early years of the first Gladstone ministry were spent in modernising ancient institutions, creating new machinery, eradicating abuses and dealing with other neglected areas of public life. It is on Gladstone's handling of a number of these issues that the reputation of the administration depends; it has widely been viewed as a brilliantly successful one, perhaps the most impressive in achievement of any in Victoria's long reign. Not for nothing is it often called a 'great reforming ministry'; certainly it was one of the greatest, and Gladstone's most successful.

The new Prime Minister approached his task with characteristic moral earnestness, recording in his diary that, 'I ascend a steepening path, with a burden ever gathering weight. The Almighty seems to sustain and spare me for some purpose of His own, deeply unworthy as I know myself to be'. His personal ascendancy was in no doubt, and his followers were united behind him in a way that was not to be the case in his future administrations. The government was a mixture of Whigs, Peelites and Radicals. As always, however, in his cabinet-making, Gladstone relied primarily on the Whigs, with whom he felt comfortable. Nonetheless, there were also representatives of the middle classes in key positions, such as Bright at the Board of Trade, Bruce at the Home Office, Cardwell at the War Office, and Forster in control of education. The last three in particular were to preside over a series of important reforms.

An examination of these reforming measures should allow an understanding of the nature of Gladstonian Liberalism to be built up.

a) Education

In a speech on education and the franchise in 1867, the Whig Robert Lowe had observed, 'From the moment you entrust the masses with power, their education becomes an important necessity ... Having placed the government of this country in the hands of the masses ... you must therefore give them an education'. Other forces combined to make a new Act necessary. W.E. Forster, the new Vice-President of the Board of Education, showed that Britain was falling behind other industrial countries, a situation attributed to the neglect of working-class education; 'We must not delay. Upon the speedy provision of elementary education depends our industrial prosperity. It is of no use trying to give technical teaching to our artisans without elementary education.'

Within the Liberal Party the more 'advanced Liberals' were strong believers in the value of education as a right which should be available to all. Many outside the party also saw the need for action, for provision in Britain lagged far behind that of some of its rivals. In 1869 popular clamour was led by the Birmingham Education League which was transformed into the National Educational League under the vigorous leadership of Joseph Chamberlain.

As with a number of reforms, Gladstone was not initially interested in the details. He left these to his ministers. However, if he did not take the initiative, he soon threw himself into the struggle, and felt that delay was more likely to damage than to further the interests of the Voluntary Schools of which he approved. Forster also admired the work of the Voluntary Societies.

In parts of the country where there was insufficient provision, Forster proposed to 'fill in the gaps' by establishing popularly-elected School Boards of five to fifteen members which would provide schools, paid for out of the local rates. A fee could be charged, though 'necessitous' children could have the fees met (via Clause 25), and education could be made compulsory. Religious teaching was to be given, but it was to be 'not distinctive of any religious denomination'.

These proposals were embodied in the Education Act of 1870, usually known as the Forster Act, the first major measure of state education, and one which brought about a national system. In terms of long-term significance, it was the greatest of the reforms of the ministry, and it bore the imprint of many things that mattered to Gladstone - a concern for the work of the Church in education and for freedom of voluntary action, as well as a distrust of compulsion. However, it was not without its defects, for the measure was a compromise and as such satisfied few people completely. In particular, it again aroused sectarian feelings, for the Nonconformists felt that Gladstone had yielded too much to pressure from Church schools. Chamberlain and the League would have preferred a system of free, compulsory, non-sectarian education, and they felt that the new proposals offered a rescue to the Anglican National Society. Some amendments were secured in the passage of the Bill, but the problems it created continued to be a cause of trouble to ministers in the coming years, for the numerous local conflicts of Anglicans and the Nonconformists were often bitter.

b) Institutional Reforms: Extending Opportunity

i) Oxbridge and the Civil Service

In the early nineteenth century, the old universities were not open to non-Anglicans, for to enrol as members a student had to subscribe to the 39 Articles of the Church of England and regularly attend an Anglican service. Since the 1850s undergraduates had been relieved of these 'religious tests' which had barred the entry of many talented young people to Oxford and Cambridge. However, Nonconformists were still denied a chance to take up teaching posts and fellowships at either institution. Gladstone felt some reluctance in tackling this question, for as an Anglican himself he tended to view the ancient universities as an Anglican preserve. However, he accepted that the Nonconformists should not be denied their claims and was prepared to remove their disabilities. He recognised not only that was it prudent to concede something which his backers wanted, but also that it was a matter of extending personal liberty, and therefore in line with Liberal thinking. Once he was committed to the cause he was determined that government policy should prevail and he was prepared to overcome strong criticism of the University Tests Bill from Anglicans as well as obstruction from the Lords.

Anglicans feared the moral consequences of allowing non-Anglicans to engage in tutoring their offspring, as well as a loss of key positions of patronage. Not surprisingly, Nonconformists were more satisfied with the proposed change which became law in 1871. For them, a key bastion of privilege had been reformed, and most Liberals shared this view. They were pleased to see the Church of England lose more of its control over education, and certainly by this Act much had been done to remove sectarian controversy from an important aspect of educational policy. In the short term, the Act benefited the middle classes, as many of his measures were to do. In the long run, however, it was of value to the rest of the community, once enough people had achieved the necessary qualifications and money to benefit from more advanced study.

Also in 1871 Gladstone's government legislated for the removal of another privilege. Entry into the Civil Service had for years been on the basis of 'whom you knew' and was essentially an aristocratic preserve. The sons of the wealthy had long been able to find well-paid sinecures (offices of profit without any significant duties involved) in public services and, however indolent, had been able to monopolise positions there. Middle-class supporters were looking for more avenues of advancement, and found in Gladstone a sympathetic ear. Back in 1855, during his days as Chancellor, he had already acted to advance the principle of open competition in the Indian Civil Service, by decreeing that successful candidates had to pass an examination ; he was now attracted by a recasting of the Home Civil Service. Officials selected on merit would improve the quality of administration, by ensuring that the most able persons could fill whatever vacancies arose. The emphasis on ability rather than connection was part of a new ethic in public life, one which meant that aptitude and talent should be the sole grounds of advancement. This stress on justice and efficiency helped to bring Britain into line with other states which had already improved the quality of their administrative systems.

No legislation was required, and an Order in Council opened up most of the civil service to competitive entry. There was some opposition to the move from within the Cabinet, but with the help of the chancellor, Robert Lowe, Gladstone was able to outmanoeuvre the opponents of reform, and achieve his goal. As a way of gaining its acceptance, he was content to help Clarendon, the Foreign Secretary, successfully plead his case for the exemption of the Foreign Office from the terms of the measure. It was true to say of the change, as Morley later wrote, that 'it placed the whole educated intellect of the country at the service and disposal of the state, that it stimulated the acquisition of knowledge, and that it rescued some of the most important duties in the life of the nation from the narrow class to whom they had hitherto been confided'.

ii) The Ballot, the Army and the Law

As we have seen, (pages 25 and 29), voting in parliamentary elections was still conducted in public on the open hustings, where the recording officer sat with the poll book in front of him. The voters mounted the platform, announced their vote and then descended to accompanying cheers and boos. The system was open to abuse and direct physical intimidation could occur on polling days, which were often characterised by rowdyism as well as sporadic acts of violence; the 1868 election had been a particularly lively one. Furthermore, employers and other interested parties knew how the vote was exercised and could apply pressure on their employees; sometimes, landlords issued 'notices to quit' upon tenants who had voted for the 'wrong' candidate.

For more than a generation Radicals had argued that the only solution to such problems was for votes to be cast confidentially. Gladstone was lukewarm in his enthusiasm for the secret ballot, and many Whigs were considerably more hostile, but Bright and the Radicals were convinced of its merits and urged legislation. Once introduced, the Prime Minister realised that failure to pass the Bill would enrage popular feelings. He was angry with the House of Lords for initially rejecting it. He felt that Peers were misusing their role, though he did not in any way wish to deny the importance of the House of Lords and of the aristocratic contribution to government.

The Bill was eventually passed in 1872 and at a stroke the Ballot Act substituted secret voting for the old system. In Ireland the beneficiaries were to be the Catholics who could in future cast a Nationalist vote for the home-rule candidate without considering the adverse consequences of their action, such as the likelihood of eviction. However, despite the beneficial changes which the Act brought about, corruption did not cease, and many old habits such as treating and personation occurred from time to time. The 1874 election saw rioting break out in Wolverhampton, just as it had done six years earlier. Further legislation was needed before traditional electoral malpractices could be stamped out. But the increase in the number of voters and the introduction of the ballot at least put an end to direct interference in people's voting behaviour.

Meanwhile, the Secretary for War, Cardwell, was busily engaged in another significant reform. He was one of the few remaining Peelites in the party, and he shared Gladstone's zeal for economy and efficiency. He was given the task of a major overhaul of the army, the need for which had been evident for several years. He was determined both to expand and reform the fighting forces, and the changes he introduced over the period resulted in far more modern and professional armed services. Among other things, flogging was abolished in peace-time, the length of service was cut to six years with six in reserve, a new breech-loading Martini-Henry rifle was adopted, and a system of 'linked battalions' allowed a more rapid interchange of service at home and overseas. By these measures, Cardwell hoped to attract a superior type of recruit and to ensure that the army operated on a more professional basis. They shaped the development of the late-Victorian army, but were not followed up in future years by other reforms necessary to improve recruitment and training.

However, it was the attack on the purchase of commissions in the army which aroused so much antagonism. As with the Civil Service, entry had previously been on the basis of a person's status and acquaintances, a system which had taken deep root in aristocratic society. Commissions had been seen as sinecures, and though attempts had been made to regulate the practice of purchase, there was a strong tide of service opinion which still favoured its retention. On the other side of the argument, many Liberals rallied to the anti-privilege argument, and were fond of quoting specific examples of those who had benefited from it - often ones which were rather out of date, for the system was not widespread in 1870.

As a class, Officers were generally well-rewarded whatever the quality of their contribution. Cardwell urged that 'officers shall be made for the Army' rather than the other way round, and was intent on improving a system which was believed to be a cause of military inefficiency. There had been examples in the Crimean War of the army being badly led, and the point of his plan to abolish the purchase of commissions and promotion was to substitute merit as the means of advancement.

Within the Establishment, there were again fears that the Government was interfering with property rights for the aristocracy whose members tended to view senior positions in the civil service and the army as their monopoly. Gladstone knew this and observed that 'in attacking purchase in the army, we were perfectly well aware that we were assailing class interest in its favourite and most formidable stronghold'. Though he disliked the measure, Disraeli was wary about making it a major point of contention, for he recognised that the Liberals had popular opinion on their side. He left much of the argument to those more interested in service matters, and the opposition came from a small band of Tory colonels in the Commons and from Peers in the House of Lords.

Opponents objected not only to the proposal, but also to the plan to bring it in by Royal Warrant and thereby bypass parliamentary opposition. The use of the warrant was justified by Ministers on the grounds that the original regulations establishing rights of purchase had been established by this means. Because of this and in spite of the opposition of her cousin, the Duke of Cambridge, who was Commander-in-Chief of the army, the Queen raised no objection either to the measure or to the means of implementing it. A united Cabinet pushed the proposal through, and succeeded in portraying any opposition as selfish and unscrupulous. However, this assault on privilege was not forgotten by those whose interests had been disturbed.

In 1873 Lord Selbourne's Judicature Act reformed the highly complex legal system. Several types of law had developed over the centuries, and there was a range of courts with different jurisdictions; there was an overlap in their functions and a diversity in their procedures. Two legal systems existed side by side, one based on common law and the other on equity. Common law was based on ancient customs and practices and was not written down, so that there existed no authoritative text containing the whole of such law. It was a pragmatic system which developed according to need, and hence had been unsystematic in its development. A loose body of rules was brought together in resolving a single case, and it common law grew out of the decisions of judges delivered on various occasions - hence, it is sometimes referred to as judge-made law. Equity was a more rigid body of rules grafted on to the legal system in late mediaeval times to fill in the gaps left by reliance on custom; it provided a remedy where none previously existed. Equity overrode common law, but was administered in separate courts.

The whole structure was remodeled between 1873 and 1875. As a result of Selborne's reform the two types of law were to be applied in every court, and where their rules conflicted, those of equity were made to prevail. But the Act did more, and remodelled the whole system of courts. The existing courts were merged under a Supreme Court of Judicature, under which there was a High Court with three separate divisions as well as a Court of Appeal. By a bold stroke, the amazingly complex system had been streamlined along more intelligible lines. Writing early in the twentieth century, Sir Robert Ensor (England 1870-1914) felt able to claim that this was a piece of tidying up 'on the largest scale, in a field littered with the most venerable survivals from the middle ages'. The changes passed into law with little controversy, for there was all-party support for this overdue overhaul of the judicial system. Its author was well-pleased with his work, which he described as 'the work of my own hand, without any assistance beyond what I derived from the labours of my predecessors; and it passed substantially in the form in which I proposed it'.

iii) Reforms Affecting the Working Classes: Trade Unions and Drink

Gladstone had long appreciated the importance of labour in society and had spoken of the 'responsible' sections of the working class and of the merits of the artisans. But though he was willing to concede new rights he was unwilling to offer unions a privileged position in law. In his Trade Union (Protection of Funds) Act of 1871 the formation of unions was allowed, and they were enabled to register with the Registrar of Friendly Societies and thereby gain protection for their funds. Trade union officials could 'bring or defend ... any action, suit, prosecution or complaint in any court of law or equity, touching or concerning the property, rights or claims to the property of the trade union'. The right to strike was acknowledged.

However, what had been conceded with one hand was removed by the other, for on the same day a second statute, the Criminal Law Amendment Act, eroded the position of workmen. If strike action was legalised, molestation or obstruction was not, so that a worker who used peaceful picketing to seek to persuade colleagues not to work would be liable for imprisonment. Gladstone was aware of the importance of organised labour, and his approach to parliamentary reform had indicated that he admired the qualities of the industrious artisan. He believed that unions should exist as legal entities, with the protection that the law could offer; he also supported the notion of free collective bargaining between representatives of unions and management. He felt that there was justice in removing a restriction (i.e., by providing workers with a right to strike), but having recognised the merits and utility of union activity he shrank from conceding too many rights. He did not think it was the state's role to interfere in the workings of *laissez-faire* by stepping in to give unions a privileged position in law. He was worried lest 'the labouring classes should like other classes be led to exaggerate their own rights in such a matter'. His principle was 'to punish violence; and in all economical matters the law to take no part'.

Trade unions saw the matter differently. For them, the second measure was a clear limit on the efficacy of the strike weapon, and between 1871-3 several magistrates interpreted it in a more restrictive manner than had been intended. There was much bitterness over the issue, and the recently-formed Trades Union Congress pressed for modification. Gladstone tended to leave labour matters to the relevant minister, and in the words of his biographer, H.C.G. Matthew, he acted as 'the coordinator rather than initiator' in 1873, when the issue became highly topical. As the new Home Secretary in 1873, Lowe was willing to make concessions, and recent research indicates that the Cabinet was moving by the end of the year towards some relaxation of the law on picketing. However, few Liberal MPs had shown much willingness to campaign for a change in the 1871 laws, and the Government fell before anything was done about it.

Drunkenness was a major problem in Victorian society and there was much controversy over whether the state should intervene to restrict the sale of alcoholic drink. Some Liberals such as Mill believed that drinking was a matter of individual inclination, but others urged control because of the social problems it posed. There was a strong temperance movement which sought to persuade people to renounce alcohol and it urged measures to remove temptation by curbing the number of public houses and restricting their opening times. Nonconformists were keen to see temperance (by which most meant abstinence) extended, but Gladstone was no enthusiast for the cause. Nonetheless, ministers were aware of the strength of the movement, and the Home Secretary Bruce produced a measure which was dealt with by the House largely on a non-party basis.

The Licensing Act of 1872 was the first limitation on the number of ale houses and beer shops, and on the number of hours they could be open. It created a new licensing authority in each town, and henceforth no premises could sell liquor without its approval. The authority fixed the hours of opening, and was encouraged to use the new system to ensure that there would be an overall reduction in the number of drinking-houses.

Brewers and licensees were incensed, though Robert Blake has found little evidence to support the frequently made claim that they soon went over to the other side and reinforced the membership and finance of the Conservative Party. The passage of the Act enabled opponents to condemn the Liberals for a further attack on property, and contributed to the public reaction against the government. The Liberals were to become increasingly identified with anti-drink legislation in the public mind.

3 Ireland and its Problems

There was common agreement among politicians and the public that there was an Irish problem, although there was far less concord over what it was. The country was governed via Dublin Castle under the Act of Union of 1800. It was overwhelmingly agricultural, and those who owned the land were mainly Protestant landlords, some of whom were absentees though many lived on or near their estates. Tenants rented the land and often sublet it to other tenants, so that those at the bottom of the pile could have many landlords above them in the chain. Cultivated in small plots, often almost entirely by hand, the land was unproductive and it was difficult for anyone to make a good living from it. Such a backward agrarian economy was unable to sustain the entire Irish population, and since 1800 several million people had moved across to mainland Britain or had emigrated to North America or Australia.

A further element in the problem was the status of the Church of Ireland (the Irish arm of the Protestant Church of England) in a country which was predominantly Catholic; the issue continued to cause much resentment. As the century progressed, these Irish problems gained greater urgency. The campaign for Repeal of the Union had been growing in strength since the 1840s and in the 1860s the Fenian Movement for Irish Independence had staged several uprisings in the United States, Canada and in Ireland itself. In 1867 a bomb explosion at Clerkenwell prison in London killed over 100 people and made Gladstone aware of the importance of tackling discontents across the water.

We have seen how Gladstone took up the issue of Disestablishment in 1868 (see page 78), for reasons of expediency as well as of belief; by so doing, he had placed Disraeli uncomfortably on the defensive and exploited Conservative difficulties on the topic. As Prime Minister after

1868, having announced in a much-quoted phrase that his 'mission was to pacify Ireland', he acted to draw up a Bill for Disestablishment of the Irish Church and for its partial disendowment - its property would be reduced to a value of £10 million. After a struggle with the House of Lords, where there was much feeling against the measure, it became law; the only change was that the Church retained £13 million in property.

At this stage, Gladstone's understanding of Irish affairs was based primarily upon his broad liberal outlook, rather than upon a detailed appreciation of the issues involved. However, he laboured long hours over the complexities of the land problem, believing that the goal was 'to give peace and security to Ireland, and through Ireland to the Empire'. He acted in two ways: to make funds available to assist tenants to purchase their land, and (of significance to far more of them) to curtail the landlord's freedom of action by restricting his rights of eviction. He would be forced to pay compensation for any improvements made by the tenant, should eviction be carried out. This was a controversial area, for property rights were generally viewed as sacrosanct, and some Liberals were unhappy.

The 1870 Land Act which embodied these proposals was useful but inadequate, for it did not go far enough to protect the tenants against excessive rents. As an agricultural depression set in the mid-1870s, many of them were to be unable to pay the rents, and further action was necessary. However, by then the Gladstone administration had fallen.

4 Decline of the Ministry

In 1872 Disraeli described the Liberal Front Bench as a 'row of exhausted volcanoes'. Indeed, the ministry had by then accomplished most of its useful work, and over the next year it became increasingly disunited. The Cabinet became restive and Gladstone's skills of party management appeared to have deserted him. It was only his personality and his powers of persuasion which kept it together. However, the strain of office was beginning to show in his own performance which lacked its former vigour. He found that life was becoming out of balance; he was unable to detach himself from his work and spoke of retirement.

By-election defeats had begun in 1870 and had increased in numbers as the years went by. By 1874 there had been 27 Conservative gains in 47 months, and the Liberal Home Rule majority was halved. In these circumstances, Gladstone attempted to resign in March 1873. However, Disraeli was too wily to accept office, for his position in the Commons would have been too weak to ensure survival. Gladstone continued as Prime Minister, but his party seemed accident-prone and continued to lose ground and in January 1874 he called a general election. Despite the promise of a reduction in income tax and of its eventual complete abolition, he was defeated and the Liberals went into opposition.

The years up to 1872 were ones of constructive achievement, and proved to be the most successful ones of Gladstone's long career as Prime Minister. His powers of work were prodigious and his considerable parliamentary skills were displayed to full advantage. On several issues he had thrown his full weight and prestige into skirmishes at Westminster, and this had proved decisive. He did not often take the initiative in proposing innovations, but he was prepared to back ministers in need of assistance. He did not have the grasp which Peel had possessed of every government department, but he was skilful in directing the attention of his fellow MPs on issues which he took up.

The reforms did much to create the administrative structure of a modern state, and enable it to cope with the growing business of government. Professor Annan has referred to the period of 1870-1 as the time when there was a 'glorious revolution' in the administrative system, and in these years the measures did do much to bring about an end to patronage and privilege. Much of Gladstone's attention was directed to attacking manifestations of unfair advantage and prejudice, and the nepotism of the past gave way to a new emphasis on equality of opportunity in which appointments and promotions were based upon merit alone.

R.M. McCallum put it well in his history of *The Liberal Party From Earl Grey To Asquith,* in which he noted that the reforms were about the 'improvement in the method and art of government, and the removal of any restriction or disqualification that fell on any particular class or sect'. In that spirit, new opportunities were opened up, and the civil service, the old universities and the legal system all benefited from this review. The work on behalf of the army was particularly impressive.

John Morley, Gladstone's biographer, wrote that 'The most marked administrative performance of [his] great government was the reform and reorganisation of the Army. In Mr Cardwell he was fortunate to have a public servant of the finest order. Before he had been a month at the War Office the new Secretary of State submitted his ideas of a plan that would give us an effective defence at a greatly reduced cost'. In some ways it seems ironic that the Liberals, the anti-militarist party, should be the one to modernise the British army; but their emphasis was upon efficiency and value for money, and the military was a suitable arena for such treatment.

John Bright was able to offer an approving verdict on the ministry in October 1873 when he told his Birmingham audience that,

1 These five years are memorable years and its measures will bear comparison with those of any government which has ever preceded it. A few years ago it was thought an impossible thing to remove an Established Church, and yet an Established Church - I speak of the
5 political institution only - has been removed, while the Church remains.

> Another great principle has been established - that office, authority and dignity in service of the State shall not henceforth be bought by the rich to the exclusion of those that are less rich, or are
> 10 poor. The corruption market is closed for ever in departments of public service.
> There is another principle that has been established which must interest many here, and that is that the franchise is the right of the electors; whether we win elections or lose them, I am for the ballot
> 15 ... The State has admitted its responsibility for the education of the people by public grants, by public rates and the partial application of the power of compulsion. The education of the children of the country is henceforward to be provided for by the State.

Much had been accomplished and if the Front Bench was 'a row of exhausted volcanoes' it was in reality a gibe which contained an unintended compliment. It was exhausted because ministers had completed a major programme of reform, which until it petered out in 1872-3 had transformed important aspects of public life.

The reforms were effective in extending opportunity to the middle classes, but in the short term they did not help the working classes very much. Of course, the increase in educational opportunities was directly beneficial to them, but there was little by way of social improvement to help the lowly-paid, the badly-housed, the sick or the unemployed, or to improve working conditions. Nor was there likely to be for the Liberal Party believed that it was not the role of government to regulate social and economic life, and *laissez-faire* philosophy combined with a deep aversion to increasing government expenditure and a preference for low taxation made social provision unlikely. Clearing the slums was costly, limiting the opening hours of public houses or increasing the opportunities for advancement in the civil service was not.

The trade union legislation was similarly inexpensive, and legalising union activity was a step forward. However, the limitations placed on the right to strike were a blow to working people, which suggested that the government had an ambiguous attitude to organised labour, on the one hand accepting its existence, on the other showing anxiety lest it become too powerful. Indeed, it achieved the worst of both worlds, for among the middle classes there were some who were uneasy about the recognition of unions, and felt that ministers had made an error; yet for the working people whom the legislation was supposed to help, the limitations on peaceful picketing were a serious drawback.

Some members of the Liberal Party would have liked to see the reforming zeal extended more widely so that it had more impact on the social life of the working classes. An article in *Fraser's Magazine* in March 1874 showed the differing emphases of members of the Liberal Party.

1 The Liberals of the old school - those who, as the late election has so plainly shown, represent far more truly than their extreme associates the genuine feeling of the nation - were bent upon the maintenance of peace and the enforcement of honest retrenchment
5 for the sake of the preservation of our ancient institutions. They have achieved their objects, and are contented.

They see Liberals of a new school striving vehemently and dictatorially for a variety of changes, which are not in their creed, and they are alarmed. They are not disposed to flirt with Home
10 Rule, to try questionable experiments in education, to relieve the bulk of the nation from fair contributions to the revenue, to endure the dictation of Trades Unions; still less are they disposed to permit for an instant any tampering with the just rights of property - and they think they discern in the attitudes, and still more in the
15 character, of Mr Gladstone, a probability that he may be led in the direction of all these things.

To opponents, it was all too much. Many vested interests had been upset, and it was hardly surprising that the wealthy and most privileged section of the community should feel aggrieved by the concerted attack upon the bastions of influence which they once monopolised. For the propertied classes Gladstone was undermining a style of life to which they had become accustomed, and whether it was in the army, the Church, the civil service and the colleges at Oxbridge, things for them would never be the same again. Disraeli was correct in his belief that many people were tired of a policy of 'plundering and blundering', and ready for a period of consolidation after the Liberals' 'over-hasty' changes. In 1873 he argued that; 'For nearly five years the present Ministry has harassed every trade, worried every profession and assailed or menaced every class, institution and species of property in the country ... the country has, I think, made up its mind to close this career of plundering and blundering.'

Many of the people most harmed by the changes might not have been disposed to vote for Gladstone anyway, and perhaps more serious was the way in which his measures antagonised more traditional Liberal supporters - labourers, radicals and Nonconformists. The working classes had no reason to thank Gladstone for his licensing and trade union legislation, the former having upset both those who disliked the limitations on their opportunities for drinking and the brewers who had found the Liberals so unsympathetic to their interests. The latter had caused bitter resentment, the more so as in a series of legal cases it was clear that the law was being stringently applied. As the unions campaigned for repeal of the Criminal Law Amendment Act, they became increasingly hostile to the Liberal Party and its middle-class ethos, and in 1874 some of them campaigned on behalf of the Conservatives, or ran their own candidates.

More serious was the Nonconformist revolt. For Dissenters, the Education Act was a bitter blow, both because it preserved the Anglican-dominated system of voluntary schools and because, via Clause 25, it enabled them to gain some rate-aid as well. Chamberlain felt especially bitter, and argued that 'The Government has chosen deliberately to defy us ... This conduct leaves us no alternative ... The 'Nonconformist Revolt' long threatened has at last begun'.

It is difficult to gauge how much this 'revolt' contributed to the defeat in 1874, but the historian of the National Educational League, Francis Adams, has made clear that the timing of the election caught Nonconformists by surprise and in a state of unpreparedness. Some of its spokesmen such as Joseph Chamberlain, then a candidate for Sheffield were defeated, and the concentration of the Nonconformist vote was in the North where there were proportionately fewer parliamentary constituencies than the population would have merited. He calculates a loss of 20 seats brought about by Nonconformist abstentions, a serious setback but not quite enough to account for defeat.

The defeat when it came was a decisive one, and Gladstone saw it as 'the greatest expression of public disapprobation of a Government that he ever remembered'. In a memorable phrase, he claimed that the party had been 'borne down in a torrent of gin and beer', and he was right to pinpoint the unpopularity of the Licensing Act, even if the mass desertion of the brewers and their funds to the Conservative side has been exaggerated. The loss of trade union sympathy did not help and probably provoked some abstention or pro-Conservative voting, and poor organisation magnified its extent. The Liberals were vulnerable to attacks on their patriotism, and accusations of a weak and spineless foreign policy (see pages 115-16) and of 'selling short on British interests' did not help. But beyond this there was the fact that Disraeli had caught the public mood by the skill of his attack on the government. Armed with a revived organisation and a clearer identity following his speeches of the early 1870s, he was able to draw attention to exploit the government's 'achilles heel', and the middle classes, fearful of Gladstone's radicalism, were in no mood for further experimentation.

5 In Opposition, 1874-80

In January 1875, Gladstone decided to relinquish the leadership, explaining his decision to Lord Granville in this way; 'I see no advantage in my continuing to act as the leader of the Liberal Party and at the age of sixty-five, and after forty-two years of a laborious public life, I think myself entitled to retire as the best method of spending the closing years of my life'. Granville and then Hartington led the party in these years in opposition, and the Liberals suffered from a lack of direction. Radicals such as Morley and Chamberlain used the pages of the *Fortnightly Review* to develop the idea of a 'third force' in British politics, with its own distinctive strategy. Chamberlain, in particular, having entered the House of Commons in 1876, began to widen the basis of his interests, recognising that education was but one of a number of social injustices and that 'Education for the Ignorant cannot have the same meaning that belonged to Bread for the Starving'.

It was the issue of the Bulgarian Atrocities that brought Gladstone back into public prominence once again. When the Bulgars revolted against their Turkish rulers in May 1876 the rising was suppressed with great brutality by irregular Turkish troops known as the Bashi-bazouks whose techniques included rape and arson, as well as mass repression. The Liberal *Daily News* reported the massacre of some 10,000 women and children, and, though the pro-Turkish Disraelian government appeared not to take the account seriously, the Liberal conscience was outraged. Gladstone was not quick to get in the forefront of the campaign, but once he did the effect was dramatic.

Here was another of his 'volcanic eruptions', and he condemned the iniquity of the government's behaviour as well as the brutality of the atrocities, observing that 'Under the authority of Turkey to which all the time we have been giving the strongest moral and material support, outrages so vast in scale as to exceed all modern example' had occurred. His denunciations breathed new life into a somnulent party leadership, and Chamberlain, who had not shown much interest in foreign questions previously, now saw the opportunity of providing his Radical creed with an ethical dimension; he allied himself firmly with Gladstone.

On other issues of overseas policy, Gladstone savaged the government front bench, culminating in his attack on the wars in the Transvaal and in Afghanistan. He stood for what was 'right' and 'just' on matters of foreign policy, whereas Disraeli emphasised national honour and self-interest. Of course, it was relatively easy for an opposition spokesmen, freed from governmental responsibility, to assume the lofty moral 'high ground', but it is on the basis of his sentiments and outbursts that Gladstone's belief in the importance of morality in political life becomes so apparent.

Gladstone's two Midlothian Campaigns of late 1879 and early 1880 showed his righteous indignation at its most effective. He was challenging to re-enter Parliament by winning the seat held by the Earl of Dalkeith, the son of the grandest Conservative landowner in Scotland, and in his whirlwind tours he launched into a remarkable series of public meetings in which in addition to condemning the impiety of Disraeli's approach he outlined his ideas on the just conduct of Britain's relations with the rest of the world. He managed to equate the cause of empire with not only incompetence and waste, but also with evil.

In the election campaign Disraeli, old and weary, was no match for Gladstone and could never have sustained such an arduous programme. In addition to problems overseas, the administration had run into difficulties at home, and more than anything else it was 'hard times', which lost the Conservatives the election. At a time of growing economic depression and mounting unemployment, Disraeli was unable to offer any way forward to lead the country out of its difficulties, and in the event the Liberals won a handsome victory - aided by the effective organisation which Chamberlain had been so instrumental in setting up (see page 104).

The Colossus of Words, *1879, by Tenniel*

6 The Second Gladstone Ministry, 1880-85

Although Hartington was still the nominal leader of the party, Gladstone was the only person who had the authority to form the new administration; he *was* the Liberal Party. Despite his earlier doubts, even Chamberlain had come to recognise that Gladstone was 'our best card

... If he were to come back for a few years (he can't continue in public life for very much longer) he would probably do much for us and pave the way for me'.

In 1880 there were high expectations that, armed with a substantial majority of 46 over the Conservatives and the Irish, there would be another period of effective and reforming government. Gladstone seemed to be reinvigorated, and saw his victory as a divine judgement - 'I do believe that the Almighty has employed me for His purpose in a manner larger or more special than before'. Post-Midlothian his own personal prestige was at a height and there were several able men around him. In addition, the party at Westminster was backed by a formidable organisation around the country. But things were not the same as in 1868. Then Gladstone had led a cohesive party and a united Cabinet. After 1880, there was to be regular schism, vacillation and continuous unpopularity.

To please the Whigs who disliked the more ambitious Radicals and their growing 'demagogy', in his Cabinet-making Gladstone relied on the predominantly Whig 'old guard'. They occupied the majority of posts and only the ageing Bright and Joseph Chamberlain were there to represent the other side. But the Radicals would never allow Gladstone to forget their importance in the election victory, and they watched him with growing suspicion. He failed to settle ministerial feuds by imposing strong leadership and Chamberlain took to unilateral action to maintain Radical influence - in particular, through press releases and attacks on some of his Whig colleagues. From the beginning, the Speaker of the House of Commons noted that Gladstone had a 'difficult team to drive'.

Apart from divisions at the top, the new Liberal government suffered from the fact that the party had no definite political philosophy or agreed programme. The ministry had gained power largely because of the depression and the reaction against Beaconsfieldism (Disraeli had become the Earl of Beaconsfield in 1878). It was united only on the negative issue of denouncing Disraeli's foreign and imperial policies. As Gladstone had put it; 'All our heads are still in a whirl from the great events of the last few weeks which have given joy, I am convinced, to the large majority of the civilised world. The downfall of Beaconsfieldism is like the vanishing of some vast magnificent castle in an Italian romance'.

No-one had worked out a scheme of principles to meet the new age, and the Liberals had no definite programme to offer. As Beatrice Webb, an influential early socialist thinker and writer, put it; 'Mr Gladstone's administration of 1880-85 ... wandered in and out of the trenches of the old individualists and the scouting parties of the new Socialists with an "absence of mind" concerning social and economic questions that became, in the following decades, the characteristic feature of Liberal statesmanship'. The root cause of the ministry's malaise lay in the composition of the Liberal Party. For a long time it had prided itself on the strength afforded by diversity. In Gladstone's first administration there had been little discord, but it became increasingly obvious that the divisions of Whig-Radical, Right-Left, were becoming unbridgeable. Gladstone had appointed a conservative Cabinet at a time when the party was becoming more radical and the divided team was unable to prove an effective instrument of government. Within the party as a whole, tensions and differences on personality and policy were too great. What Morley said of the Cabinet was true of the whole party; it was not only a coalition, 'but a coalition of that vexatious kind where those who happened not to agree sometimes seemed to be almost as well pleased with contention as with harmony'.

a) Problems at Home

The government was beset with problems at home and abroad (see page 117), and an issue soon arose which was to prove an incubus throughout the ministry. Charles Bradlaugh, a committed atheist, republican and pioneer of birth control, was elected as a Radical MP. As a non-believer, he refused to take the Parliamentary Oath which implied a belief in the Almighty which he did not possess. He offered to affirm his allegiance, as certain other groups were allowed to do. The Speaker unwisely allowed the issue to be debated and then referred to a Select Committee which ruled against Bradlaugh. Neither would it allow him to take the Oath, so that he was unable to take up his parliamentary seat.

Gladstone was at his best in that he forsook any opportunity to seek popularity or party advantage and stressed the cause of religious liberty to which over the years he had become deeply committed. The issue was much exploited by his opponents, particularly the young Lord Randolph Churchill who urged him not to allow 'an avowed atheist and a professedly disloyal person' on to the Liberal benches, and denounced 'Bradlaugh and Blasphemy'. He enjoyed watching the unusual spectacle of the Grand Old Man being seen to defend one whose views were so personally abhorrent to him. The issue dragged on for the lifetime of the ministry, consuming time and energy, and Bradlaugh only entered the Chamber in 1886.

Lord Randolph was to prove difficult to handle. His official Tory leader was Northcote who had once worked for Gladstone and treated him with deference and caution; it was he who had coined the label 'Grand Old Man'. Churchill mocked Northcote unmercifully, but along with his colleagues in the 'Fourth Party' (a ginger group committed to the Disraelian legacy) he was also able to make life difficult for ministers. Bitingly sarcastic, he was able to goad Gladstone into losing his temper so that the Prime Minister seemed not to be in control of events. Gladstone took Churchill's antics seriously and recognised him as a formidable opponent. Over the five years of its existence, opportunities were effectively used by the Fourth Party, and whether it was over Ireland or some colonial problem, the government front bench was much harassed and embarrassed.

b) Irish Events

Irish affairs proved to be particularly difficult to handle, and in the face of mounting misery and violence policy veered between coercion and kindness. The second Land Act of 1881 provided tenants with new rights, the so-called 'three Fs' - Fair Rents, Fixity of Tenure and Free Sale - benefits which had been demanded over several years. The Act brought a degree of peace to the countryside, for evictions were much reduced and so was disorder. However, the Coercion Act which had preceded it by a few months and which gave the authorities special powers of arrest, had provoked the Irish representatives at Westminster to furious obstruction of Commons' business, and this poisoned the atmosphere when the Land Act was passed.

Charles Stewart Parnell, who was the leader of the Irish Home Rule contingent at Westminster, had considerable influence over his fellow-countrymen. His family was anti-British and he shared its outlook. He was a resourceful parliamentary performer who exploited the political situation of the early 1880s with much success. The militant posture he and his fellow Home Rulers had adopted had won concessions from the government. But his championing of anti-English activity in Ireland and of obstruction at Westminster led to his imprisonment at Kilmainham Gaol, in Dublin. He was released a few months later (April 1882), for his imprisonment had not reduced the number of outrages in the island, and there was little point in his detention. The government seemed to be turning from coercion, and prospects temporarily seemed brighter. However, the murder a few weeks later of a new Chief Secretary, Cavendish, and his Under-Secretary in Phoenix Park, Dublin, changed the picture dramatically, for the assassinations aroused a sense of horror in England. Many Whigs were especially appalled, for Cavendish was a brother of Lord Hartington, and a senior figure in Whig society.

Gladstone found himself in a very difficult situation, for there was a wide variety of attitudes on Irish problems within his party. The Whigs were hostile to much 'improving' legislation for they were shocked by evidence of agitation and disorder. At the other extreme, Radicals such as Chamberlain and Bright were uneasy about resorting to repression and wanted to see remedial measures to tackle legitimate grievances; they believed that coercion alone could never settle the situation. Home Rule, the policy to which Gladstone eventually turned, was to achieve the improbable feat of uniting these formerly distinct groups in opposition to his leadership.

c) Legislation 1880-85

The legislation passed by the ministry lacked a coherent theme such as the destruction of unfair privilege and advantage that had been so evident in the first administration. The measures were in line with Liberal attitudes, but did not constitute such a memorable overall programme. Several of the reforms were in themselves useful, but they were of limited scope and significance. The first two listed below fall into this category.

In 1880 the Burials Act removed a grievance of the Nonconformists by permitting them to bury their dead in parish churchyards, with religious forms selected by themselves, or without any at all.

The Ground Game Act of the same year, popularly known as the 'Hares and Rabbits' Act, allowed tenant farmers to protect their crops from vermin and to share the sport of their landlords.

Also in 1880 Mundella's Education Act completed the journey towards compulsion in elementary education. In 1876, where there were no School Boards, districts had been ordered to set up School Attendance Committees with compulsory powers of attendance. Now attendance was made compulsory for all children to an age not exceeding 13. In 1870, Forster had presided over a major first step by the state into the field of education; thereafter, governments, including this one, began to show greater interest in its development.

In 1881 flogging was abolished in the army and navy, and a year later the Settled Land Act gave tenants of an estate the right to grant further leases. Also in 1882, the Married Women's Property Act, following on from a measure in the first Gladstone administration, allowed women to own property in law for the first time. The earlier Act of 1870 allowed women to keep their earnings; this one granted them the same rights over their property as single women. This was a move fully in line with the Liberal outlook, in that it enhanced individual rights for a section of the community on whom a serious disadvantage had fallen. The law had previously emphasised the subordination of women in a male-dominated society, and the two pieces of legislation were of particular consequence to middle-class women who were more likely to have worthwhile and valuable possessions.

The two most important reforms concerned the method of voting. The Corrupt Practices Act of 1883 may be compared to the Ballot Act as one of the laws that has done most to make Britain an effective democracy. It defined precisely the amount of money that could be spent on each electoral campaign, ruled out every form of bribery and undue influence, even laying down the number of conveyances that could be used for bringing voters to the polls. It went a long way to removing electoral corruption, although isolated cases of it still occurred from time to time.

The most important measure of the period was the Third Reform Act of 1884-5. The previous measure in 1867 had granted the vote to workingmen in the boroughs but not in the counties, and most Liberals were committed to campaigning for equality of treatment between town and country. Bright was in the forefront of the campaign and Chamberlain was active in the struggle. On the Whig side, Hartington was uneasy for he saw that a further measure would lead to the election of a large number of Irish Nationalist MPs.

By the Bill, the franchise was extended to householders in the country, thereby adding more than two million voters to the electoral roll and bringing the total number of voters in the United Kingdom to well over five million. Such an enfranchisement of the agricultural labourers was deemed to be favourable to Liberal prospects, and Lord Salisbury used the Conservative majority in the Lords to block the proposal. It was allowed to pass only when it was agreed that it be followed by a Redistribution Bill (1885). This effected a radical change, and deprived 79 small towns (under 15,000) of any separate representation and ensured that those of under 50,000 had only one representative. Most constituencies, other than those between 50,000 and 165,000, were now to be single-member constituences.

The effects of such redrawing of the boundaries were considerable. Within the Liberal Party the Whigs lost influence for whereas before some constituencies had returned a Radical and a Whig representative, now most selected a Radical one; the already-declining Whig element in the Commons was further reduced. The Conservatives had gained out of the redistribution in that in future they were often victorious in the single-member, middle-class suburbs where the phenomenon of 'Villa Toryism' became a potent feature.

d) Assessment of the Reforms of Gladstone's Second Ministry

Taken in conjunction with the legislation of the earlier ministry, the effect of these changes was to make a concerted attack on prejudice and privilege which was the essence of Gladstonian Liberalism. His support for, among other things, the Disestablishment of the Irish Church, two Land Acts, civil service reform, the extension of the franchise and the elimination of electoral abuses, aroused the ire of the propertied classes who saw him as an ogre who was attacking the very fundamentals of society as they knew them. The reforms indicate the extent to which the Liberals under Gladstone were ceasing to be a party of 'the establishment'. Indeed, to the more cautious amongst them, he was exhibiting a dangerous radicalism. Hartington feared that he was driving 'our best men, or at all events the Whigs' into the Tory camp, for he had placed the aristocracy firmly in opposition to him.

In the second ministry the amount of reform was not inconsiderable but most of the changes were relatively small-scale, useful but not far-reaching in their implications. Of course there were exceptions, and granting the vote to agricultural labourers was an important step which did the party some good in the 1885 elections. That measure, and the Corrupt Practices

Act, moved the country substantially forwards on the road to becoming a political democracy. Nonetheless, compared with the expectations in 1880 the outcome was less impressive than had been anticipated. Hence the observation of Sir Robert Ensor that 'Never has a triumphant House of Commons achieved so little'. In different circumstances, and at a time of looser party alignments, Palmerston's ministry of 1859-65 had produced only very modest innovation, but the essential implication of Ensor's comment is true enough. Perhaps it was Winston Churchill who got it right when he observed; 'Few periods of office have begun with higher hopes; none has been more disappointing in its outcome'.

7 Chamberlain and the Radical Challenge

The ministry had been undermined from the beginning by disharmony within the party and as Gladstone's son Herbert recognised, 'Whigs and Radicals fought, if not to a finish ... yet to an advanced stage on the way to it'. The cement which kept it together was provided by Gladstone, and considering the difficulties with which he was beset it was a considerable achievement to keep the 'show on the road'. As Harcourt wrote to him in 1885, 'You are the Party and your acts are its acts'. Clearly he was pivotal in keeping the disparate combination together.

But those tensions had been apparent from the first parliamentary session, when the Radicals were unhappy about the composition of the Cabinet and the Whigs disapproved of elements of the legislative programme. Whigs were generally uneasy about the Ground Game Act and its assault on the exclusive rights of landed property; they continued to show alarm at other changes, most notably over the passing of the Third Reform Bill. Hartington threatened resignation over the measure, but was frightened into staying on, lest the influence of the left-wing Radical element in the party should be strengthened. He often spoke of retirement and claimed to yearn for a life back on his estates. But he remained in office despite his uneasy relationship with Gladstone, and his presence was reassuring to those who shared his fear of Radicalism.

Hartington and other Whigs were much irritated by the behaviour of Joseph Chamberlain in the government for he proved a disloyal colleague, much prone to leaking information to his press associates and, on occasion, to writing unsigned articles attacking his more conservative ministerial colleagues. Chamberlain was caustic in his observations about the role of the aristocracy, and he and other Radicals were impatient with the Whigs who were a barrier to progress and reform. Henry Labouchere spoke for many of them when he wrote in 1885 that; 'A distant view of the promised land, and a few grapes from it, will not suffice us. We must possess the land at once. We are not prepared to suit our pace to the heavy lumbering coach of Whiggism.' Of all those unwilling to wait for the 'lumbering coach of Whiggism', the most impatient was 'Brummagem Joe', the earnest spokesmen of provincial radicalism. Chamberlain had been an innovative Mayor of Birmingham between 1873 and 1876, and on entering the House of Commons as one of the city's MPs, (in company with John Bright), he had sought to establish a reputation as a politician equipped with a broad reforming programme.

Chamberlain was also an innovator in the field of party organisation. Having been active in his local Liberal association and in campaigning for a nation-wide system of education, he proceeded to effect a transformation in the central party machinery. He was instrumental in setting up the National Liberal Federation in 1877, a body which would provide the Liberals with a means of galvanising support across the country and also, he hoped, demonstrate the strength of radical feeling among the rank and file.

After 1880 Chamberlain was in the Cabinet, although without the influence to which he felt entitled. His interests extended well beyond his official responsibilities at the Board of Trade and his articles and speeches over a whole range of topics much irritated fellow-members of the Cabinet. He was active in denouncing the House of Lords for obstruction over the passage of the Reform Bill, and was relentlessly critical of representatives of the landed class, such as Lord Salisbury, who was seen as typical of that section of society who 'toil not, neither do they spin'. But members of his own party did not escape the lashing of a venomous tongue. Lord Hartington was likened to 'Rip Van Winkle', the fictional character who went to sleep for 20 years.

Conceptions of Reform

The Whig Approach

Lord Hartington wrote complacently of the Whig attitude to progress, in 1883.

The Whigs are not the leaders in popular movements, but ... have been able, as I think, to the great advantage of the country, to direct, and guide, and moderate those popular movements. They have formed a connecting link between the advanced party and those classes which, possessing property, power and influence, are naturally averse to change, and I think I may claim that it is greatly owing to their guidance and to their action that the great and beneficial changes, which have been made in the direction of popular reform in this country, have been made not by the shock of revolutionary agitation, but by the calm and peaceful process of constitutional acts.

The Radical Approach

Joseph Chamberlain wrote to his colleague Sir Charles Dilke expressing his exasperation with the Whig presence in the party.

The business of the Radicals is to lead great popular movements and if they are fortunate enough to stir the hearts of the people ... then it will be the high-born prerogative of the great Whig noble who has been waiting round the corner to direct and guide and moderate the movement he has done all in his power to prevent and discourage.

In 1884-5 Chamberlain articulated an alternative programme to that of the official party, and crowds flocked to hear him proclaim his views and launch savage attacks on the aristocracy and their privileges. However, if enthusiasm in the country was such that he was once announced as 'Your coming Prime Minister', his enemies were roused to fury. They were especially disturbed by his adoption of the notion of 'ransom', by which he meant that the rich deserved to pay heavily in taxation to compensate for the privileges which they enjoyed. The term sounded menacing, although, as was often the case, the rhetoric was more threatening than the actuality of what was proposed.

To Gladstone, Chamberlain was a socialist. Chamberlain occasionally used the word himself for 'every kindly act of legislation by which the community has sought to discharge its responsibilities and its obligations to the poor is Socialism and is none the worse for that'. The term was much used at the time, and can create a confusing impression. Chamberlain distinguished his creed from Marxism which he abhorred as class warfare; he 'opposed confiscation in every shape and form'. His general belief in the redistribution of wealth was far short of what is meant by socialism in its usual definition. He was too much the enterprising businessman and believer in individual effort and initiative to easily accommodate himself to collectivist ideas which stressed an ever-widening role for the state.

8 The Fall of the Second Gladstone Government; the 1885 Election

By early 1885 there was much disagreement within the government over Ireland (see pages 100 and 109) and other issues. Chamberlain was keen to see some form of self-government across the water, though one well short of Home Rule; he favoured 'National Councils' for the four parts of the United Kingdom which would have substantial domestic responsibilities. His colleagues were generally unimpressed by his ideas, and he resigned in frustration and general disillusion with the Liberal performance. Soon afterwards, in June 1885 the government was defeated and resigned.

Elections were to be held later in the year on the new register once it was ready for use, and meanwhile in the summer Chamberlain published a collection of this thoughts of recent months in *The Radical*

Programme, a campaigning document. A Whig colleague, for so the Whigs officially were, referred to the contents of Chamberlain's handbook as 'the unauthorised programme', a label which stuck. His personal manifesto was bold and imaginative; the official (authorised) one of Gladstone was by comparison lack-lustre and non-committal.

Main Contents of the Liberal Manifestoes of 1885

Unauthorised Programme	Official Programme
Reform of Lords	Possible Lords changes
Triennial Parliaments	Reform of Commons procedure
Payment of MPs	Attempts to boost voter registration
Manhood Suffrage	Local Government reform
Disestablishment of State Church	Modest changes in land registration
Democratic Local Government	No commitment on Ireland
National Councils for England Scotland, Wales and Ireland	Vague references to tax changes
Free elementary education	
Graduated tax on property	
Help foragricultural labourers	

Making notes on *'Liberalism, 1868-85'*

This is a very familiar topic and you need thorough notes on these two ministries. You would do well to know the results and some data relating to the election victories of 1868 and 1880, and the reasons for the Liberal defeat in 1874.

On the first administration, a good knowledge of seven or eight reforms is likely to be sufficient. The Education Act is a basic reform, and you should also see that your notes include at least two concerned with the extension of opportunity (e.g., civil service, Oxbridge), one or two with the reform of institutions (e.g., army and judiciary) and one with the pursuit of political equality (e.g., the ballot). Reforms which contributed to the government's unpopularity (e.g., Licensing, and Criminal Law Amendment Act) are worth a section. Information on the two Irish measures is important, despite the fact that many questions on this ministry exclude Ireland.

For each reform, ask yourself why it was needed, who wanted it and how useful it was. Try to assess how it fitted into the pattern of basic Liberal attitudes.

On the Second Ministry, these headings will be useful:
Internal divisions in the Cabinet and party
The Radical approach of Chamberlain
Bradlaugh

The Fourth Party
Irish difficulties
Reforms; (especially those on education and voting)
Assessment; (you might equip yourself with one or two useful quotes concerning the difficulties of the ministry and its record)

Answering essay questions on *'Liberalism, 1868-85'*

Essays are frequently set on Gladstonian Liberalism, often on the first ministry, sometimes on the second, and more occasionally on a combination of the two. In an essay discussing whether the 1868-74 one was 'a great reforming ministry', you would need to assess the merits of some key reforms used as examples to illustrate the reforming drive; comment on their strengths and limitations. Note that there were few social reforms, but then Gladstone, most Liberals and most contemporaries believed in the prevailing ideas of *laissez-faire* and minimum government regulation. Even on trade union reform which would have been cheap, little was offered. The reforms were of a different type, and were all about modernising institutions, extending opportunities and promoting political equality.

You might be asked why Gladstone lost in 1874. Apart from mentioning the scale of defeat, you would need to consider where the Liberals had lost support and among which groups. The impact of the attacks on 'vested interests' (e.g., brewers and aristocracy), the public mood, disappointment with foreign policy and the resurgence of the Conservatives are all relevant.

A likely question might ask you to comment on the view that the reforming impetus of Gladstonian Liberalism was exhausted by 1874 (though extending the period of the question to 1885); another might ask you to compare the two ministries directly. The plan gives an example of how such a question might be tackled. Such a visual plan is clear and, if done on a separate sheet, can be kept in front of you. It can be filled with as much information as you wish to remind yourself of; you may just choose to use headings, or perhaps to add one or two examples. If you think of more points as you are writing, they can easily be inserted. Above all, what it does is to help you write a well-organised essay, in which points logically flow from the Introduction to the Conclusion. Remember that each paragraph should contribute something identifiable to the argument.

Source-based questions on *'Liberalism, 1868-85'*

1 Gladstone's First Ministry

Refer to the assessments of Bright, Disraeli and *Fraser's Magazine* (see pages 92-3 and 94). Answer the following questions.

a) Bright refers to the removal of an 'Established Church' and to the

'corruption market'. Explain both references. (4 marks)
b) Compare the views expressed by Bright and Disraeli on the impact of the legislative changes of 1868-74. (6 marks)
c) In the article from *Fraser's Magazine,* a reference is made to 'Liberals of the old school'. Who might these have been and how do you think they would have reacted to Bright's defence of the Liberal record? (5 marks)
d) Frederick Harrison, a Radical, wrote in the *Fortnightly Review* in March 1874 that 'the real truth if that the middle class has swung round to Conservatism ... of a vague and negative kind ... its practical effect is an undefined preference for leaving well alone'. What evidence is there in the extracts from Disraeli and the magazine of such a change in the public mood by 1874? (5 marks)
e) To what extent do the documents reveal evidence of any 'tensions and differences' in Liberalism? (5 marks)

2 The Radical Challenge
Consider the comments of Gladstone, Hartington, Labouchere Chamberlain and the Webbs, and the official and Radical platforms of 1886 (see pages 98, 102, 103 and 104-5). Answer the following questions.
a) What evidence is there in the extracts from Gladstone and the Webbs to suggest that the Liberals had no clear policy after 1880? (4 marks)
b) What did Hartington, Labouchere and Chamberlain see as the roles of their respective groups within the Liberal Party? (6 marks)
c) What were the main elements of Chamberlain's radical diagnosis of society and in what ways was his approach different from that of official Liberalism? (7 marks)
d) Gladstone once described Radicals as 'Liberals in earnest'. In what ways does a study of the evidence presented suggest that this was true? (4 marks)
e) What evidence is there in the extracts to suggest that Gladstone did have 'a difficult team to drive'? (4 marks)

The Age of Gladstone, 1868-95

Part B: The Direction of Liberal Politics

Despite the disappointments of the period from 1880-5, the period of Gladstone's predominance had some distinguished achievements to its credit. Liberalism had shown itself to be a reforming creed. After 1885, there was little domestic innovation brought about by governments under his leadership, and the third (1886) and fourth (1892-4) ministries were overwhelmingly concerned with his Irish preoccupation.

Having no enthusiasm for the politics of social improvement, he was happy to immerse himself in his crusade to bring justice to Ireland. However, that crusade was to bring him no glittering trophies, and was to undermine the fragile basis of unity within the Liberal Party.

1 Gladstone, Chamberlain and Home Rule

The demand for Home Rule, a degree of self-government involving the creation of an Irish parliament in Dublin, had been articulated by the moderate Home Rule Association since 1870. However, it was only when the astute and resolute Parnell assumed control of the Irish Nationalist cause that it made a serious impact. He was determined to achieve Home Rule from whichever party he could secure it, and his influence was to become a major factor in the House of Commons. He was to hold the balance between the parties in 1885-6.

Gladstone's policy of pacification had not worked, and he began to consider the Irish Question as more than a collection of accumulated of social and economic ills which could be addressed by reasonable legislative concessions. It was the very existence of British rule which was at the heart of the matter and no solution which did not embrace this objection would stand a chance of success. The Irish believed that they could govern Ireland better than Britain was able to do, and demanded the right to so do.

In coming to recognise this situation, Gladstone was seeing the Irish problem in a European context. As a Liberal he could sympathise with the rights of peoples struggling for their freedom, and had often supported their endeavours. Yet on his doorstep the government was denying this right to a nation close at hand. This was the key to Gladstone's change of mind; he could recognise the element of nationality in the Irish struggle.

Other Liberals also championed the rights of struggling peoples, but not all were able to detect this element in the situation they confronted. Many of them were prepared to see amelioration of living conditions, but some baulked at self-government. The Whig element was increasingly uneasy about events in Ireland, especially after Phoenix Park; Hartington and others saw the murders as further evidence that the Irish were irresponsible and unfit to govern themselves. They were unhappy about even moderate constitutional reform.

The ageing Radical, John Bright, who had never had a very flattering view of Irishmen, was out of sympathy with home rule. As a Protestant Nonconformist, he firmly believed that 'Home Rule will be Rome Rule', and did not want to see the hand of the Papacy guiding the conduct of policy in a Dublin parliament. However, of greater significance was the attitude of Joseph Chamberlain, for here was a Radical who had in 1880 a genuine wish to see a constructive solution. He realised that preoccupation with Irish problems and Nationalist obstruction at

Westminster was blocking the way to far-reaching Liberal changes in Britain, but beyond this tactical consideration, he recognised that the Irish had 'just discontents'. As an exponent of social reform he was attracted by the prospect of achieving a satisfactory answer to a seemingly intractable problem, and argued that 'it may be the work of the Tories to crush out discontent. It is the better and higher work of the Liberals to find out the cause of disaffection and remove it'.

However, he strongly opposed the terrorism of the Irish countryside and supported strong measures to deal with it, remarking that; 'I hate coercion. I hate the name. I hate the thing ... But I hate disorder more'. He was prepared to go some way along the road to self-government and could support a federal scheme for the government of the United Kingdom - with legislative councils for the four components of the UK - but was unwilling to contemplate home rule which he believed to be tantamount to its break up. Ultimately, he was one of nature's imperialists, not a separatist. His attitude was crucial, for between them Gladstone and Chamberlain had more to offer in the solution of the Irish situation than any other politicians; the one had insight, the other was a proven and practical reformer. Their failure to reach accommodation was fatal to the chances of achieving home rule, and highly damaging to the future of the Liberal Party.

Gladstone came out in favour of Home Rule in December 1885, his son Herbert having leaked news of his conversion to the press. Probably he was 'flying a kite' (the Hawarden Kite, as the incident was known) to gauge reactions to a policy change which would have the merit of winning the Parnellites over to the Liberal side and enabling Gladstone to form a new administration. The minority Conservative government was brought down on a Chamberlainite amendment to the Queen's Speech in January 1886, and the Liberal leader was back in power, committed to Home Rule to which the Conservatives were strongly opposed.

a) The Third Gladstone Administration, 1886: the First Home Rule Bill

Gladstone did not have the support of Bright and Hartington in his new administration, but Chamberlain agreed to serve, though with some reluctance. His resignation was always likely, for inevitably he would find the Home Rule Bill difficult to swallow. Indeed, the omens for the government were in some ways unpropitious, for there was little indication of firm backing for the Prime Minister. One historian has noted that the Liberals seemed 'no longer to have a clear agreed understanding as to what made them all Liberals, or what they ought to be doing together in politics'.

In March the Bill appeared and on seeing its terms Chamberlain departed. He objected to the absence of Irish representation from the House of Commons which would have been evidence of the ultimate supremacy of Westminster over Irish affairs; he saw Home Rule as being but a step away from separation and independence, though the moderate Gladstonian proposal was designed to stave off that possibility by conceding enough self-government to assuage Irish discontents.

Gladstone proposed to establish an Irish parliament and an executive in Dublin which would have powers over a whole range of domestic affairs, though there were to be certain 'reserved powers' retained at Westminster; these exclusions covered such areas as foreign relations, defence, international trade, customs and coinage. Irish representation at Westminster was to be at an end, thus putting an end to the possibility of further obstructionist tactics by the Nationalists or of them again holding a balance and hence a bargaining position between the parties.

In the debates between April and June, Chamberlain also used the problem of Ulster as an element in his opposition to the Bill. No provision was made to safeguard the position of the majority Protestant population who feared being submerged in an all-Irish and predominantly Catholic legislature.

The debates over Home Rule were among the most dramatic and memorable in the annals of parliamentary history. Gladstone was at his most impassioned and impressive, warning the House of Commons that 'Ireland stands at your bar, expectant, hopeful and almost suppliant ... she asks a blessed oblivion of the past, and in that oblivion our interest is deeper than even hers'. Such a 'blessed oblivion' was not to come about, for the Liberal Party was seriously split, and in the crucial division the Bill was lost by 30 votes. Ninety-three MPs, most of them Whigs under the influence of Lord Hartington, but also including the Radicals most associated with Joseph Chamberlain, were in the 'No' lobby.

These opponents of Home Rule were known as Liberal Unionists because of their desire to preserve the Act of Union; they were to become increasingly allied with the Conservatives in the coming years, though complete organisational fusion did not occur until 1911. Chamberlain's Radical days were over and in his personal contacts and political outlook there was to be a growing rapport with the supporters of Lord Salisbury whom he had once so reviled. With his departure went also many of the hopes of a more constructive Liberal approach to the issue of social reform with which he had made himself so identified.

Gladstone had never shown much liking for Chamberlain who had proved such a difficult colleague in the second ministry. He saw him as a presumptuous upstart, and he always had difficulty in acclimatising himself to the new breed of professional politician whose values and background were so different to his own. Beyond a mutual personal antipathy, however, there was a clear line of division between the two men. Chamberlain ultimately saw Ireland and its problems as a distraction from his main cause of social reform and suspected that

Gladstone was content to use his immersion in such complexities as a reason for not pursuing the more constructive policies of which he anyway disapproved. Such disagreements were about more than Irish issues alone; Chamberlain wanted the Liberal Party to veer to the left and embrace a more electorally appealing programme, whilst to Gladstone the Liberal mission lay in the 'politics of passion', of occasional bursts of moral enthusiasm.

Whatever the reasons for their failure to co-operate harmoniously, the outcome was disastrous for Liberalism. Attempts at any Liberal Unionist reunion with the Gladstonian Liberals broke down with the failure of the Round Table talks in early 1887. The desertion of the defectors among MPs was matched by a similar exodus of most of the remaining Whig aristocracy in the House of Lords, and a consequent loss of income from the element which had contributed most generously to party funds. Much of the formerly sympathetic press also ceased to support the Liberals, and the loss of sources of influence and money were almost as serious as the secession of key personnel.

Home Rule almost completed the process of separating the parties along class lines, for it carried off into the Unionist camp most of the last great Whig families; thereafter, Society contained few Liberal sympathisers. Of course Chamberlain had been identified with the progressive forces in British politics and his desertion confused the scene, but ultimately his commitment to the integrity of the United Kingdom and to imperialism proved to be stronger than his enthusiasm for radicalism. From 1886 the Conservative Party increasingly represented a defensive alliance of the forces of property, landed and business, and the Liberals were a party of appeal to some traditionally Liberal elements within the manufacturing and professional community, and to working people in the towns and many, but not all, of the cities.

Gladstone retained control of the National Liberal Federation (NLF - see page 104), but around the country the party organisation often suffered from division, especially in Chamberlainite Birmingham. From now on the Liberals were committed to Home Rule. Before the great schism of 1886, it had seemed not only a just but also a wise policy for the Liberals, as they sought to remove the Irish incubus from British politics. They were now stuck with it, still recognising its essential justice but also the immense difficulties of it practical fulfilment.

b) Gladstone's Fourth Ministry, 1892-4: Home Rule Again

Gladstone's control over the Liberal machine was strengthened in 1891 by his general if not wholehearted endorsement of the Newcastle Programme, which reflected many of the policies favoured by the NLF which had steadily grown in influence. The statement contained several resolutions concerning the need for Radical reform to tackle such issues as the power of the House of Lords, Welsh and Scottish Disestablishment, the land laws, factory reform and personal taxation. Over Home Rule, the Programme looked 'with unshaken confidence to Mr Gladstone' to push through a measure which would leave the House of Commons 'free to attend to the pressing claims of Great Britain for its own reforms'.

There was much interest in the 1892 election campaign, as indicated by the low number of uncontested seats. The Liberals had a majority of about 40 over the combined strength of the Conservatives and Liberal Unionists, if they could count on Irish support. Yet this performance was disappointing, for they won only four more seats than the official Conservatives, and there was little sign of popular enthusiasm for Home Rule.

Gladstone was now almost 83 and his eyesight and hearing were failing. Yet his mental power remained prodigious and undimmed, and he was determined to complete his mission to bring justice to the Irish people. It was an obsession - if by that we mean a haunting preoccupation fixed in the mind. He quickly produced a new Bill for Home Rule, and on its introduction there ensued a further momentous clash between the elderly titan who remained in the House day after day, brilliantly piloting his measure through its Commons' passage. He was, in the words of the young Winston Churchill, 'like a great white eagle at once fierce and splendid', as he fended off amendments. Against him, the opposition was again led by his former colleague, Chamberlain, not yet 60 and looking considerably younger. The arguments were much the same as they had been in 1886 for the content of the measure was little different save only in one regard; this time there was to be Irish representation at Westminster.

This time, Gladstone was successful in getting the Bill through the House of Commons, but when it reached the Lords it was effectively assaulted by the former Lord Hartington, now the Duke of Devonshire, among a series of other critics. It was overwhelmingly rejected in September 1893, and the futility of a Liberal government faced with a hostile upper chamber was again exposed. There was little interest in the Cabinet for dissolving the House of Commons and fighting on a 'Peers versus the People' platform; after all, in 1886 and six years later there was no indication that the British public was very sympathetic to the cause of Irish self-government and the likelihood of victory seemed remote.

Gladstone always felt that the Cabinet should have resolutely tackled the powers of the upper chamber, and hoped that members would come round to his viewpoint. He could not adjust to their way of thinking when it was proposed to embark upon an increase in defence expenditure, and denounced the 'monstrous scheme of the Admirals' for more battleships. He felt that the dead - 'Peel, Cobden, Bright, Aberdeen' - were with him, and because he was so out of sympathy with the proposed changes he resigned in March 1894. In his last speech as

Prime Minister, he attacked the onesidedness of the House of Lords and called for a revision of its powers. After that, he translated some of Horace's love odes before tending his resignation to Queen Victoria, thus ending a most remarkable parliamentary career.

Home Rule was a great historic cause and Gladstone had dedicated himself to achieving this final resolution of Irish demands. He had not succeeded and in the process had spent much of the time and energy of fellow-Liberals, and divided them from each other. On his resignation, there were Liberals who would gladly have dropped the policy altogether. Most recognised the impossibility of its early achievement, and were content to relegate the issue to the back burner. Lord Rosebery, Gladstone's successor, lacked a serious interest in the question, and faced by the apparent coolness of the electorate, most Liberals could agree that it should remain as a nominal aspiration.

2 Foreign Policy: Gladstone's Early Ideas and Events, 1868-74

Before 1868 Gladstone had only intermittently concerned himself with questions of foreign policy. He had attacked Palmerston's policy in the First and Second Chinese Wars, arguing in 1840 that, 'we the enlightened and civilised Christians, are pursuing objects at variance both with justice and with religion'. He also opposed Palmerston in the Don Pacifico debate (see pages 60-1), and in a major speech on the conduct of foreign policy lambasted his approach. Towards his conclusion, he attempted to define the desirable foundations of British policy, expressing disapproval of Palmerston's 'spirit of interference'. He concluded that, 'interference in foreign countries, should be rare, deliberate, decisive in character, and effectual for its end'. He did, however, share Palmerston's sympathy with European liberal movements, as over Italy (see page 73).

We are not primarily concerned with the detail of foreign policy in this volume, but a review of some of the incidents which arose in Gladstone's tenure of office illustrates something of his approach to political life, and to his view of the role of morality in the conduct of affairs.

When he took office in 1868, British influence in the world was already being eroded. As Bismarck came to dominate European diplomacy more and more, Britain was on the defensive in many episodes, and the appearance of such a strong rival power meant that British hegemony was at an end; there would not be the diplomatic triumphs of the early Palmerstonian era. There was more uncertainty in the direction of British policy, and in the Gladstone administration of 1868-74 the public were to be starved of the sort of 'successes' to which they had been used in bygone days.

During the Franco-Prussian War of 1870-1 Britain remained on the sidelines, and when Russia took advantage of the conflict to renounce its treaty obligations over the naval de-militarisation of the Black Sea unilaterally, Britain acquiesced. Yet both cases say something about the Gladstonian approach. When the Prussians were victorious in the former, Gladstone was appalled by the incorporation of Alsace-Lorraine into Germany, a transfer of land without the consent of its inhabitants, 'a violent laceration'. Over the second issue, he emphasised the importance of international law by summoning a European Conference to discuss the issue.

He himself abided by international law in 1872 over the Alabama Question. A British-built 'ironclad', the Alabama, had been ordered from Britain by the Confederate South, and had done great damage against the Northern states in the American Civil War. After the North had emerged triumphant in the struggle, the United States wanted compensation. The matter had gone to arbitration and in 1872 Britain agreed to pay $15 million in compensation. Disraeli, in opposition, was able to make much political capital out of the settlement, condemning it as an unjustified surrender to an improper claim. The settlement may have been a significant step forward in the resolution of international conflicts, but it cost Gladstone popularity.

The British public had been used to a different, nationalistic approach by Palmerston, and Disraeli caught the public mood with a new assertive attitude to Britain's role. He condemned the Liberals for their efforts 'so continuous, so subtle, supported by so much energy, and carried on with so much ability and acumen, to effect the disintegration of the Empire of England' and added that 'It would have been better for us all if there had been a little more energy in our foreign policy, and a little less in our domestic legislation'. To Gladstone, it was a just settlement of a difficult issue.

a) His Outlook in Opposition; the Basis of Foreign Policy

In opposition after 1874, we have seen how Gladstone returned to political activity over the question of Bulgaria and proceeded to challenge Disraeli's imperial and foreign policy as it unfolded. In his Midlothian tours, his speeches stirred the political consciousness of the country. He was greeted with extraordinary enthusiasm as he castigated his rival, and he produced some of his most ringing declarations. He particularly criticised British policy over Afghanistan, where Britain was adopting a 'forward role' in its bid to prevent Russian advance. His words stressed his view of the rights of subject peoples.

> Remember the rights of the savage, as we call him. Remember that the happiness of his humble home, remember that the sanctity of life in the hill villages of Afghanistan is as inviolable in the eyes of almighty God as can be your own.

In a speech at West Calder, he laid down six leading principles of foreign policy. It was rare for anyone to attempt to define fundamental and underlying tenets, and whatever their practical limitations, their enunciation was in itself an act of constructive statesmanship. The six principles were:

1. 'To foster the strength of the Empire ... and to reserve it for great and worthy occasions'. This would be done not by displays of bluff and bluster, not by aggression and the use of force but by 'just legislation and economy at home'.
2. 'To preserve to the nations ... the blessings of peace'.
3. 'To strive to cultivate and maintain to the utmost the Concert of Europe', because you thus 'neutralise and fetter the selfish aims of each'; 'Common action can alone unite the Great Powers for the common good'. (He often spoke of the Concert of Europe, by which he meant regular gatherings of European statesmen to resolve disputes - though there was not any formal machinery for such discourse).
4. 'To avoid needless and entangling engagements which only reduce the power and independence of the Empire'.
5. 'To acknowledge the rights of all nations'. He warned of the danger of a 'pharisaical superiority' if you elevate your country above all others.
6. That foreign policy 'should always be inspired by love of freedom'. It should be about the 'maintenance and extension of liberty'.

b) Second Ministry, 1880-85

On his election in 1880, Gladstone inherited a number of difficult colonial problems from his predecessor, Disraeli, whose policies he had condemned in his Midlothian speeches, and was unable to impart to the conduct of foreign policy the principles he had embraced. Indeed, the Disraelian criticism of 'more energy in our foreign policy' would have been endorsed by a large section of the public in 1885. Many people were affronted by his failure to send a relief force to rescue the British soldier, General Gordon, when he was stranded in Khartoum in the Sudan; the force which was eventually sent arrived too late, and Gordon was killed in January 1885. There was public outrage, and some critics suggested that Gladstone's popular nickname of the initials GOM stood for 'Gordon's Own Murderer' rather than 'Grand Old Man'.

c) Summary of Gladstone's Approach to Issues of Foreign Policy

In foreign policy as in other fields of political activity Gladstone sought to practise Christian ideals. He thought that states should observe the same ethical standards as individuals. He had a genuine horror of bloodshed and disliked increases in armaments; yet he was not a pacifist, and had been a member of the Cabinet which declared war on Russia in 1854 (the Crimean War).

From the time of his visit to Naples in 1851 he was conscious of the liberal aspirations in many countries. This led to his sympathy for nationalist movements, 'the cause of nations rightly struggling to be free'. He was always insistent on the right of self-determination (Alsace-Lorraine 1870-1) and fiercely attacked cruelty and oppression by those in authority (the treatment of political prisoners in Naples, the Bulgarian atrocities). To the end of his life, his dislike of oppression was manifested in his public utterances, and in his last speech, when he was 87, he came out of retirement to denounce the Armenian Atrocities, and made the memorable observation that, 'the ground on which we stand is not British, nor European but it is human'.

He recognised Britain's commitments to the colonies, but was opposed to further expansion. He was completely hostile to Disraelian Imperialism, both on the grounds of additional expense and the annexation of unwilling populations (Transvaal, 1877).

Gladstone's stress on the importance of morality in foreign affairs was unusual for a politician, even if the attacks he made were often those of an opposition spokesman. Many may find it expedient to adopt a lofty tone, but few have expressed their view with such moral fervour or have taken the time to elaborate a set of ideas concerning the basis of appropriate conduct in dealing with other nations. Of course, when in office, he found himself expected to act in defence of British interests and was unable to detach himself entirely from such considerations. Indeed, Philip Magnus, a sympathetic biographer, has observed that 'Gladstone never understood that high moral principles, in their application to foreign policy, are often more destructive of political stability than motives of national self-interest'.

It was fashionable in the years after the appalling bloodshed of the First World War for historians to be much impressed by this emphasis on doing what was right. The results of the unfettered pursuit of national interest had proved destructive, and the emphasis then was upon international conciliation via the machinery of the League of Nations. R.W. Seton-Watson praised Gladstone for an internationalist approach, and placed him in a tradition running from Castlereagh through to then-current ideals - for his notion of the Concert of Europe seemed to be in line with the preference of internationalists for diplomacy by conference rather than resort to bluster, threats and the pursuit of national advantage.

3 Assessment of Gladstone

Gladstone's career spanned almost the entire period of Victorian England and he was the archetype of Victorian liberalism, one who reflected its strengths and limitations. He represented its characteristic belief in human progress and reform, and yet in his outlook showed why it was a creed which was difficult to adapt to the needs of a mass electorate in the new century. He remained till the end what one writer has called a 'Peelite imbued with Benthamism'.

When he retired there was a huge void in the party he represented for he had come to be identified with the Liberal Party, moulding its pattern and development. He dominated the era of late Victorian England and no person could rival his individual ascendancy. He was beyond many contemporaries in talent and achievement, and his towering personality and enormous impact were such that they are not easily dealt with in a short space.

The task is the more difficult because he was himself a mass of contradictions - the deeply God-fearing person who anguished over his own sexual desires, the Flintshire landowner and self-confessed inequalitarian who nonetheless believed in opening opportunities for everybody, the committed Anglican who won the acclaim of English Nonconformity, the cautious conservative with a reverence for tradition who ended his career with a bold and risky attempt to resolve the Irish problem.

Not surprisingly, assessments of him have varied, and broadly those written nearer to his death were the more favourable, although they continued to be generally supportive until the last two decades. More recently, critical works of scholarship have appeared which take note of the contents of Gladstone's lengthy Diaries. Those writing contemporarily or soon after knew of his reputation at first hand and understood his moral impact and the 'politics of passion' which he represented. More recently, his motives have been questioned and there has been more stress upon his role in the decline and near disappearance of the Liberal Party. He has been blamed for its fall.

a) Gladstone the Man and the Politician

Gladstone was prodigious in his labours, with immense physical and mental agility, a man of massive intelligence and scholarly interest, a writer and pamphleteer. Yet for all this he was also at times a man of engaging simplicity whose behaviour could be astonishingly naive. From the 1840s, for one evening every week, he performed 'rescue' work on behalf of London prostitutes, whose souls he sought to redeem. For his labours, he was mocked and there were even attempts at blackmail. As a politician, he was playing with fire by being seen in the twilight zones where prostitution flourished. Ribald contemporaries nicknamed him 'Old Gladeye', indicating the suspicions of some who saw him at work.

As a parliamentarian his abilities were remarkable and he often left his hearers transfixed. Into very old age he astounded those around him with the strength and vitality of his performance, and he could rise effortlessly to the occasion in moments of great parliamentary drama. On the public platform there was no-one quite like him for he could hold an audience in thrall. The crowds were in awe of the great man and received him with warmth and affection. His speeches could be taxing for them to follow for his sentences were often long and complex, and his precise meaning could be obscure - but like a revivalist preacher he held sway. The audience loved his style and he gained enormous satisfaction and strength from their enthusiastic and loyal support. He appealed to the people's better nature, directing his appeal to their religious and moral instincts, rather than solely to their self-interests. He in turn found them a welcome tonic, their attitude being in marked contrast to what he viewed as the selfishness of the privileged landed classes.

As a party leader, he was not at his best when it came to leading a team. Unlike Disraeli, he did not have a facility for surrounding himself with younger and more stimulating minds, preferring the company of those he knew well. He lacked a good understanding of men and could be insensitive in dealing with colleagues. He certainly showed the least generous side of his nature in dealings with Joseph Chamberlain, failing to recognise the qualities which he had to offer. On occasions, Gladstone could be unbending and unwilling to accept the vanities and idiosyncrasies of men, so important in the art of party management.

b) Gladstone and Morality

No survey of Gladstone can ignore the strength of his religious conviction nor the considerable impact that they had on his behaviour and attitudes. Indeed Gladstone cannot be understood without reference to his view of the importance of right conduct in public as well as in personal life. His first choice of career was to become an Anglican priest and to the end of his life he pursued his quest for a close relationship with the Almighty, wishing to be a 'doorkeeper in the House of my God'. He knew - or believed he knew - what was right, and often presented his policies in Christian/moral terminology. Politics for him served a moral purpose; political questions were moral ones. He claimed to represent the moral high-ground.

Of course, in presenting his outlook in these stark terms he was open to mockery when his motives or behaviour seemed strangely worldly. Disraeli found him a self-righteous prig; others noticed his capacity for self-deception, hence the observation that he not merely kept the ace of trumps up his sleeve but maintained that Almighty God had put it there!

Politics was for him a Christian duty which he took up with a fervour which astonished those around him. In an age when outbursts of moral feeling could engulf the country, he was the politician most prone to gusts of moral explosion. Hence Blake's depiction of his 'formidable, indeed terrifying effect, as of some Old Testament prophet'.

On a variety of issues from Italy to Bulgaria, from Ireland to Armenia, he presented major issues in passionate crusades which made his case seem impossible to answer. To deny his case seemed to be denying his God, and few felt safe when Gladstone claimed to be acting in a virtuous cause. Lord Randolph Churchill was one of the few who by unrelenting ridicule was able to needle him and draw out his wrath.

His approach to foreign policy particularly was much affected by morality and this appealed to the Liberal way of thinking, for contemporary Liberals tended to portray their outlook as being based on right conduct. Whereas in their view the Conservatives thought in terms of what was in the national interest (expediency), Liberals reacted according to what was the appropriate thing to do; theirs' was a conscience-searching attitude. Nonconformity was a telling influence upon Liberals who warmed to expressions of moral commitment such as that of one of the Methodist leaders, Hugh Price Jones, who said that 'Nothing that is morally wrong can be politically right'.

c) Gladstone and the Liberal Party

The Liberal Party had an abiding attachment to civil and political liberty, and to equality of opportunity. From the 1830s some of its members had used the phrase 'Peace, Retrenchment and Reform', and the Gladstone of later years embodied these traditional party beliefs. He shared the commitment to a non-aggressive foreign policy, the wish to show care in administering the national finances, and to the Benthamite desire for the modernisation of institutions he added the Peelite emphasis on good administration, efficiency and moderate reform. The added-extra ingredient in the Gladstonian Liberal Party was the moral input, and if the party Radicals found his preoccupation a distraction or a liability, Liberals in the country liked his adoption of uplifting causes. Most of his famous pronouncements, whether on Ireland or the franchise, were couched in such terms, and politics was presented as a simple choice between right and wrong.

That he personified much of what Liberalism in late Victorian England represented is clear enough, but already by the 1870s there were elements within the party who were dissatisfied with the direction it was taking - notably Chamberlain and his followers. In 1886, the division in the party which had gathered pace in the early part of the decade burst wide open over Home Rule. At this point there was, in Southgate's phrase 'a divorce between Whiggery and Liberalism', even though a few Whigs remained Gladstonian.

When the Lords rejected his Second Home Rule Bill in 1893 by a majority of ten to one, of those who spoke Devonshire, Argyll, Northbrook and Selbourne had held office in his cabinets and others had served in his administrations. Missing from his side were the vast majority of Whig peers, and even 38 of the 62 peers he had nominated. As he told the Queen, he had been 'deserted by the upper and more prosperous classes of the community'. Ultimately, it was his action over Home Rule which brought about the final break between Whiggery and Liberalism.

The gulf between his outlook and that of most of the party had been apparent before then. His actions had often seemed to threaten the rights of property, and sometimes alienated the innate conservatism of many of the middle classes. Home Rule clarified the division in the Liberal Party and provided the occasion, for some the excuse, to separate themselves from their former home. In their eyes, they were not deserters but rather the aggrieved.

Home Rule was a key issue but not the only one, and Dicey, a distinguished writer on the Constitution, linked as his causes of secession the inability to trust Liberal leaders to resist socialism, the fatuous folly that Ireland must be governed by Irish ideas, and the failure to uphold Britain's imperial mission. The Earl of Fife wrote in *The Times* of Irish separation 'and illogical and insincere tamperings with socialistic doctrines'. By providing a dramatic issue, Home Rule turned the growing trickle of seceders into a flood.

At the same time the Liberals lost not only the cautious Whigs but also their practically-minded demagogues, and diverted the party from a radical mission into a political cul-de-sac. Liberalism lost the chance to become a party of the masses as distinct from one of two for which the masses might vote. It lost sight of the 'condition of England' question under Gladstone, and then soon after his passing was to split asunder on Imperialism.

By the time of his death in 1898, Gladstone's approach was becoming obsolete, and he increasingly felt disenchanted with what he felt to be the narrow-mindedness and self-interest of politicians around him. The age of party had dawned and for a man who could not easily compromise in the interests of unity the routine business of party management had for him a low priority.

Arguably, he had already lived too long and his longevity crippled his party; his values, the essence of his strength, seemed increasingly less relevant towards the end of the century when patriotic fervour on one side and the coming creed of socialism on the other were becoming the dominant influences in political life.

Ultimately assessments are inevitably coloured by the feelings of those who write them and whatever may be said about his motives and effectiveness in the many events of his life, the final verdict depends to some extent on the view taken of his moral stand. For some that stand is difficult to accept and sounds too sanctimonious in a more secular age in which organised religion has lost much of its earlier hold and most people do not spend their life pursuing in an ardent quest in search of their God. Others, religious or otherwise, admire his attempt to place the higher dictates of morality at the forefront of his behaviour, even if they recognise that on occasions he could deceive himself about his motives - for them, he raised the standard and tone of public life.

If Gladstone thought that an issue was right or just, he was prepared to take it up. He was often not the first to see where justice lay and, as with other people, when he did so his motives were normally a mixture of the noble and the self-interested. In the pursuit of his moral objects he sometimes did things which detracted from the image. But the attempt was to get the strategy right, and he did not flinch from the cost and unpopularity of his behaviour, as over Home Rule.

In some ways Gladstone was more important for what he was than for what he did. There is a grandeur in him, something caught well in the following contemporary verse:

> Tis justice that inspires our fire,
> To do the right is our desire,
> The Old Man's voice the trumpet call;
> Come, old and young; come, one and all.

That concept of morality was the basis of his Liberal belief in the rights of the individual, whether in Ireland or elsewhere. He believed in the value and dignity of the human spirit and that is why, to his supporters, his life had, in Robert Rhode James's admirably pithy summary, 'a nobility which transcended all defects and which expunges all errors and failures'.

Making notes on 'The Direction of Liberal Politics'

We are not here primarily concerned with a detailed investigation of Irish and foreign policy - detailed notes on these topics are likely to be made from other books in the series. In both cases, however, you would do well to write two or three paragraphs explaining Gladstone's general approach to such matters, illustrating how this related to the approach of other Liberals.

You might find it helpful to make a list of what you think are the good and bad points of Gladstonian Liberalism in practice. In the light of information provided earlier in the book, consider the extent to which his Liberalism was a departure from, or in line with, nineteenth-century Liberal principles and conduct.

Answering essay questions on 'The Direction of Liberal Politics'

We have already seen that many questions are set by examiners either on the first or the second Gladstone ministries. Here, we are concerned with ones which attempt to consider his life and work in more general terms. Consider the following questions.

1 Comment on the view that 'without Gladstone, the Liberal Party was nothing'.
2 To what extent did Gladstone determine the priorities of the late nineteenth-century Liberal Party?
3 Gladstone claimed to have been 'a learner all his life'. Does a study of his political career support his verdict?
4 'In his career, Gladstone began as a Tory and ended up as an advanced Liberal.' How did this transformation come about?

Do not forget that you may challenge the basis of the underlying assumptions in any question. As a broad guide, you are wise to adopt a cautiously sceptical approach. Full-hearted endorsement of a view expressed in a quotation might suggest that you have no ideas of your own. Total disagreement might be risky, unless you are very sure of your ground; examiners do not invent observations which are deliberately misleading purely to try to catch you out. 'Agreement but' can be a sound policy. Certainly you are wise to think critically about key words in the quotation, even if you broadly endorse the view that it presents.

***Source-based questions on** 'The Direction of Liberal Politics'*

1 Peace, Retrenchment and Reform

Study the cartoon on page 97, the two quotations on pages 104-5 and the two manifestoes of 1886 on page 106. Answer the following questions.

a) What were the main differences in the programmes put forward by Gladstone and Chamberlain in 1886? (6 marks)
b) In the light of his manifesto, how do you think Chamberlain would have viewed the Gladstone programme as shown in the cartoon? (5 marks)
c) With which quotation, that of Hartington or Chamberlain, do you think Gladstone would have found himself in greater sympathy? (4 marks)
d) Were the Gladstonian reforms more in line with the thinking of Hartington or of Chamberlain? (6 marks)
e) Gladstone is depicted in the cartoon as a 'colossus' who 'straddled the Victorian era'. How appropriate do you think this portrayal of him was? (4 marks)

CHAPTER 6

Liberalism, 1894-1914

1 Introduction

After Gladstone's death there was a vacuum at the top of the Liberal Party. Professor Hamer, in *Liberal Politics in the Age of Gladstone and Rosebery,* has noted that 'the sudden removal of the two factors which had disciplined and concentrated Liberal politics over the eight years since 1886, Gladstone's leadership and the preoccupation with clearing the Irish 'obstruction', restored to view the basic disorganisation of Liberal politics. Sectionalism re-emerged rampant and uncontrollable'. There was indeed a problem for the Liberals; they had to rediscover their identity. Having lost their leader and their mission, what was to be their new focus in the post-Gladstonian world?

For several years it was difficult to find one, and in the circumstances the Liberals fell back upon their traditional faddism, in which a variety of groups ranging from land reformers, temperance reformers, Dissenters who wished to disestablish the Scottish and Welsh state Churches, and other sectionalists, tried to push their programme to the forefront. Herbert Gladstone felt that the Liberals were 'plagued with obstinate faddists who are too strong for the leaders, and except for Ireland I could wish to get rid of them through defeat'. No-one could provide the necessary leadership to hold the diverse elements of the party together. The task was difficult for there were serious divisions within the party. However, the failings of the Conservative government in the years immediately before 1905 not only damaged the Tory reputation but as a by-product had the effect of reuniting the Liberal Party which won a handsome victory in the general election of 1906.

It is on the basis of the work done over the next eight years that Liberals could make their oft-repeated claim to be the 'fathers of the Welfare State'. The inspiration for the reforming impetus owes much to the New Liberalism, and especially to its leading representatives, Winston Churchill and David Lloyd George. Controversy continues over the content of the New Liberalism and whether it marked a development of, or a departure from, the older variety. For some historians, New Liberalism was a desperate response to the challenge of Labour, and indeed the Liberal-Labour relationship presented the government with a major challenge after 1906.

Several writers - particularly those of a left-wing persuasion - have seen Liberalism as an essentially middle-class creed which was quite unable to reach out and offer a broad appeal to new working-class voters. It has been argued that because of this Liberalism was fundamentally doomed, and that the threats to parliamentary government in the period after 1909 were an indication of its limitations in dealing with groups unwilling to abide by the niceties of the democratic process. The argument is that it lacked those roots in the community which would have provided a source of authority in handling discontent. Therefore, there has been talk of what one writer has called the 'strange death of Liberal England' - a demise which as yet did not affect Scotland and Wales, where Nonconformity in religion and Liberalism in politics still held sway.

When Gladstone retired he was not consulted by the Queen about the choice of his successor. The obvious contender was the Chancellor of the Exchequer, Harcourt, who was the senior figure in the House of Commons, but he was known to be unpopular with his Cabinet colleagues who found him too abrasive. The Earl of Rosebery took over the leadership; he was an immensely rich aristocrat who displayed an easy charm on the public platform and in private conversation. The situation was a difficult one, for the two rivals could not work together in harmony and it was anyway, in Churchill's phrase, a 'bleak, precarious, wasting inheritance'. From the beginning, the Cabinet and the party were so divided that when defeat came in 1895 it was, in Rosebery's view, a 'great blessing for the Liberal Party'. He became increasingly identified with the Old Liberals over the following years, and was concerned to fend off radical initiatives in Liberal policy. He resigned in 1896, and after an uneasy partnership between Harcourt and Morley, Sir James Henry Campbell-Bannerman assumed the leadership in 1899.

Campbell-Bannerman was lacking in charisma or dynamism, but after an uneasy start he grew into the position and displayed some astuteness in appeasing the various factions in the party. His initial difficulties concerned party attitudes towards the Boer War (1899-1902), over which the Liberals split three ways. The Liberal Imperialists (Asquith, Grey and Rosebery among them) wholeheartedly supported the position of the Conservative government and approved the conduct of the war. The 'Limps', as the Liberal Imperialists were unflatteringly known, denounced the Radical Liberals, who in Lloyd George's phrase found the war 'senseless and unnecessary'. This group were labelled by their opponents as Little Englanders, or at worst, pro-Boer. In between were the centre Liberals who, in Herbert Gladstone's phrase, were 'anti-Joe [Chamberlain] but never pro-Kruger'. They echoed the leader's view that in principle the war was right, but they disapproved of what he called the 'methods of barbarism [i.e., concentration camps]' used in the winning of it. *The Annual Register* for 1900 listed 62 Liberal MPs as Limps, 68 as pro-Boer, 30 as Campbell-Bannerman supporters, and the remainder (27) as uncertain.

With such disunity in their midst, the Liberal opposition could not perform effectively, and the party was decisively defeated in the Khaki election of 1900. However, after 1902 it was the distinctive contribution of Balfour as Tory Prime Minister to pursue policies which succeeded in rallying the divided Liberal Party and enable it to regain a unity it had not possessed for many years. All Liberal factions could agree in their denunciation of the 1902 Education Act which offended the Nonconformists because it provided aid from the rates for Church schools. With even greater passion they could campaign in defence of free trade, a traditional Liberal cause. Joseph Chamberlain, a Unionist minister until 1903, left the government to tour the country, whipping up support in his crusade for tariff reform or modified protection. The effect of his policy would have been to make goods from outside the Empire more expensive. Because much of our wheat was imported from America, this would have increased the price of bread. The working classes were unlikely to support the 'small loaf' of the tariff reformers when they could have the larger one which Liberal policy would allow them to buy.

The Liberals did themselves some good in the short term by making an electoral pact with the emerging Labour Representation Committee in 1903, so that candidates of the two parties would not oppose each other in the next general election, and this was to contribute to the scale of the Conservative defeat when polling took place. Balfour resigned in December 1905 and the new Liberal administration of Campbell-Bannerman quickly dissolved Parliament. The result of the election in January 1906 was a landslide Liberal victory. The Conservative vote per candidate was actually much the same as it had been in 1900, but the Liberal/Labour vote per candidate averaged 25 per cent higher. The Liberals gained a massive majority, winning 377 seats, as against 157 for the Conservatives. With Irish (83) support and that of the LRC/Lib-Lab MPs (53), the government looked invincible.

2 The Liberals Take Over: New Emphasis on Social Reform

The Liberals had a strong cabinet which reflected all shades of party opinion and mixed old with new. But in the election of January 1906 which sweepingly endorsed the change of government, little had been proposed by way of a programme of social improvement. Campbell-Bannerman had hinted at land and poor law reform, and mitigation of the 'evils of non-employment', but there was no early sign that social reform would become the Liberal response to tariff reform. Indeed, he had extolled the virtues of retrenchment. Herbert Gladstone congratulated him on the preponderance of 'centre' Liberals among the party backbenchers, and the 'Review of Reviews' in February 1906 noted that the Liberals in parliament included 176 Nonconformists - mostly middle-class men 'whose sympathies are more with the employer than the employed'.

Yet over the next few years there was to be a burst of reforming measures, particularly after 1908. Several factors created a momentum in favour of measures, one of which was a disturbing amount of recent evidence about the scale of poverty, distress and sickness. There was plenty of evidence which pointed to the destitution that existed. Charles

Booth's four-volumned *Life and Labour of the People in London* (1889-1907) was the first and most impressive indictment. It showed that 30 per cent of the population lived below his 'poverty line' and that 10 per cent fell into his lowest class, as labourers only occasionally employed, loafers and semi-criminals. A new and quantified sense of the amount of poverty existing was not the only result. A simultaneous change of attitude about the causes of poverty began to carry an important section of educated opinion far away from the assumptions of the past. Booth emphasised old age - the unavoidable growing beyond the capacity to earn an income - as a cause of destitution.

Rowntree's surveys in York showed that 28 per cent of the population never earned income sufficient to maintain their physical effectiveness, or had incomes so small that, by failing to apportion their expenditure properly, they fell into want. Other investigations also pointed to the existence of 10 per cent of the population living in a perpetual state of chronic want. Some of the evidence pointed to the connection between poverty and ill-health. Recruitment to the Boer War showed evidence of physical deterioration in the health of the community. In Manchester, in 1899, of 12,000 men who offered themselves as recruits, 8,000 were rejected straight away and only 1,200 men were considered fully fit, though requirements were the lowest since Waterloo. In the decade after 1893, some 34.6 per cent of would-be recruits had been rejected throughout the country and, in addition, many more had been considered not to be worth examining. This sort of evidence was surprising and troubling to respectable opinion, which it appeared had been content to found its convictions on an extensive ignorance of the facts. Such findings and the social concern they engendered were the driving force behind the Liberal reforms.

Another reason why reform was taken up concerned competition with Germany. Mentally and physically, the German people were in a fitter state than their British counterparts. At a time of intense international friction, when Germany was a possible military rival, was it wise for Britain to lag behind? When introducing health insurance, Lloyd George spoke enthusiastically of the continental example, and added 'we must put ourselves on a level with Germany ... I hope our competition ... will not be in armaments alone'.

New social doctrines were then being advanced. Chief among them was Socialism, which was concerned with people's quality of life and the need for a more just and equitable society. If socialist ideas were not widely held at that time, more tangible was the presence in the House of Commons after 1906 of 53 working men as MPs, some of whom reflected such thinking; others were less moved by ideology and more by their experience of poor living and working conditions. They were to be a pressure group for social change and pressed particularly hard for the provision of school meals and improvements in the position of organised labour. Their presence heightened awareness of social problems.

Above all, and especially relevant to the changes which followed, there were in the House a number of members on the progressive wing of the Liberal Party who held more advanced opinions on social issues and were aware of the need to prevent the Labour contingent from making all the running on them. They wished to see Liberalism divert into new courses, partly out of political necessity and partly out of their own genuine sense of compassion. They were committed to the New Liberalism. Among them, were a number of intellectual radicals, and politicians such as C.F.G. Masterman, a rising young minister and perceptive commentator who wrote widely on social questions, Winston Churchill and David Lloyd George.

It was Masterman who, writing on *The Heart of the Empire; Realities at Home* in 1901, stated that the Liberals were 'ripe for a new departure in constructive Radicalism after the sterile futilities of the Irish diversion'.

3 The New Liberalism

New Liberalism was at the heart of the debate over social change in Edwardian England, for many writers have seen this as the theme which characterised the reforms after 1906, and more especially after 1908. Before we examine these changes, we need to be clear about what the New Liberals were proposing which was different from the more traditional Gladstonian view. Gladstone had stated his opinion on the role of government back in 1884.

> 1 There is a disposition to think that the Government ought to do ... everything. If the Government takes into its hand that which the man ought to do for himself, it will inflict upon him greater mischiefs than all the benefits he will have received ... The spirit of
> 5 self-reliance should be preserved in the minds of the masses of the people, in the minds of every member of that class.

In the 1880s and 1890s a number of Liberals began to reinterpret the doctrine of Liberalism and call for increased legislative action. They were still concerned to maintain individual liberty, promote individual enterprise and attack monopoly and privilege, but they were beginning to see a greater role for the state in protecting the weak. Why did this interest in government intervention develop?

Thirty years before, one could believe that economic growth might absorb unemployment and poverty, but by the time of the 'Great Depression' of the late nineteenth century it was difficult to be confident about further industrial expansion. Poverty was at a depressingly high level. This caused T.H. Green, the Oxford philosopher, to advocate more positive use of state intervention, and by the turn of the century an impressive body of academics and publicists were reinterpreting

Liberalism. L.T. Hobhouse, a prominent Liberal thinker and writer, urged 'collective action for mutual advantage', and Green, though seeing capitalism as broadly good, wanted state legislation to protect those lacking the opportunity to show entrepreneurial enterprise. J. Hobson, the most famous propagandist of the New Liberalism, urged the state to maintain a minimum national standard of living for all its citizens.

In the 1890s several small groups of intellectual radicals - such as the Rainbow Circle formed in 1893 by Hobson, Herbert Samuel and Charles Trevelyan, with the support of Fabian socialists such as MacDonald - had tried to formulate a revised creed. But though their influence spread gradually within the party, it was not strong in its official organs. Not until 1903 did the National Liberal Federation pass a motion in support of greater social radicalism. Given the leadership of Campbell-Bannerman, any new progressive stance was unlikely. It was traditional Liberal causes - free trade and Nonconformity - that reunited the Liberals, not a commitment to social amelioration.

However, the main intellectual spokesmen of the party were overwhelmingly committed. In 1909 J. Hobson spoke of a 'crisis in Liberalism' in which the old distinctions between Liberalism and Socialism 'must of necessity become blurred'. He claimed that the old *laissez-faire* Liberalism was dead. Charles Masterman's *Condition of England* published in the same year was an eloquent statement by a junior minister and close confidant of Lloyd George of the gulf that existed between the 'conquerors' in 'suburban villadom' and the spiritual and social destitution of the 'prisoners' in urban slums. Social Christianity was also becoming more fashionable in a number of Nonconformist chapels, and in the face of social evils many young Christians wanted to marry the idea of Christian witness and social concern. Instead of an emphasis on old-style individualism, they and others were in the words of a young Fabian, Sidney Webb, 'thinking in communities'.

Basic to the new emphasis was the idea that taxation was not inherently bad, as most Liberals had traditionally believed, but that it could be used for positive and beneficial purposes. Old Liberals had viewed the uneven distribution of wealth as both necessary and desirable; diverting money to the masses via social programmes was seen as detrimental to business development. But New Liberals argued that the uneven distribution of wealth actually harmed the economy because it deprived the mass of the population of the capacity to buy goods. They argued that the real weakness in the economy was underconsumption and that this could be remedied by a reallocation of purchasing power through taxation and social welfare; rising demand would thus stimulate economic growth, making the economy more productive. In other words, expenditure on reform would not be burdensome but would be of advantage to the country's economic future.

Some of the new thinking was to be found in Herbert Samuel's slim volume on Liberalism, published in 1909. He argued that the ministries of 1892-5 had already adopted a more positive approach to the role of the state, and, influenced by Hobhouse, Hobson and others, he wished to see further development along interventionist lines. In his view there were limits to the state's intrusion into the economic and social sphere, for he disapproved of the socialist idea that 'the state is to be the sole capitalist', but the work reflected the growing belief that individualism was not enough. Collective action to eradicate injustice and redress the social balance was in vogue, and Samuel articulated clearly the difference between the Old and the New Liberalism.

> 1 To many among the fathers of modern Liberalism, government action was anathema. They held, as we hold, that the first and final object of the State is to develop the capacities and raise the standard of living of its citizens; but they held also that the best
> 5 means towards this object was the self-effacement of the State ... Liberalism became a negative policy ... its positive policies were constitutional [only] ... Three causes ... combined to convert Liberalism from the principle of State abstention ... It was seen that the State had become more efficient and its legislation more
> 10 competent, and laws of regulation were found by experiment neither to lessen prosperity nor to weaken self-reliance in the manner foretold. It was realised that the conditions of society were in many respects so bad that to tolerate them longer was impossible, and that the laissez-faire policy was not likely to bring
> 15 the cure. And it was realised that extensions of law need not imply diminutions of freedom, but on the contrary would often enlarge freedom.

Younger Liberal politicians began to pick up some of the new ideas, which circulated in magazines such as *Nation*, and social radicals thought that it was time to move away from old Gladstonian preoccupations and attitudes. No leading member of the Cabinet was at this time committed to the New Liberalism and even Lloyd George for all his recognition of the needs of labour after the election, was still essentially committed to the old causes - temperance, Church disestablishment, local Home Rule and land reform - not a programme particularly in tune with the needs of the working-class electorate. As Kenneth Morgan in *The Age of Lloyd George* has explained,

> 1 [He] had been in the van of the fight for the old causes; indeed, it was they that had brought him to national prominence ... [But] more than most backbench radicals, he was a pragmatist, and his years of office after 1905 were to show how the old creed and the

> 5 new could be reconciled, how individual libertarianism and state intervention could make common cause.

He came to see things differently and the concern of the Liberal programme as it eventually took shape was with the prevention of the poverty that Booth and others had so glaringly revealed - poverty that was not due to drink or moral inferiority, as many in the nineteenth century had uncritically believed, but as Lloyd George said, 'to old age, sickness, the death of a breadwinner or unemployment'. It did not seem to him that extreme measures were called for to remedy these ills. The traditional Liberal respect for the freedom of the individual could coexist with a limited degree of collective control in order to protect those who had been shown to be unable to protect themselves. The necessary steps could be taken without violent upheaval.

It was, for Lloyd George, vital that the Liberal Party made the necessary adaptation, for he had learnt the lesson of the failure of continental Liberals to change their approach;

> 1 The Liberalism of the Continent concerned itself exclusively with mending and perfecting the machinery which was to grind corn for the people. It forgot that the people had to live whilst the process was going on, and people saw their lives pass away without 5 anything being accomplished. British Liberalism has been better advised. It has not abandoned the traditional ambition of the Liberal Party to establish freedom and equality; but side by side with this effort it promotes measures for ameliorating the conditions of life for the multitude.

It was not a matter of controlling wealth but of ensuring that all received an adequate minimum, so that whatever the extremes of affluence none should be in actual want. As Churchill put it, 'we want to draw a line below which we will not allow persons to live and labour'. This was Liberalism echoing the doctrines of the Webbs and other Fabians but it was far removed from any form of socialism which stood for the removal of the capitalist system; the aim was not to transform the system of private ownership, but to make it work to the advantage of a larger section of the community.

By the early twentieth century, progressive Liberals were abandoning Gladstonian retrenchment. They accepted that the state had a wide responsibility for welfare, and that this must be financed by limited redistributive taxation; a fair contribution should be made by those best able to pay. Increasingly, Liberals were differentiating their party from the Conservatives, who still favoured indirect taxation, disliked graduated direct tax on principle and wished to restrict government expenditure to a very limited range of functions.

Not all Liberals liked the new emphasis and, although by 1914 it represented the mainstream of party thinking, there was always tension between Old and New Liberals. Traditional members, at Westminster and in the country, could not easily adjust, and some wealthy patrons left the party around 1900 finding the new gospel excessively radical. As time went by, others were to have misgivings about the policies which were pursued, and many would not have travelled even as far as they did without the dynamic impetus of Lloyd George and Churchill to drive them onwards. Many of the Cabinet were out of step with the new collectivist creed, Grey, McKenna and Runciman among them, and Asquith was not the man to provide new initiatives. However, Lloyd George and Churchill were impatient with the priorities of the Old Liberalism and particularly after 1910-11 it was to be the former who made the running.

4 The Campbell-Bannerman Administration, 1906-08; Asquith's Takeover

Campbell-Bannerman never thought in terms of widespread social reform, which he deemed to be too expensive, and Asquith spent his first year at the Treasury in restoring Gladstonian standards without any hint of a revolution in public finance. There were some changes, as we shall see, but the cause of reform did not flourish. Hence the disappointment of the New Liberals. Social radicals looked in despair at the leadership of 'C-B', and requests from the constituencies for action received scant sympathy. Not only was he by inclination conservative on such matters; he also feared that radical reforms might reopen the divisions in a party which had recently been torn by disagreement. Masterman observed that social reform had 'not gone beyond the rhetorical stage'.

During the 1906 session legislative attention was concentrated upon the Education Bill which was intended to eliminate Anglican influence in single-school rural areas. It was eventually emasculated by the Lords and withdrawn. A further Education Bill in 1908 proved unsatisfactory even to Nonconformists and thereafter the Liberal government tacitly accepted the 1902 reorganisation.

The change came with C-B's departure in 1908. Asquith (1858-1928) became Prime Minister. He was not the man to supply new initiatives, but his arrival marked a dramatic change in the tone and approach of the Liberal administration. He had come to the fore as the skilful exponent of free trade who at every opportunity demolished the case in favour of tariff reform for which Joseph Chamberlain campaigned. At the Exchequer he had made the first provision for old age pensions, before succeeding to the premiership in April 1908. He had exceptional capacity for administration and the transaction of business, and when it came to defending his policies in Parliament he was most effective. He inherited and remodelled a talented if not always harmonious Cabinet, and led it with considerable adroitness for much of the time. He was willing to back his ministers when they needed support, and could expound their case with lucidity and conviction.

The new Chancellor of the Exchequer was Lloyd George and Churchill took over at the Board of Trade. Their promotion indicated that Liberalism was moving into a new phase, for only the previous month Churchill had written in *Nation* calling for his party to move forwards from the campaign for political liberty to the cause of economic and social freedom. He advocated a 'new constructive policy' applying scientific remedies to such evils as pauperism and lack of employment - he was even prepared to support measures such as the public acquisition of railways and canals. All this would, he believed, strengthen and preserve capitalism. He now had the chance to champion such policies from within the Cabinet.

At last the government was catching up with the intellectual currents that had swept it to power. That summer Churchill urged a 'slice of Bismarckianism' on his colleagues, including labour exchanges, unemployment and health insurance, and modernisation of the old poor law. He did not believe that the victims of such evils as illness and poverty should be left to the arbitrary ravages of nature. In 1910-11, with this in mind, he applied his immense energies and powers of advocacy to persuade his colleagues of the urgency of redirecting the efforts of the ministry. Forty or so backbenchers pressed regularly for new social measures, often voting with the Labour Party on them.

5 The Liberal Social Reforms

a) Those Affecting the Young

In Edwardian England there was widespread concern about the health of the young and an interdepartmental Committee on Physical Deterioration (1904) urged the case for free school meals and medical inspection. The idea of school meals was not entirely novel, for on occasion local charities had made money available to provide them in times of distress. The Committee observed that,

> 1 With scarcely an exception, there was a general consensus that the time has come when the State should realise the necessity of ensuring adequate nourishment to children in attendance at school; it was said to be the height of cruelty to subject half-starved
> 5 children to the process of education, besides being a short-sighted policy, in that the progress of such children is inadequate and disappointing.

A Labour MP introduced a Bill to provide for school meals, and with government support it passed into law as the Education (Provision of

Meals) Act, 1906. The Act was not compulsory but after a slow start 96 local authorities provided a total of 9 million meals per school day by 1910; by 1914, 14 million were provided. There was unease at what one member called this 'grave social departure', and the report of *The Times* on the parliamentary debate of March 1906 indicated the heart-searching involved.

1 *Dr MacNamara.* He used to think that the proper way to deal with the question should be by charitable organisation, but he had been driven from that position by the hard facts of the case. Charity fluctuated and it could never cover the ground.
5 *Mr Bowles.* This Bill would be most mischievous in the interests of the country, and particularly in the interests of the working classes. How often was the local authority to resolve that a particular child was underfed, and how were they to make their enquiries? ... This would be setting up a system of inquisition which the working
10 classes would much resent. The Bill ... would be a tremendous burden on the rates, and relief so given must pauperise the recipients. The well-known dangers which attended all forms of Socialism belonged in a particularly virulent form to this measure.
Mr Cox. The Bill would create a large body of working men who ...
15 would be sponging on their fellow workers ... The parental duty of providing for the child was one of the strongest means of keeping up a high home standard.

The following year a clause to provide for medical inspection was slipped into the Education (Administrative Provisions) Act to allow visits to elementary schools. The architect of this advance was a civil servant, Sir Robert Morant, the Permanent Secretary to the Board of Education. He knew that several Liberals, among them a few ministers, were less than enthusiastic, hence the need to disguise it; the proposal was not made mandatory. Yet, taken with the previous change, it did mark a 'social departure' for the state was now accepting a responsibility for what had been viewed as a purely family problem.

A significant reform was the all-embracing Children's Act, a codifying measure which consolidated 39 previous statutes related to children into one measure known popularly as the 'Children's Charter'. Among other things, it defined negligence and cruelty, tackled the problem of young offenders, established borstals - as an alternative to prison - and special juvenile courts, and made it illegal for children to beg or smoke.

b) Those Affecting the Old

Britain was slow to introduce old age pensions. Germany and New Zealand had pioneered these in the 1880s, and other countries had followed their example. Several committees had examined the issue and had concluded that old age was a frequent cause of poverty. However, like Joseph Chamberlain, another advocate, they had run up against a barrier in the form of the Treasury, for cost was seen as an obstacle. So also was the opposition of the Charity Organisation, which feared that pensions would undermine personal thrift. The body had been set up in 1869, largely because many middle-class people were anxious that too much charitable assistance was being given to those who did not deserve it; there was a lack of any clear objective about the purpose of such assistance. The Charity Organisation was intent on ensuring that the poor would ultimately be able to help themselves and become self-reliant. To this end, it preferred private to state action, perhaps administered via the Friendly Societies.

By 1906 opinion was changing, and when Asquith introduced the proposal in his 1908 Budget it provided for a non-contributory scheme which would provide five shillings (25p) a week to the over 70s (7/6d for a married couple) whose income did not exceed £31 a year. The amount was small and was never intended as a substitute for saving, hence Churchill's observation that, 'We have not pretended to carry the toiler to dry land. What we have done is to strap a lifebelt around him'. The measure was immediately popular with the working class after its inception in 1909, and Lloyd George who was Chancellor when it was introduced 'sold it' with passion.

Despite the modest cost of under £10 million in a full year, there was opposition within the Liberal Party, and Rosebery saw the scheme as 'so prodigal of expenditure' that it constituted 'a mortal blow to the whole fabric of the Empire'.

c) Those Affecting the Sick

We have already seen that there was anxiety about the health of the nation, and sickness was seen as another cause of poverty. The British Medical Association saw a need for some kind of scheme to cover those who did not gain assistance under the Poor Law, and argued the case for preventive medicine. Lloyd George was attracted to some form of insurance along the lines of the German pattern with which he was 'tremendously impressed'.

His exuberance and energy were assets in producing and carrying his proposal in the teeth of some furious opposition. His plans involved everyone earning up to £160 a year. A sum of 4d was to be deducted from the wage as a contribution to the scheme. Employers would pay 3d and the state 2d, hence his claim that it offered 'ninepence for fourpence'. Those participating in the scheme received ten shillings a week in benefit if they fell ill, in addition to free medical care from a doctor on the panel of local general practitioners.

There was massive political opposition to the scheme from the convinced socialists such as Keir Hardie, the leader of the Labour MPs, who saw it as a 'porous plaster to cover the disease which poverty causes' and wanted to tackle the underlying problem with its deep roots in the capitalist system. Others on the left, including unions, disliked compulsory deductions from wages. The vested interests disliked the administration of the scheme and its compulsion; in particular, the doctors saw it a threat to their independence and felt ill-rewarded, while insurance companies and friendly societies saw it as the state intruding into their affairs.

Lloyd George's success in getting the bill passed was a prodigious feat and, attacked on all sides, he was passionate in his scheme's defence. He portrayed himself as the saviour of the working classes.

1 I am in the ambulance corps. I am engaged to drive a waggon through the twisting and turnings of the parliamentary road. There are men who tell me that I have overloaded the waggon ... There are those who say my waggon is half-empty. I say it it as much as I
5 can carry. I am rather in a hurry, for I can hear the moanings of the wounded, and I want to carry relief to them in the alleys, in the homes where they lie stricken.

When passed, the plans constituted Part One of the National Insurance Act, described by J.L. Garvin, a prominent contemporary journalist, as 'the greatest scheme of social reconstruction ever yet attempted'. Many others saw it as one of the boldest and most innovative social reforms yet on the statute book. It produced a striking change which by using the insurance principle was made acceptable to many of those who had traditional views on providing for oneself.

d) Those Affecting Workers and Those Without Work

Little was done before 1905 to help those in poverty because of the lack of work. Local Distress Bureaux had a limited responsibility for locating jobs, but the time was ripe for a more comprehensive arrangement such as Germany already possessed. The economist, William Beveridge, helped to devise a plan for a national system of Labour Exchanges, which Winston Churchill piloted through the House of Commons. It would enable 'men to go at once where they are wanted, but at the same time [discourage] movement to places where they are not wanted'. By February 1910, 83 centres were open, and they proved valuable in helping people to find work if it was available to be had.

Help was also needed where there was no opportunity for work. Part Two of the National Insurance Act was designed to insure the family 'against catastrophe which otherwise would smash them up for ever'. 2.5 million workers were compulsorily insured in another contributory scheme in which employers and employees each paid $2^1/_2$d a week, and the state slightly less. The benefits were deliberately modest, seven shillings (35p) a week for a maximum of 15 weeks, for Liberal ministers did not wish to subsidise 'work-shy malingerers' who might abuse the provisions. People were still expected to make their own provision, so that the amount was less than was necessary to sustain a family through the bad times.

There was much less antagonism associated with this part of the National Insurance Act, the need for which was widely appreciated. As an insurance scheme, it enabled a man to pool his luck with that of his fellow workers. Moreover, because it was introduced at a time of rising employment, there was a £3 million surplus in the fund by 1914, so it was not seen as a drain on the Exchequer. Limited in scope though it was, it covered a number of industries and trades, such as shipbuilding, which were especially vulnerable to fluctuations in employment.

Other measures helped those in employment, but whose conditions were poor. In 1906, a Workers Compensation Act enabled workers who were injured at work to claim compensation from their employers not only for accidents but also for ailments which resulted from their occupation. In 1908, directly attributable to the parliamentary pressure of 16 mining MPs, the miners secured an eight-hour day by the first statute which regulated just men's hours of work. Four years later, a minimum wage was conceded to the same group during the prolonged industrial stoppage. The level was not decided on a national basis but was agreed district by district. In 1911, shopworkers benefited from the Shops Act which allowed for a weekly half-day holiday.

For workers in the 'sweated industries', mainly women who worked in occupations such as tailoring and lacemaking, there was some relief of their dreadful working conditions. They were one of the worst exploited and least organised groups, and protection was offered in the form of minimum wages and maximum hours of employment laid down by new Trade Boards.

The organised working-class vote in Parliament was instrumental in persuading the government to improve the rights of trade unionists. The Trade Disputes Act reversed the Taff Vale Judgement of 1901 so that in future trade unions were no longer held liable for the payment of damages as a consequence of organised strike action - thus removing a grievance of many working people and their representatives. The Trade Union Act of 1913 clarified the legal position. It restored the political power of the unions, and the financial position of the Labour Party. The unions were to be allowed to use their funds to support a party, but this money must be kept in a special 'political fund' from which anyone who was so inclined might opt out. This last clause was not popular with union officials, but they recognised that it was the 'most we could extract from them'.

e) Meeting the Costs; the People's Budget of 1909

The government needed to increase its revenue to meet the growing costs of its programme. As the international situation worsened, a programme to build more Dreadnoughts (a new class of British battleship) was initiated, and the cost of the eight ships wanted by the Admiralty was £15 million; in addition, there were the social reforms to finance. Lloyd George as Chancellor had to find the money, a task which he relished for he portrayed his proposals as a 'war budget' to tackle 'poverty and squalidness'. He was not unaware of Liberal losses in recent by-elections and of the need to rouse flagging morale, and so he framed a provocative Budget which aimed to 'hit the rich'.

Many extra duties were raised, such as those on liquor licensing, spirits and tobacco, and new ones on cars and petrol were introduced. Whereas an Income Tax allowance of £10 a year was given to those earning less than £500, tax was increased at the higher levels and was complemented by a new Supertax on incomes over £500. Death Duties were increased as was the rate of tax on unearned income. But what really provoked controversy was the policy adopted towards land ownership, notably a 20 per cent revenue tax on the unearned increment in land values and a capital

Lloyd George was the Liberal giant who issued the challenge

tax on the value of undeveloped land and minerals.

Landowners were able to make great profits if their land became valuable as a result of building development or because minerals were discovered beneath it. Such a bonus was not a result of any effort on their part, but resulted from fortunate circumstances beyond their control. Lloyd George thought it reasonable that they should yield some of their profits to the community. His opponents thought his proposals were the beginning of an onslaught on established property rights. Moreover, to assess liability for such taxation, a survey of land ownership would be necessary, and this would expose who owned the land and how much an individual possessed; this would be useful information to those on the left who wished to exploit inequalities in the ownership of wealth and property.

The Budget was not just about raising money, it was an instrument of political and social policy. Hitting the rich would be politically popular, and if the wealthy peers in the House of Lords were provoked into rejecting the proposals, in breach of past precedent, Lloyd George would then be able to use his considerable rhetoric to denounce the aristocracy as privileged people content to live off the rest of society in a 'Peers versus People' campaign. Whether or not he deliberately set out to goad members of the second chamber into rejection is difficult to say. But he must have realised that controversy was inevitable and that rejection would almost certainly advance the Liberal cause more than acceptance. Even those members of the Cabinet who were not fully behind Lloyd George, especially over the land proposals, recognised that there could be an electoral bonus.

Lloyd George was portrayed in *Punch* as a philanthropist who wanted to tackle the 'idle rich who pass by in their new motor vehicles; "I'll make 'em pity the aged poor" '. He attacked the Peers as parasites whose function was 'stately consumption of wealth produced by others'. He and Churchill launched a series of verbal assaults against unearned advantage, and at Limehouse in July 1909 and elsewhere, his invective was devastating. At Newcastle, in another hard-hitting speech, he suggested that,

1 A fully-equipped duke costs as much to keep up as two Dreadnoughts; and the dukes are just as great a terror and they last longer. [He wondered whether] 500 men, ordinary men, chosen accidentally from among the unemployed, [should] override the
5 judgement ... of millions of people who are engaged in the industry which makes the wealth of the country ... Who ordained that a few should have the land of Britain as a perquisite, who made 10,000 people owners of the soil and the rest of us trespassers in the land of our birth; who is it - who is responsible for the scheme of things
10 whereby one man is engaged through life in grinding labour, to win a bare and precarious subsistence for himself, and when at the end

> of his days he claims at the hands of the community he served a poor pension of 8d a day he can only get it through revolution, and another man who does not toil receives every hour of the day, every
> 15 hour of the night, whilst he slumbers, more than his poor neighbour receives in a whole year of toil?

The furious opposition of the Lords to the Lloyd George proposals induced them to make the tactical mistake of rejecting the Budget. They thereby played into the Liberals' hands, for they had forced an issue on which they were almost certain to lose. Their action was a defiance of a long-standing tradition that the House of Commons had primacy in matters of finance. Left untackled, it would have made it impossible for ministers to have administered their declared policies. This is why Asquith and his colleagues decided to trim the powers of the House of Lords, as explained in the section on the Constitutional Crisis (see pages 145-7). The budget was finally passed in April 1910, after a general election had been fought not just on the merits of the proposals, but on the behaviour of the Upper House.

f) The Effectiveness of the Liberal Social Reforms

The comprehensive Welfare State, with its large-scale governmental intervention in the life of the individual, lay in the future. It was to embrace the idea of an optimum level of provision which would be sufficient for people to live an adequate existence, rather than the notion of a basic minimum which is what the pre-war Liberals were concerned with. Yet these Liberals pioneered the route towards that more all-embracing social service state that emerged after 1945, and their action just about entitles them to make their oft-trumpeted claim to be 'fathers of the Welfare State'.

In truth, the reality of what was available in 1914 was some way short of the Welfare State as we know it today. Ministers had not formulated a creed and a programme which could provide a comprehensive answer to the problems of society, about which so much more was now known, if only because several ministers were still committed to old nineteenth-century attitudes. They thought in terms of restraining government expenditure and therefore could only make a limited impact on the social problems of Edwardian England. Moreover, they were constrained by their general philosophy and approach. They preferred minimum government intervention, and, although they recognised that certain problems required legislative action, they were content where possible to avoid its necessity. Inevitably then, changes were often modest in scope and there were a number of areas which remained unreformed. Little was done for housing and local government, and above all the old Victorian Poor Law with its use of workhouses remained untouched.

Typical of this approach was John Burns, a workingman who occupied the key post at the Local Government Board, a position which he retained throughout the period. He was lacking in imagination and boldness, and proved to be a less than competent choice. If he was among the most conspicuous examples of the old thinking, others doubted the value or efficacy of wholesale reform. They tackled matters of interest and concern on an individual basis, some of them more actively and enthusiastically than others. A right-wing politician and historian, Robert Rhode James, in *The British Revolution; British Politics, 1880-1939,* has observed of the government's handling of events:

> 1 It tinkered - often very effectively with social problems on the classic nineteenth-century pattern; at no point did it deal with fundamental social problems; at root, it was emphatically a Free Trade and Laissez-Faire Government. It moved slowly and
> 5 carefully, under a leader whose conservatism was deeply ingrained, who distrusted enthusiasm, who dealt with matters as they arose ... The vital feature of the Welfare State - massive State intervention in the life of the individual - was conspicuously absent in the pre-1914 government, and no assaults on Socialism were more
> 10 trenchant and swingeing than those delivered by Lloyd George and Churchill. In its approach, if not in some of its measures, this was a government of which Mr Gladstone would have been proud.

More often the attack has come from those on the left who have sought to demonstrate that Liberals were not committed to reform and that therefore a Labour Party was necessary to produce schemes of social progress. The indictment has usually followed similar lines: that on the one hand the reforms were narrow in range, a far cry from the mid twentieth-century conception of welfare, and that most of them were only half-hearted and only made a very tentative beginning. As such, they reveal the limitations of the Liberal outlook. The implication is that this was a traditional Liberal government different only from most previous administrations in the amount, rather than the nature, of reform it introduced.

Critics also argue that the reforms were the work of only the two leading radicals in the government, Churchill and Lloyd George, both of whom revealed a certain skill in adapting Liberalism to the challenge of the 'condition of the people' question. In so doing, they retained some middle-class support and made a bid for the loyalty of the working classes. They were acting out of political necessity, for social improvement offered a route which was an alternative to the challenging creed of socialism. Doubters might also stress that a number of reforms were passed only as a response to political bargaining or outside pressure, the actions of the miners in 1908 and 1912 and of Labour over school meals being useful examples.

A socialist poster; a souvenir for May Day, 1907

The criticism is not without foundation, and overblown claims for the Liberals as pioneers of the modern system need to be viewed with some scepticism. There were Gladstonians in the administration and several ministers had a foot in both camps, sometimes echoing the approach of their forebears, and sometimes looking to the future. Yet because of the lack of conviction of some of them, it is easy to concentrate on what they did not do and to lose sight of the considerable extent of the overall achievement. Much had been accomplished, certainly more than any other government to this date.

Of course, there was a desire to secure working-class support, and shrewd politicians such as Lloyd George, were alive to the danger of Liberals being outflanked on the left. Opportunism and principle are often combined in political life. But though their measures were in some cases too modest and inadequate to be an answer to the problems of the time and unsatisfactory to some more radical than themselves who had stronger convictions than they did, in fairness neither Lloyd George or Churchill considered that they had done all that needed to be done to eliminate poverty and insecurity. They had other proposals in mind, and Churchill spoke of building 'an unbroken bridge or causeway, as it were, along which the whole body of the people may move with ... security and safety against hazards and misfortunes'.

They both accepted heavy expenditure as a necessity and were prepared to finance it through increased taxation, a far cry from the Gladstonian wish to leave money 'to fructify in the pockets of the individuals'. Their approach certainly convinced some committed reformers of the day, for Beatrice Webb, a leading Fabian socialist, was able to write in 1910, in *Our Partnership,* that; 'The big thing that has happened in the last two years is that Lloyd George and Winston Churchill have practically taken the limelight, not merely from their own colleagues, but from the Labour party. They stand out as advanced politicians.' Some ministers were notably effective and, although they were concerned to distance themselves from socialism which many of them abhorred, nonetheless they were keen and able to show that the concept of Liberalism could be stretched to embrace far-reaching change. If the government as a whole lacked an overall strategy for removing social disadvantage, Churchill and Lloyd George did enough to demonstrate their concern to equip Liberalism with a new dynamism. They were willing to look beyond the political liberty of yesterday with its emphasis on the freedom of the individual and *laissez faire,* and to seek to adapt it to tackle the grave social problems of the larger industrial centres.

The way in which state intervention was employed marked a distinctly new departure in Liberal thinking. There was a greater emphasis upon collectivism for it was recognised that, without some governmental regulation to eliminate poverty and injustice, the individual, the traditional target of Liberal concern, could not lead a full and satisfactory life. Whilst Liberals such as Churchill still stressed the limited goal of protecting the weakest from life's hazards rather than providing a fully-fledged welfare service, nonetheless there is in the changes introduced a greater emphasis on the role of the state. As Donald Read has remarked, 'whereas in the Victorian era the rule of *laissez-faire* in economic and political life had never ... been practised without qualification ... [now] there were as many exceptions as applications'. The political philosopher, Sir Ernest Barker, could write in 1914 that, 'While in 1864 orthodoxy meant distrust of the State, and heresy took the form of a belief in paternal government, in 1914 orthodoxy means belief in the state, and heresy takes the form of mild excursions into anarchy'.

As to precisely how the New Liberalism fitted in with the new creed of socialism, opinions differed. The Webbs clearly did not see a strong distinction, and neither did Churchill feel that it was necessary to spend too long agonising over the issue. He felt that Liberalism was particularly suited to the task of necessary reform, for,

> 1 It supplies at once the highest impulse and the practical path. By sentiments of generosity and humanity, by the process of moderation ... Liberalism enlists on the side of progress hundreds

of thousands whom a militant Socialist party would drive into
5 violent Tory reaction. It is through the agency of the Liberal party
alone that Society will in the course of time slide forward almost
painlessly ... We are all agreed that the State must concern itself
with the care of the sick, of the aged and, above all, of the children.
10 I do not want to limit the vigour of competition, but to mitigate the
consequences of failure.

Two years later, in 1908, he was able to make the distinction that 'Socialism wants to pull down wealth, Liberalism seeks to raise up poverty ... Socialism assails the maximum pre-eminence of the individual - Liberalism seeks to build up the maximum standard of the masses'. If by Socialism, a full state programme of intervention to embrace wholesale change in the capitalist system was implied, then he wanted none of it. In as much as socialist values were concerned with social progress, he shared a commitment, but Liberals such as he and Lloyd George in their measures attached some importance to keeping benefits sufficiently low to ensure that thrift was practised and that people were encouraged to help themselves. Hence their belief in the insurance principle whilst many socialists were less convinced of its merits and preferred non-contributory schemes.

6 Problems of Late-Edwardian England

The Liberals had lost support in several by-elections in 1908-9, but there was popular backing for their People's Budget which galvanised interest in Liberal politics, although it did not do the party much good in the elections of 1910. Thereafter, the Liberals were faced by a series of daunting problems. The immediate one concerned the House of Lords and the Budget rejection, but in addition the suffragettes, industrial militancy, extremism in Ulster, and the imminence of war in Europe cast a gloomy shadow over the administration.

In 1911 party bitterness was acute, and fierce controversy raged over the Peers and the Ulstermen, made worse by the arrival in that year of the dour and uncompromising Bonar Law as the new Conservative leader. Balfour was too quiescent and many Conservatives were pleased to see his replacement by a more partisan figure who brought a new acerbity to the leadership. *The National Review* expressed the extreme anti-Liberal sentiments of the right in its denunciation of ministers for promoting 'national anarchy', and it was Lloyd George in particular who was singled out for attack. His Limehouse and other speeches raised the temperature of political debate, and 'Limehouse' became a word popularly used to convey hatred and loathing.

The Bill to disestablish the Welsh Church was another cause of contention between the parties. Gladstone had succeeded in disestablishing the Anglican Church in Ireland in 1869, and Welsh Liberals awaited a similar measure. The majority of their constituents were Nonconformists and there was considerable pressure on MPs to keep the issue near the top of the Liberal agenda. The Conservatives were appalled at the prospect of any legislation on the subject, for they equated disestablishment with paganism. In a conversation with Asquith, Law even suggested that his backbenchers would prefer Irish Home Rule to any move affecting the status of the Church. Their fears were confirmed when, after stormy debate, the Welsh Disestablishment Bill was passed into law at the third attempt, on the eve of war and under the terms of the Parliament Act (see page 146).

On Welsh Disestablishment, the party battle between Lloyd George and Lord Hugh Cecil was intense, but at least in this case it was a violence of rhetoric rather than reality. In other problems which faced the Liberals, the hostility sometimes took a more dramatic form.

Lloyd George provided an opportunity for his opponents when in 1912-13 allegations were made that he and Sir Rufus Isaacs had personally benefited from government dealings with the British Marconi Company which pioneered the development of the wireless. As the affair unfolded, it centred upon the failure of the two men to disclose their private financial transactions to the House when they had a personal connection with matters being discussed. Lloyd George was able to extricate himself and even later claim that his honour had been maligned. In a supreme irony, he was defended in court by F.E. Smith and Sir Edward Carson, two men who were revealing extreme hostility to the government and whipping up the temperature over events in Ulster.

The pursuit of the ministers by the Conservatives revealed the extreme hostility between the parties, yet of all people it was Lloyd George, the demon of the People's Budget, who in the midst of party rancour over the Constitutional Crisis could soar above the contemporary hostilities and (with Churchill's approval) propose the establishment of an all-party coalition. He was impatient with the squabbles of the day and seemingly keen to see a constructive partnership to solve some of the leading issues. Some new centre party seemed to him an obvious way forward but at a time when Liberals were railing against the privileges of the Lords and the Unionists were adamant in their defence of Ulster Protestants there was an air of unreality about the proposition.

a) The Clash With the House of Lords

The House of Lords had long been dominated by the Conservatives, and Liberal governments from the time of Gladstone had been frustrated by the opposition of the second chamber. Clashes had occurred over Home Rule, the extension of the vote and other proposals, but the long period of Conservative rule in the late nineteenth century limited the amount of disagreement. The anti-Liberal bias became more evident after 1906, for in the light of the massive victory the Conservative leader Balfour remarked that 'no matter which Party sat on those benches [pointing to the government side] the Unionist Party will always rule the country' through the power of the House of Lords. He saw the Lords as having important delaying powers to curb hasty, ill-considered legislation. Liberals took a different view and believed that Balfour was denying the people's wishes as expressed in the election. As Lloyd George remarked, 'the House of Lords is not the watchdog of the Constitution; it is Mr Balfour's poodle'.

The Lords began to reject or severely amend Liberal proposals on education and licensing, but it was the 'People's Budget' that proved to be the cause of intense controversy. By tradition, the second chamber did not a block a money Bill but on this occasion it had done so, and the outcome was a full constitutional crisis. Asquith declared their behaviour to be 'a breach of the Constitution' and resolved to put the issue to the electorate. Parliament was dissolved and elections held, but the Liberals did much less well than in 1906 and won only 275 seats, two more than the Conservatives. They were dependent on Irish and Labour support, but with this firm backing they decided to go ahead with a Parliament Bill to trim the powers of the second chamber, even though the Lords belatedly allowed the Budget proposals to pass into law.

A new king, George V, attempted to mediate between Liberal and Conservative leaders, but discussion was futile and he indicated that if the issue was put to the electorate on a second occasion, he would be willing to create enough Liberal peers to allow the Bill to pass through the Upper House. The second elections followed in December 1910 and produced an almost identical result. After a struggle, the Conservative peers relented and narrowly passed the Parliament Bill (131-114) as the lesser of two evils; the alternative was to hold out and see their chamber swamped with new Liberal peers. If that had happened, the Bill would pass anyway and the new members would be able to use their position to advance the progress of other Liberal proposals.

As a result of the Parliament Act the Lords lost their power to reject money Bills and in future they would only be able to delay other forms of legislation. If a Bill passed the Commons in three successive parliamentary sessions, it would automatically pass into law; thus, the Lords would be able to postpone but not permanently to veto any Bill, however controversial. From 1911 onwards, a government with a clear majority and in its early life, could get its programme through Parliament and on to the statute book - a measure of momentous consequence for future developments in Ireland and Wales in the short term, and for the country as a whole over a longer period.

The Act was a substantial Liberal achievement and it resolved a problem which had beset past progressive administrations. As such it was much to the credit of ministers, though the energy and time spent in tackling the Lords exhausted much of its reforming impetus. It was unfortunate that the issue of the powers of the second chamber had not been tackled before the Liberals had lost electoral support. Even when action did become necessary Asquith seemed at first reluctant to move. He tended to prefer words to action and to assume that others shared his basic respect for the constitution and established institutions. He found difficulty in coming to terms with the ferocity of the Unionist opposition in its zeal to inflict damage on the elected government. Neither was he easily able to handle the two kings involved in the constitutional crisis, both of whom failed to respond to his sometimes ambiguous verbal subtleties. However, when he did decide to press ahead with a measure to curb the second chamber then he kept to his task and saw the objective through to completion.

b) The Suffragettes

Another challenge to the government was presented by the suffragettes. Their campaign for 'Votes for Women' was but one aspect of the campaign for female emancipation which had been developing in the mid-to-late nineteenth century. Some progress had been made in securing rights in education, medicine and the law, and women could vote in local elections. But their right to participate in parliamentary elections was still denied.

John Stuart Mill had set out their case during the debates over the 1867 Reform Bill, and subsequently the National Union of Women's Suffrage Societies had campaigned for the cause. Many Liberal women were involved in its network of local associations, but at Westminster male MPs, including many Liberals, were unmoved. In 1897, a Bill had been 'talked out' by opponents and the moderate methods of persuasion via leaflets and meetings seemed to have achieved little. In 1903, Mrs Emmeline Pankhurst launched a more formidable organisation, the Women's Social and Political Union (WSPU), which was prepared to adopt a more challenging and direct approach. Its members became known as the suffragettes, the moderates then being referred to as suffragists.

In the election campaign of 1906, Campbell-Bannerman seemed to be sympathetic, as did several Liberal candidates, but after their electoral triumph little happened to benefit the cause. Women were allowed to sit on county and borough councils, and to serve as mayors, as a result of the Qualification of Women Act (1907), but there was no indication that sympathy for the female franchise was being translated into legislative action. The WSPU stepped up its campaigning, and particularly from 1909 onwards was prepared to use organised lawlessness to gain attention for the claims which were denied them. Apart from interrupting speeches of politicians and disrupting parliamentary debates, as part of their direct action they chained themselves to railings, set fire to post boxes, and even slashed pictures in the National Gallery. By 1913, defiance of the law had taken a more violent turn, and even included suicide when Emily Davidson made a martyr of herself in a self-inflicted death at the Derby.

The response of the authorities was severe, with the police and some of the public treating the suffragettes roughly. In prison, they were forcibly fed if on hunger-strike and were handled most unceremoniously. The government resorted to passing a Prisoners (Temporary Discharge) Act, popularly known as the Cat and Mouse Act, which allowed prison governors to release prisoners who were near to death through hunger; they could then be re-arrested when they had recovered, and re-released if they went on hunger-strike again. It seemed a very illiberal way to react and reflected the desperation of ministers when faced with defiance of their authority.

'Votes for Women' should have been a good Liberal issue. Liberals prided themselves on their record of parliamentary reform; moreover, their doctrines stressed equal rights and the removal of disqualifications which fell on particular groups. Liberal women were involved in the movement, and some Liberal men around the country could see the justice of their claim. Yet at the top, the leadership of the party was unmoved. Gladstone had been an opponent of female voting, and Asquith was also unyielding in his opposition. It seemed illogical that ministers were upholding male privilege and denying political equality to women at the same time as they were willing to attack the privileged position of peers.

In 1911 and 1912 Women's Suffrage Bills were eventually introduced to allow some women to vote, but they were lost in parliamentary manoeuvres. Voting was not conducted on a party basis, and the outcome revealed the extent of support for women in the House of Commons. On the second occasion, 117 Liberals supported women and 73 opposed them. The measure was defeated by 222-208, Labour MPs having overwhelmingly backed it and the majority of Conservatives having been opposed. *Why did the Liberals deny the womens' claims?*

Partly, their position was a reflection of Asquith's personal hostility, for he felt that women did not generally want or need the vote, and that issues of state were not their sphere of decision-making. He also felt that to concede their claim would be a political blunder, for it raised the question of which women should vote. This was a concern of many MPs. If all women had the vote, then this would necessitate remaining males being granted the franchise also. This was not seriously on the cards. If voting rights had been granted on the same basis as men, most wives not being property-owners, would have been excluded, and the likelihood was that a substantial number of better-off women would have been the beneficiaries - a likely reinforcement to the Conservative Party. Finally, the methods of the suffragettes outraged many people who felt that they showed that women were unfit to exercise the vote. They attacked the government whose support they needed to win, and whilst Asquith was a convinced opponent, some ministers such as Lloyd George were personally sympathetic.

Lloyd George was particularly surprised that he was the victim of suffragette attacks for he was the person most likely to argue the women's case in Cabinet. 'Why don't they go for their enemies?,' he asked on one occasion. By 1913, he felt that Christabel Pankhurst was 'mad' and had mislaid 'all sense of proportion and of reality', particularly with her cry of 'Votes for Women and Chastity for Men', a reflection of her suggestion that women should deny husbands their marital pleasures as a means of persuading them to back claims for female suffrage.

He was a politician who needed to be encouraged and influenced, rather than to be intimidated and the suffragists realised this. However, neither the moderate nor the more extreme approach had proved successful when war broke out. Women proved their worth in their contribution to the war effort. It was Lloyd George, by then Prime Minister, who presided over the first step on female enfranchisement in 1918.

c) Militancy in the Unions

Late-Edwardian England, using the term in its broadest sense to include the period up to the outbreak of the First World War, was a time of intense conflict between employers and their workers. Until 1907 industrial relations were reasonably tranquil, and the number of working days lost through strike action ranged between 1.5 and 4 million a year. Thereafter the strike weapon was more frequently employed, and over the next few years the number averaged 11 million, with a particularly bad year in 1912 when, primarily because of the prolonged coal stoppage, 41m days were lost. By then, the country was engulfed in an industrial crisis.

Militancy was most marked in the period after 1909, for a number of reasons. Whereas until that year wage increases had kept in line with price increases, they no longer did so afterwards and for many working people there was serious pressure on their weekly budget. Britain was losing its share of world trade and manufacturers were consequently cutting back on employment; they were unwilling to grant pay increases. Another factor in the growing dissatisfaction of trade unionism was disillusion with the performance of the Liberal government which they saw as disappointing in its social legislation. But they were particularly frustrated with the performance of the new Labour element in the House of Commons which seemed to be ineffectual when faced with a reforming administration. Labour MPs were meant to protect working-class interests but they were often divided and leaderless, and only rarely did they have a significant impact on social issues. Their lack of impact encouraged some trade unionists to abandon the parliamen-

THE RIGHT DISHONOURABLE DOUBLE-FACE ASQUITH.

LIBERTY
EQUALITY

A. PATRIOT.

Citizen Asq—th: "Down with privilege of birth —up with democratic rule!"

Monseigneur Asq—th: "The rights of Government belong to the aristocrats by birth—men. No liberty or equality for women!"

Privilege and equality

tary process as a means of achieving their ends.

There was a further factor in union unrest, and that was the growing influence of Syndicalism, a doctrine which derived from overseas theorists. Daniel de Leon, an American, believed in the concept of class warfare, while Georges Sorel, a French philosopher, was committed to the idea of a general strike of workers. Both men, as well as other syndicalists, were committed to a more revolutionary stance. They wanted to see large trade unions flex their industrial muscle to bring about a socialist state by means of a trade union takeover following a breakdown of governmental authority. The strike weapon was no longer merely a means of coercing an employer but a way of bringing the whole of society to heel and winning control of the state.

Older union leaders were opposed to many of the political aims of the syndicalists, who were only ever supported by a small minority of workers, but they were under pressure from their rapidly growing membership for strong leadership and a more determined stand against their employers. Labour relations markedly deteriorated in 1910, and following a rail strike and a dispute in the cotton industry there was prolonged and sometimes riotous action by the miners of the Rhondda which resulted in the Hussars patrolling the valleys to ensure that peace was preserved. At Tonypandy, a miner was killed by their action, an incident which did lasting damage to Home Secretary Churchill's reputation in the area.

In the years 1911-14, the movement towards larger unions and the decline in support for traditional parliamentary methods of pursuing objectives gained momentum. A serious rail dispute was ended only after ministerial intervention, and the following year the National Union of Railwaymen was formed to embrace the vast majority of rail workers. A strike of the miners in 1912 involved some 850,000 members of the largest union in a long stoppage. Other unions joined in the spreading unrest, and action occurred in many areas - on the docks, among the weavers and in the transport industry. Such action occurred against a background of growing union membership and a trend towards amalgamation. Unions were becoming a formidable power in the land, and the Triple Alliance of miners, railwaymen and transport workers (1913) was a recognition of the strength possessed if the individual demands of unions could be backed by supportive action from other industrial workers.

The government struggled to cope with this new dimension of industrial unrest, and was ill at ease in its reaction to the growing challenge of organised labour. Ministers varied in their attitudes, but most were unsympathetic to unions and their spokesmen. Churchill's sympathy with the workers diminished as every month passed, and his earlier reforming ardour markedly cooled. The Labour Party became sharply antagonistic to him and attacked his belligerent approach to workers. When the industrial situation was at its most critical in 1912,

Lucy Masterman, the wife of the junior Liberal minister, confided to her diary that 'Winston ... was becoming less and less radical in his sympathy and was practically in a "shoot-'em-down" attitude ... The Prime Minister is not fond of Labour at any time'. Faced with this hostility, her husband was forced to 'wonder whether I am really a Liberal at all'.

Lloyd George was sympathetic to the Labour cause and enjoyed a working relationship with several of its leaders, even if he was personally cool to Hardie who he found ineffective. He was by nature a conciliator, and used his arbitrating skill to help resolve the railway strike in 1912. By emphasising the imminent danger of war with Germany, he was able to get company representatives and unionists around a negotiating table and bring about a settlement. In 1912, faced with the massive stoppage in the mines, the government conciliated again, by making concessions on a minimum wage. In the most serious disputes, therefore, ministerial intervention to force the employers to meet and make concessions might occur, but such intervention was rare and undertaken with reluctance. There were, after all, still employers within the Liberal Party, and major industrial interests - coalowners, shipbuilders among others - still providing it with financial support.

The government was uncertain in its response to agitation which it did not fully comprehend and to which it was by instinct unsympathetic; many of its members recoiled from the militancy shown by organised labour. Ministers found it difficult to handle new class pressures which threatened to overwhelm them. Keir Hardie pointed to the failure of Liberalism in this regard.

> My friends and comrades, you cannot mix oil and water. There are some men in the meeting who are half Liberal and half Labour - who want to be friends with both parties; the thing cannot be done.

d) Ireland

The problem of the future of Ireland had remained unsolved following the failure of Gladstone's attempts at Home Rule. It received little attention in the Liberal programme in 1906, but it loomed larger in the contests four years later. After their close shave, the Liberals remained in power only with the support of Labour and of the Irish nationalists, then led by John Redmond. With the constitutional crisis out of the way, ministers knew that Home Rule must be on the agenda for the House of Lords could pose no long-term threat to future legislation.

They had little relish for their task, but any backsliding was out of the question. As Redmond pointed out; 'Unless an official declaration on the question of Home Rule be made, not only will it be impossible for us to support Liberal candidates in England, but we will most unquestionably have to ask our friends to vote against them ... as you know very well, the opposition of Irish voters in Lancashire, Yorkshire, and other places including Scotland, would certainly mean the loss of many seats'. Asquith introduced a Third Home Rule Bill in 1912 which was in many respects similar to the earlier ones, but unlike that of 1886 there was to be provision for limited Irish representation at Westminster. The parliamentary debates on the Bill were to be marked by much rancour and acrimony.

The main problem with the Bill was its failure to cater for the special difficulty caused by the problem of the Ulster Protestants. The economic, social and religious life of the nine northern counties was different from that of the rest of the island; they were more industrialised, agriculture was often more efficient and the people were broadly contented. The Protestants, (a majority there, but a minority in the whole of Ireland), had no wish to be ruled from the south and to be outnumbered in a predominantly Catholic Parliament. They were determined to remain as part of the United Kingdom, and their antipathy to Catholic rule and to Rome was captured by Kipling in his poem, Ulster, in 1912.

We know the hells prepared
For such as serve not Rome -
The terror, threats and dread
In market, hearth and field -
We know, where all is said,
We perish if we yield ...

What answer from the North?
One law, one Land, one Throne.
If England drives us forth
We shall not fall alone!

Liberals had been aware of the difficulty posed by Ulster for many years, but had not been able to come up with any solution. They knew that nationalists disliked the idea of partition, for they saw the resources of the north-eastern counties and of Belfast, with the largest shipyard in the world, as being crucial to the success of devolved government in Ireland. Asquith therefore presented the new Bill as a means of catering for national aspirations and providing more efficient government, and thereby fending off any movement towards a separatist solution for Ireland. As the Bill made its passage through Parliament, twice rejected by the House of Lords, the prospect of civil war in Ireland became a very real one, for in Ulster there was growing resistance to Home Rule being imposed upon the northern counties.

e) Ulster Resistance

It was Lord Randolph Churchill who had said that 'Ulster will fight, and Ulster will be right' during the debates on Gladstone's first Home Rule Bill. For years the threat had not materialised for Home Rule did not seem an imminent possibility. In the years before 1914, it suddenly became a likely reality. Bitter antagonism developed, and steps were taken by Sir Edward Carson and others to organise resistance. After the mass signing of a Solemn Covenant in 1912 pledging 'never to recognise a Dublin Parliament' and to use 'all means which may be found necessary to defeat the present conspiracy to set up a Home Rule Parliament in Ireland', steps were taken to form an army force, the Ulster Volunteers. It was highly organised and arms were being landed in semi-secrecy from Germany to help them.

When Bonar Law took over the Conservative leadership, he echoed Lord Randolph Churchill's sentiments and encouraged Carson and others to use any means of revolt. He took a dangerous line for a parliamentary spokesmen, and said that he could 'imagine no length of resistance to which Ulster can go in which I should not be prepared to support them, and in which ... they will not be supported by the overwhelming majority of the British people'. It sounded like active encouragement for Ulstermen to defy the law, the more so when he darkly stated that 'there are things stronger than parliamentary majorities'.

In Asquith's phrase, Tory speeches over the next two years provided a 'complete grammar of anarchy'. Winston Churchill was inclined to dismiss the 'frothings of Sir Edward Carson. I daresay when the worst comes to the worst we shall find that civil war evaporates in uncivil words'. But in March 1914, the situation did seem to be degenerating into civil war, with volunteers being recruited by the nationalists (the Irish Volunteers) as well as by the Protestants. Characteristically, Lloyd George tried to find a middle way by which Ulster might be temporarily excluded from the operation of Home Rule.

The situation was changed with the news that the government had ordered military movements to meet possible violence in the North. This provoked a spate of 58 resignations among army officers, in the famous or infamous Curragh Mutiny. Troops from the Curragh barracks in Dublin were likely to be used in any coercion of Ulster, and the incident showed the unreliability of the army in the acutely difficult circumstances which could arise. Everyone knew that under the passage of the Parliament Act, Home Rule would be on the statute book later that year, and that violent resistance might ensue.

On the nationalist side, they had only to stand firm in their resolve for their aims to be realised, They knew that the Bill was going through, though a younger generation was unimpressed by Redmond and his moderate constitutional leadership, and was more attracted to Sinn Fein

(Ourselves Alone) which wanted not devolution but separation, and was active in the Irish Volunteers. Asquith was prepared to adopt the Lloyd Georgian compromise and postpone the application of devolution to Ulster for six years, but this pleased no-one, certainly not the nationalists who saw it as a betrayal, and the Ulstermen who in Carson's words did 'not want sentence of death with a stay of execution for six years'. By August 1914, Ireland was on the verge of a complete breakdown of law and order. At that point, mercifully for Ireland, if not for the world, war broke out on the continent of Europe. A month later, in September, the Home Rule passed into law, but its application was postponed for the duration of international hostilities.

Ireland had presented an acute problem for the administration, and there was uncertainty in its approach to the use of force to coerce Ulster. Initially, ministers had hoped that Carson was bluffing, but soon they privately recognised that he was not, and that concessions might be necessary. Churchill sounded characteristically belligerent and remarked that there were 'worse things than bloodshed', and added that Parliament could not be intimidated by the crude use of force. Asquith's attitude to the use of troops to enforce Home Rule was ambiguous; having seemed to support a more drastic policy, he then backed down and was unprepared to crush political opposition. Meanwhile he waited for the Bill to became law to see how events then unfolded. He felt that public sympathy would not be with the side which fired the first shots. Any state trial of Carson for sedition or even treason would almost certainly have aggravated the situation. In the circumstances, it was understandable to 'wait and see'.

7 The Dangerfield Analysis

That Edwardian England was a period of violence and of extreme passions is evident. The Liberal government was in serious difficulty and some historians have been tempted to connect the diverse components of this troubled period and construct a theory to suggest that Liberalism itself was found wanting, past its sell-by date. In a brilliant and provocative study, *The Strange Death of Liberal England* (1936), Graham Dangerfield propounded such a thesis. He suggested that the political and industrial crises showed that the party was ill-equipped to cope.

He claimed that the Liberals had no answer to the various problems, and that this was because they were an essentially middle-class party, with an outdated creed. Their values were essentially those of reasoned discussion, and compromise; they adhered to the constitution, to order, and to the rule of law. When those values were under duress, the creed cracked. Faced with a pattern of violence, sometimes of rhetoric but more often of a physical kind, in which people were prepared to threaten parliamentary government, Liberalism was incapable of decisive action. This was not just because of any failings in the leadership of Asquith.

The party was bankrupt of ideas, and lacked popular roots in the community which would have enabled it to withstand the assault upon its cherished traditions and attitudes.

Other historians have latched on to this theory and adapted it to suit their particular ends; in so doing, they have sought to demonstrate that the Liberals were ceasing to govern, indeed that they were incapable of so doing. Left-wing historians have an interest in demonstrating that the replacement of Liberalism by Labour was an inexorable development, and several have taken up and amplified the thesis. They see 1906 as a freak election result, based largely on Conservative mistakes and the temporary revival of the Nonconformist and working-class vote for the Liberals. Thus Henry Pelling, in *Popular Politics and Society in Late Victorian Britain* and other works, claims that Liberals were not able 'to take advantage of twentieth-century political conditions', and that Labour taking over from the Liberals was an inevitable process.

McKibbin in his *Evolution of the Labour Party* (1975) dismisses Dangerfield's analysis as 'literary confetti', clever, stimulating but essentially misleading. Trevor Wilson, in *The Downfall of the Liberal Party, 1914-1935* (1966), has argued that the Liberals in 1914 were still essentially sound, and that they had on occasion, as with the New Liberals, demonstrated a capacity for renewal and regeneration. Liberalism had problems of personnel and ideology in adapting to changed conditions, but that does not mean that the task was impossible.

Wilson argued that, rather than being related by a common thread, the attacks on parliamentary government were an 'accidental convergence of unrelated events'. Some of the problems were passing; the Upper House had been put in its place, and the strike wave appeared to be waning. The other problems were not manifestly insoluble, though the Irish one was exceedingly complex. The Liberals had indeed struggled to cope with the situation, but if Liberalism seemed rather stale in 1914, after a long and active period in office, there were Liberals planning new initiatives - such as Lloyd George with his plans for education and an extension of national insurance. It was true that there were problems in developing the appropriate relationship with Labour; it was true that in Europe as a whole Liberalism was a declining force, and that more left-wing parties were benefiting from the growth of organised labour. That does not mean that a reforming Liberal Party was inevitably incapable of the necessary adaptation.

Dangerfield's was ultimately an unconvincing thesis, harsh in its verdict on Liberal rule. The 'crises' of the period were not a failing of Liberalism as such. The assaults were directed at parliamentary government, at the whole constitutional system rather than specifically the Liberal ministers. Faced by unfamiliar and very demanding challenges, those ministers seemed to have lost their way, but this was not to detract from the range of their achievement. If they were unable to assuage the discontent of those who rejected the established order, nonetheless their work in laying the early foundations of state welfare, in tackling the ills of labour, and in putting a Parliament Act and Irish Home rule finally on the statute book is a tribute to their reforming zeal. It was not a sign that they were moribund, nor faced with extinction.

Making notes on 'Liberalism, 1894-1914'

Two aspects of this topic are especially important as far as examinations are concerned - the Liberals as social reformers and the political and social problems faced by ministers, particularly in the years 1909-14.

On the Liberals as social reformers you should make notes on the following:
1 The reasons for the prominence of social reform; 2 The approach of Campbell-Bannerman and Asquith; 3 The meaning of New Liberalism; 4 A selection of reforms

The reforms can be noted chronologically, but you may find it yields better notes to revise from if you list them by category. Key ones concern:
1 School meals; 2 Old age pensions; 3 Trade Boards; 4 Labour exchanges; 5 National Insurance; 6 Trade unions

For each reform try to include in your notes an explanation of i) why it was passed, ii) how effective it was, and iii) how it fits into the pattern of the New Liberalism.

On the problems you should cover:

1 The People's Budget - motives, contents, rejection by Lords and ensuing constitutional crisis
2 Votes for Women - Suffragists, Suffragettes, the Liberal attitude and handling of events
3 Trade unions - reasons for militancy, main outbreaks of unrest, reactions of ministers
4 Ulster - nature of problem, progress of Home Rule Bill, deterioration of situation, Liberal handling of events

You might assess the Liberal performance on each of the four areas, and briefly say whether it was effective or otherwise. Do the events point to a party in serious decline, as Dangerfield suggested?

Answering essay questions on 'Liberalism, 1894-1914'

Examiners are very keen on this area of British history on which several forms of question are possible. On the social reform theme, a quotation is often provided, as in this question;

> 'Fathers of the Welfare State'. Is this a valid description of the Liberal contribution to social reform in the years between 1905 and 1914?

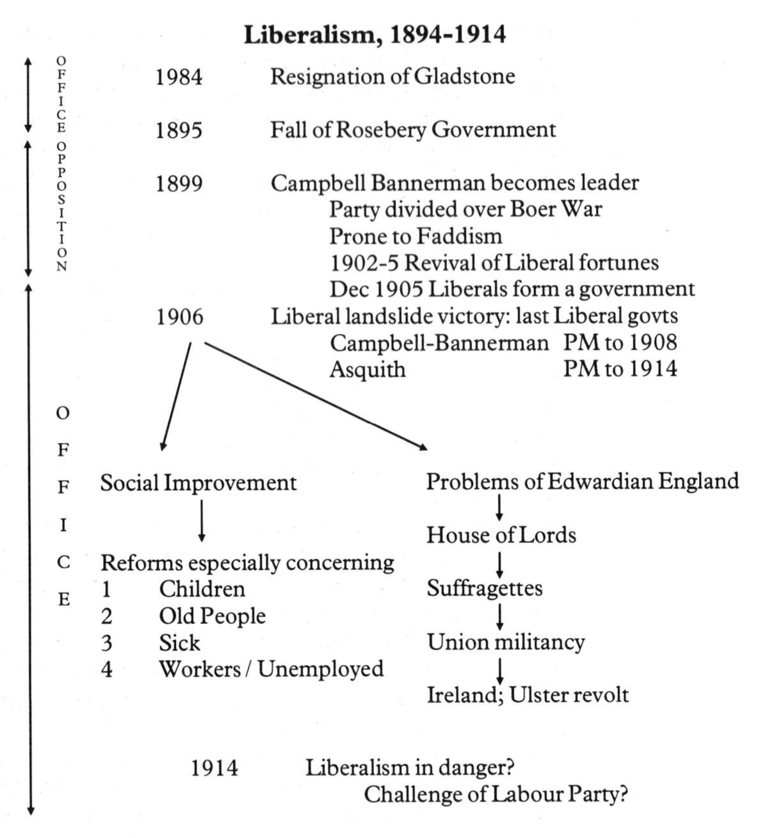

Summary - Liberalism 1894-1914

Always look out for key words. 'Fathers' implies that they were responsible for sowing the seeds of the 'Welfare State' if not for its main development. Those last two words need to be considered. What is the concept of the 'Welfare State' as we understand it today, and is it what the Liberals were launching, consciously or unconsciously?

Some questions are phrased in a straightforward manner, such as 'Assess the reforms...', and, as long as you take note of the word(s) of instruction such as 'assess', they should pose few problems if you write pertinently to the title. Others are more thought-provoking, asking 'In what ways (or 'To what extent') did the Edwardian Liberal social reforms help to raise the living standards of the working classes between 1906 and 1914?'.

The answer to such a question can easily degenerate into a catalogue of reforms, at worst ones not even assessed. Ask yourself how particular legislation assisted the living/working conditions of the working classes directly or indirectly. For instance, trade union changes in 1906 enabled the industrial leaders of the working classes to organise strike action in the knowledge that it could prove effective, as the union would not be liable for damages in court. Some reforms were less effective than others, and the important areas of the Poor Law and housing were not adequately tackled - so that deprivation still widely existed. Other things helped the working classes besides Liberal legislation - e.g., the voluntary organisations, Friendly Societies and more forward-looking local authorities. You might even mention how the rising cost of living posed problems for the working-class budget. In other words, the 'Edwardian Liberal social reforms' must not be a trigger to write down all you know about a few social improvements or to decide on whether they constituted 'the foundations of the Welfare State'. Answer the question asked.

Finally on social reform, there are more probing questions such as those asking about the New Liberalism. Think about the following two questions and devise a plan for one of them showing what you would include; 'What had the New Liberalism achieved by 1914?', and 'What was new in the New Liberalism?'.

The other type of question concentrates on the problems and unrest of the immediate pre-war period. You could be asked to 'Explain the growing unrest ...' or to decide 'How effectively did the Liberals handle the unrest ...?'. More thought-provoking is a question asking whether there was a serious threat to stability (or parliamentary government) in the years 1909-14. Sometimes questions focus on just one problem, such as the female vote or more often the Budget and constitutional crisis. Be careful not to allow yourself to be so immersed in the details of the unfolding events that you fail to provide the explanation or assessment required by a title such as 'Why did the People's Budget prove so controversial and how effectively did the Asquith government handle the issues raised by its rejection in the Upper House?'.

Finally, in the light of Dangerfield's analysis, link the episodes together and consider whether 'The crises of 1909-14 point not only to the failings of the Asquith administration but also to the relevance of Liberalism itself'. You need to emphasise the handling of the events, with due recognition of their inherent difficulty. Was there, as he suggested, a general failing of Liberalism (because the creed was no longer relevant) or were the difficulties of particular complexity which would have taxed any party in power?

Source-based questions on *'Liberalism, 1894-1914'*

1 Liberalism and Socialism

Read the extracts from Gladstone (page 128), Smiles (page 5), Churchill (pages 142, 143-4) and Beatrice Webb (page 143), and study the Socialist poster (page 142). Answer the following questions.

a) Churchill spoke of 'building an unbroken bridge or causeway'. Do you think that the contents of the Socialist poster suggest that his approach would have been adequate to satisfy socialist demands? (5 marks)

b) How similar was the approach of Beatrice Webb to that of Churchill? (3 marks)
c) Hobson argued that the 'old barriers of Liberalism and Socialism must be blurred'. Does a study of the extracts suggest that there was such a 'blurring'? (7 marks)
d) What were the similarities between the thoughts of Smiles and Gladstone? (4 marks)
e) How might Smiles and Gladstone have reacted to the poster? Explain your answer. (6 marks)

2 Liberal Thinking on the Role of the State

Read the extracts on the provision of school meals (page 134), the comments of Gladstone (page 128) and Robert Rhodes James (page 141). Answer the following questions.

a) According to Samuel, what was the role of the state in social improvement? (4 marks)
b) Would Gladstone have welcomed Samuel's analysis on the state's role? Explain your answer. (4 marks)
c) How did the speakers in the House of Commons debate differ in their approach to the state's role in the provision of social facilities? (6 marks)
d) According to Rhodes James, the Liberal government was one of which 'Mr Gladstone would have been proud'. Does the material in the other extracts suggest that this would have been the case? Explain your answer (6 marks)

3 The House of Lords and Votes for Women

Read the Newcastle speech (pages 139-40), and examine the three cartoons on pages 138 and 150. Answer the following questions.

a) Comment on the tone, style and contents of Lloyd George's speech. (7 marks)
b) What evidence do the cartoons provide about the Liberal attitude to equality? (6 marks)
c) In what ways is Partridge's cartoon giving an ambiguous message? (4 marks)
d) Why is Asquith shown as a Monseigneur (a dignitary) on one side of the cartoon and as a citizen on the other? (3 marks)
e) The two cartoons on the relationship between the constitutional crisis and the women's campaign make similar points. Explain the viewpoint they are expressing, and comment on any difference in the message. (5 marks)

CHAPTER 7

Conclusion

Liberalism was the dominant creed for much of the nineteenth century, especially in the period between 1830 and 1886 during which the Conservatives only twice won an overall majority in the House of Commons. The Gladstonian form of Liberalism, especially between 1868 and 1874, epitomised some of its most positive aspects and, until Irish problems dominated considerations, Liberalism seemed to be in good health. Although growing tensions between the party's component elements were already apparent in the early 1880s, they were disguised to some extent by Gladstone's towering personality.

In 1886 the party split asunder over the question of Ireland and lost not only its more conservative Whig element but also a large number of reform-minded Radicals. This was a devastating blow. In electoral terms the adoption of Home Rule was costly; between 1886 and 1900 the Liberals lost three out of four elections and did not win an overall majority again until 1906. Not only was Home Rule an electoral liability, but it also took away from the party most of its wealthy backers. In addition, it damaged the party organisation, causing serious splits, particularly in Birmingham.

1 Elements Within the Nineteenth-Century Party

The evolution and composition of the Liberal Party was a complex matter, for during its history it both gained and lost groups of supporters. The Gladstonian party was a different one from that which preceded it. From 1859, in addition to the Whigs and Radicals, it had an added-extra ingredient, the numerically small but very influential Peelite grouping. The Whigs were becoming increasingly anachronistic in that they represented only a small group in the community, and Gladstone was to lose much of their remaining support, especially but not exclusively over Home Rule. The Radical element was the likely one to supersede them in influence, but the departure of Chamberlain and his followers was a serious loss.

Jonathan Parry, in *The Rise and Fall of Liberal Government in Victorian Britain,* has argued that the Liberal Party, despite its divisive tendencies, had more coherence than has generally been recognised. In his examination of the strategy employed by Liberal leaders from Grey to Gladstone he suggests that there were similar attitudes shared by most Liberal politicians in the party's Victorian heyday. He portrays the Liberals as a partnership between leaders in Parliament and enlightened opinion in the country at large. He sees the role of the leaders as being to exert a moderating influence on public opinion. In his view, the leaders were essentially pragmatic rather than ideological. He concedes that Cobden and Bright were exceptions to the rule, being dogmatists of the *laissez-faire* school, but claims that their influence on the party was marginal.

Several historians have made greater claims for Bright's contribution to the creation of the Gladstonian party, and recognise that he was instrumental in building up the reputation of 'the People's William' around the country. In addition, the Manchester School was an important component in Liberal thinking. However, on Parry's main point, whilst not all writers have discerned the ideological coherence, there is more agreement that, in varying degrees, most Liberals were committed to the idea of 'progress' and reform.

2 What it Meant to be a Liberal

What did these Liberals, with their varying shades and emphases about the pace of change, believe in?

The broad outlook of those politicians claiming to be 'Liberals' has been explored in Chapter 1 and here we are concerned to draw together some threads in the light of what has followed. They were committed to the idea of 'progress'. H.J. Hanham, in his excellent study of *Elections and Party Management; Politics in the Time of Disraeli and Gladstone,* quotes Gladstone's definition of progress as something 'qualified by prudence; trust in the people above all, qualified only by that avoidance of violent ... ill-considered change which is really necessary in order to give due effect to the principles of Liberalism'. Gladstone also spoke of 'emancipation and enfranchisement' as the key aspects of the Liberal belief, and during his ascendancy over the party Liberals were proud to trumpet his opinions. In 1885, they published *Why I am a Liberal; Being Definitions and Personal Confessions of Faith by the Best Minds of the Liberal Party,* which gave an honoured priority to one of his other highly quotable observations.

> The Principle of Liberalism is Trust in the People, qualified by Prudence
> The Principle of Conservatism is Mistrust of the People, qualified by Fear.

It was a good politician's line, clear, combative and easily committed to the memory by ardent followers. It raised the issue of exactly who politicians meant by 'the people'. In the early nineteenth century, in the days of a very restricted franchise, Brougham made a telling distinction; 'If there is a mob there is the people also. I speak now of the middle classes'. He was making the contemporary distinction between the turbulent element among the working classes, and the more sober, industrious and respectable middle classes. By the end of the century there were more than five million extra voters, but essentially the distinction still stood. Gladstone would have distinguished between the people (the artisans and the middle classes) with their trustworthy behaviour, and the rootless and unintelligent mob or populace at large, whose virtue could not be so relied upon. When he spoke of his support for the 'masses against the classes', the masses to which he referred were those qualified to vote, whose merits he had extolled back in the early 1860s - those who possessed the 'self-command, self-control, respect for order, patience under suffering, confidence in the law, regard for superiors' which he so admired.

What he discerned about these 'responsible' masses was an ability to react without the selfishness of the class which owned property, wealth and influence, and which was determined to cling on to these advantages. In the absence of such benefits, it was easier for them to come to the right judgement. Seeing the issue as ever in religious terms, he asked, 'Did the Scribes and Pharisees, or did the shepherds and fishermen, yield the first, most and readiest converts to the Saviour?'.

He recognised that others in the party wished to push ahead more quickly than he did with change, and that those whom he felt it was best to exclude from 'the pale of the constitution', the unenfranchised populace, would eventually get their day, for 'when I am gone younger men who may take my place will either be far more advanced than I ever have been, or will be forced on by the extreme liberalism of the masses'.

3 Who were the Liberals in the Nineteenth Century?

a) The Parliamentary Liberals

Throughout the century MPs were unpaid and the nature of political life, based as it was in London, meant that inevitably politics was an exclusive profession. The vast bulk of MPs were comfortably off and for most of the century came from a highly privileged background. Not until 1906, in the year of the Liberal landslide, was there an overwhelmingly middle-class House of Commons.

It is not easy to give a straightforward classification of those who made up the parliamentary party, because many MPs had more than one connection. Often landed members owned business rights, and the interests of manufacturers and mine owners often overlapped with ownership of land. Until the 1880s most MPs were of a landed background, though John Vincent's research has shown that the socially-exclusive Whig element was relatively small. His figures suggest that of 456 Liberal MPs in English constituencies between 1859 and 1874, 198 were great landowners (Whigs or otherwise), and that in the 1870s and early 1880s around half of the party were still landowners or 'gentlemen of leisure'. Of the other MPs, many were related to peers, and many professional men and businessmen also owned a substantial amount of land.

Vincent shows that in the middle of the century those Liberal MPs who had business influence were not often of the Cobden and Bright type, self-made northern industrialists. Amongst others, there were railway-owners, brewers, bakers and stockbrokers. Throughout the whole of the century the industrial regions of the Midlands and North were seriously underrepresented at Westminster, so that manufacturing representation was unlikely to be extensive. However, if middle-class businessmen were numerically less significant than has often been assumed, certain professions leant themselves to membership of the House of Commons, which for most politicians was not a full-time activity.

Legal activity and political activity were easily reconciled, and the hours and lifestyle of lawyers and particularly barristers enabled them to take lucrative briefs and indulge in parliamentary work in between their work in court. Terry Jenkins, in *Gladstone, Whiggery and the Liberal Party, 1874-1886,* has estimated that in 1874, 23 per cent of Liberal MPs were lawyers. This group continued to flourish in Edwardian parliaments, and after 1906 there was also a strong representation of businessmen and writers.

By then of course, the titled Whig element had almost disappeared with the secession of such grandees over Home Rule. In fact, in the House of Commons as a whole, the landed element was on the wane, for 'land' was losing its priority in the economy, hit as it had been by the Great Depression of the last quarter of the nineteenth century. Business was a growing source of parliamentary recruits on both sides of the chamber, and as we have seen was well-represented in the Liberal ranks. By contrast, few working men graced the Liberal benches, and most who did so were there as a result of the Lib-Lab agreement.

If the character of the party in the House of Commons had undergone substantial change, this was much less true of the House of Lords where the landed element remained supreme. That element also continued to have an important role in Liberal cabinets for much of the century. In the 1830s, the Whigs monopolised the ministries and even under Gladstone, no Whig himself, preference was given to them, rather than to middle-class Radicals. However, the Liberal governments of the new century were of a contrasting type to their predecessors. The highly gifted cabinets of 1905 and 1908, in which brains rather than privilege were well-represented, were predominantly middle-class. In the Campbell-Bannerman Cabinet there were only 7 aristocrats as against 11 who came from the professional/business section of the community. One member could be described as working class. In educational attainment, 14 of the 19 had been to university (11 to Oxbridge) and 11 to public school (only 3 to Eton).

Leadership of the party had passed from the Whig magnates of the 1830s to Asquith (1908-16), a well-to-do barrister. As the dominant figure of late-century Liberalism, Gladstone represented a clear departure from the leaders of 30 to 40 years before. Too audacious or dangerous for the Whigs, he was outside the inner circle of their society, although by marriage he was related to it. As Michael Winstanley, in his booklet *Gladstone and the Liberal Party* has put it, his own chequered social background was not easy to categorise for 'he had commercial origins, married into a landed family with income from minerals, yet retained a vocation more in line with the outlook of the clerical profession'.

At the end of the period, Liberalism rested in the hands of the middle classes, and the breakdown given by Chris Cook in *A Short History of the Liberal Party 1900-1985* has shown that at the start of the last Liberal government in 1906 the parliamentary party overall had

64 Barristers
22 Serving officers
69 Gentlemen
80 Established businessmen
74 Self-made businessmen
25 Writers and Journalists
21 Solicitors
9 Teachers
8 Trade unionists
5 Doctors

Overwhelmingly they were middle-aged men of business and the professions, who had been to public school and university, had roots in the land, were often Anglican and had served in the army or navy. There were fewer gentlemen than in the Conservative Party, but the security offered by their comfortable backgrounds hardly disposed the mass of Liberal MPs to radical solutions to the social question. Much of the enterprise and vigour came from the more radical businessmen and other assorted Radicals for whom issues such as national education, the campaign against church rates, and capital punishment were important.

Yet if the parliamentary party was of this ilk, the mass of Liberal supporters was rather different, as a study of Liberal support in the country illustrates. Indeed, Parliament has never been a microcosm of the nation, and has always been far more middle class in composition than the mass of the electorate.

b) Liberal Voters

By the early twentieth century, middle-class voters had increasingly deserted the Liberal Party. Already by the 1870s, some had been alarmed at Gladstonian 'radicalism', and after the Home Rule split the forces of property, business as well as landed, were increasingly to be found in support of the local Conservative candidate and association. There was still a significant minority of the middle classes which did support the Liberals and in the untypical contest in 1906 that proportion grew sharply. Nonetheless, as Paul Thompson (*The Edwardians*) remarked, the stage had been reached when businessmen who did so could be regarded as indiscreet, and acting against their own natural class interests. Of a town councillor in Yorkshire, himself a small businessman, Thompson records that 'people used to tell him that as a businessman he had no business to be so outright a Liberal'. In general, where there was a large middle-class presence in the electorate the Tories did better as they presented themselves as the party of patriotism, true Protestantism, Church and Empire. The Liberals fared better among groups less identified with those values and where there was a larger non-middle-class element.

By the beginning of the new century the greatest strength of Liberalism was as the natural voice of the working classes, and for many labourers the Liberals were 'the workingman's party'. In Edwardian England several issues allowed them to portray themselves in this way. The Conservative failure to reverse Taff Vale, their interest in Tariff Reform, and the action of the Lords in rejecting the People's Budget, all served to identify their opponents as the party of the masses. There were some predominantly working-class areas where the Liberals did less well, but these tended to be where there had been a large immigration of Jews (East London) and Irish (in several big cities). There Liberal support for the underprivileged often produced a backlash in favour of the Tories among native-born voters.

Thompson quotes the Lancashire newsagent who summed up the popular view of the social basis of the parties with considerable accuracy. Liberalism was 'more for the workingman and the tradesman ... the Conservatives were the highbrow and the rich men'. Yet among workingmen, various factors could sway their outlook; location made a difference, as did considerations of deference and perceptions of self-interest. 'Men on railways, the goods side and drivers and firemen not brought into touch with the public are Radicals, but passenger guards and porters who are also underpaid but with funds augmented by tips and patronage of the rich, [were] Conservatives'.

The Liberals were strongest in 'ordinary, solid working-class areas', rather than in the most deprived ones. The poorest electors eligible to vote were attracted to separate labour representation, or its nearest representative - maybe a Lib-Lab candidate - the more skilled and socially ambitious, to Conservatism. Among Nonconformists, with its middle-class tone, particularly in the south, Liberals votes were also to be found, although the identification of Liberalism with religion was not as strong as it had once been, and in any case organised religion aroused less popular interest than it had done 50 years earlier.

4 The Geography of Party Support

In 1832, when the Whigs won so handsomely, their support was widespread. By the time of Gladstone's victory in 1868 there were already some signs of the villa Toryism which was to be important at the end of the century in the suburbs of the south, but the Liberal victory was widely-based. In that year, the party did particularly well in Ireland, Scotland and Wales, and made substantial gains in the big cities.

The Third Reform Act created a large number of single-member, middle-class suburban seats, and shortly afterwards the Liberals were to find themselves increasingly a party of the Celtic fringes. Home Rule shattered their strength in England, and 1885 was the last election when they gained a majority in English constituencies with the exception of their outstanding result in 1906.

	Total seats		Total seats in England	
	Lib	Con	Lib	Con
1885	319	249	238	213
1886	191	393	122	333
1892	271	314	190	261
1895	177	411	112	343
1900	183	402	121	332
1906	399	156	306	122
1910	274	272	188	233
1910	271	272	186	234

By the late nineteenth century the Conservatives were the English party. Only in the West Riding of Yorkshire and the far north of England, plus Cornwall, Devon and the East Midlands, could the Liberals be confident of always gaining the greater part of English working-class support. Elsewhere, potential Liberal voters could not be relied on to go to the polls and in the years 1885-1910 the Liberals depended on winning seats in the Celtic fringe, where 77 seats were never won by Conservatives. Even in 1895, the Liberals' worst overall result, they had a majority of 81 in those parts of the country.

In 1906, of course, such was the scale of the Liberal victory that even many Conservative strongholds fell to the pro-reform tide. Areas such as the rural shires, industrial Lancashire and parts of the south east went Liberal, and in Wales they won 28 of 34 seats, while in Scotland they won 57 of 70 seats. Only the more rural parts of the West Midlands and particularly Chamberlain's home city of Birmingham stayed solidly loyal to the Conservatives.

But 1906 is not typical because it was an election in which unlikely

Liberal areas lost their traditionally Conservative character. 1910, when the Liberals lost about 100 of the seats picked up four years earlier, is a better example; the two parties were more evenly divided, and the result gives a more accurate picture of the geography of party strength. The Liberals lost most of their gains in the agricultural south Midlands and in normally Tory rural areas of the south, such as Kent, Surrey and Sussex, and the London suburbs. As usual, Wales and Scotland (particularly eastern Scotland) were impregnable bastions of support, and they continued to fare well in the West Country, East Anglia, East Lancashire, West Yorkshire and the north east with its shipping and mining interests. Even within some regions where they usually predominated, they never did well in pockets such as in the cathedral towns of Exeter and York. They were also weak in the four largest cities - Birmingham (where they lost all 7 contests in 1910), Liverpool, Glasgow and Leeds.

5 Other Sources of Strength and Weakness

By the end of the century the Liberals were losing their hold in a number of important respects. In local government they were faced with a growing challenge from the Unionists (as the Conservatives were increasingly known) in most large cities and industrial areas, and on occasion they lost control of Glasgow, Manchester and Sheffield, and never won it in Chamberlain's fiefdom of Birmingham.

Gladstone's abolition of the taxes on knowledge (the duties on paper) had done the party much good from the early 1860s onwards, for the creation of a cheap provincial press provided the Liberals with enthusiastic support in the media. There were a number of famous Liberal newspapers such as the *Birmingham Post,* the *Leeds Mercury,* the *Manchester Guardian,* the *Newcastle Chronicle* and the *Rochdale Observer.* Liberal opinions predominated in the press until the 1880s, but thereafter, of the London morning papers, only the *Daily News* stayed with the party. The *Daily Telegraph,* relaunched in 1855, had been a keen supporter, and had at its peak a circulation greater than that of *The Times.* By the end of the century, its support was no longer forthcoming, and some provincial papers ceased to back the Liberal view.

These newspapers had ensured that the fiery speeches of Gladstone and others were quickly and widely reported, and in particular they helped to boost his popular reputation. They stimulated and informed their readers, and were overwhelmingly liberal in their general outlook, and appealed especially to the artisans who were keen to acquire them. They had been 'the epitome and guarantor of liberal Britain', and their loss was a blow, both in the capital and to provincial liberalism.

6 The Challenge on the Left

In the 1906 election a total of 53 Independent Labour and Lib/Lab MPs was returned, and to Balfour, the Conservative leader, this was a sign that the Liberals were merely 'the cork bobbing on the socialist tide', a warning of things to come. Yet over the next few years it was not easy for the 'Labour' grouping in Parliament to establish itself as effective and cohesive, for with the Liberals in reforming mood it was difficult for it to assert a separate identity. Labour MPs were also prone to division, and in the circumstances it was easy for Liberals to ignore Balfour's prediction of the threat from the Left. Liberalism seemed to be riding high.

However, there were danger signs for the Liberal Party. The trade union movement was growing as was Labour representation in local government. Socialists of whatever variety were convinced that their time would come and that Liberalism had had its day. As the newly-elected Labour MP, Philip Snowden, told a Birmingham audience, the 1906 election had 'discovered the Labour Movement ... The Liberal party which half a century ago had a reason for its existence and had work to do was a disjointed party and could not long continue to exist. They [i.e. the Labour camp] knew that just as sure as tomorrow's sun would rise so surely would socialism become a reality'.

In Birmingham in 1914, if the labour movement was far from entrenched, its main lines of future development were already being marked out. Even George Cadbury, whose family were traditional supporters of the Liberal party, had come to sympathise with the idea of an independent Labour organisation. He helped his local branch in Birmingham financially and wrote that he had no interest in the Liberal Party 'except in so far as it promotes the welfare of the millions of my fellow countrymen who are on or below the poverty line'. This was the challenge of socialism, the challenge of the left-out millions. Could Liberalism provide the answer?

7 New Liberalism

New Liberals felt that they could. They anticipated a much increased governmental involvement in the running of the economy and in tackling social issues. They did not believe that voluntary effort alone would be sufficient to eliminate the problem of urban deprivation, and wished to see Liberalism become more interventionist. They were no longer merely concerned with ensuring the absence of hindrance and restraint, they wanted to ensure that all were given more of a chance to fulfil their potential. To do this, and to make certain that the 'left-out millions' had a better quality of life, would cost money - if necessary, this must come from higher and redistributive taxation.

New Liberalism was not concerned to replace capitalism, as socialists were ultimately committed to do. Their wish was to see it operate more fairly, so that urban working-class voters might feel that it had something to offer them. J.A. Hobson articulated these feelings, and wished to see Liberalism become a 'broadly-based party of the Left', a term which had first come into general use in political conversation in the 1880s. He provided the philosophical justification for the change of emphasis, and in *The Crisis of Liberalism* (1909) portrayed the new version as a logical continuation of the Gladstonian creed, a move from the political democracy which had substantially been attained towards the creation of a social democracy; 'a fuller appreciation and realisation of individual liberty contained in the provision of equal opportunities for self-development'.

Hobson recognised that if Gladstone's departure had deprived the party of his political acumen and reputation, it had at the same time provided the opportunity for it to shed the more negative aspects of his creed and develop new ideas of a more constructive kind. He accepted the need to move on from doing away with disadvantages and restrictions to a wider commitment to equality of opportunity, and urged that 'the majority of solid Liberals in the centre, must accept the need for social reform ... Let it be clearly understood that this policy cannot consist in mere economy, in good adminstration at home, peace abroad, in minor legislation for education, temperance or even land reform'. He went on to suggest the difference between his approach and that of socialism.

> 1 Liberalism is now formally committed to a task which certainly involves a new conception of the State in its relation to individual life and to private enterprise ... From the standpoint which best presents its continuity with earlier Liberalism, it appears as a fuller
> 5 appreciation and realisation of individual liberalism contained in the provision of equal opportunities for self-development. But to this individual standpoint must be joined a just apprehension of the social, viz the insistence that these claims or rights of self-development must be adjusted to the sovereignty of social
> 10 welfare.

Here was a restatement of the meaning of nineteenth-century Liberalism in a twentieth-century context. Was it the same creed, adapted in a developing situation, as the *Manchester Guardian* asserted on the hundredth anniversary of Gladstone's birth, 'a further development not a revolution'? Gladstone had cleared the ground 'for the constructive work which is the special task of our time by the demolition of the old house of bondage'. Or was it something more, a desperate attempt by a party in decline to salvage something of the future and give itself a chance of survival in a situation not altogether to its liking?

There was uncertainty in the Liberal Party about the answer. Like many other New Liberals and many socialists, Churchill was much attracted by the contemporary notion of the 'national minimum'. He wanted to 'draw a line below which we will not allow persons to live and labour, yet above which they may compete with all the strength of their manhood'. Older Liberals were less convinced that the measures of the reforming Liberals after 1906 were animated by true adherence to the Liberal principles and attitudes in which they had been brought up to believe.

8 The Decline of the Liberal Party

Some historians have argued that the decline of the Liberal Party had begun at the time of Gladstone. In their view, he was crucial to Liberal success and embodied what Liberalism represented. Without him, the party would have been nothing, for he had helped to create it and shape its character. If, instead of pursuing his Irish 'obsession', he had adopted the more constructive reforming route followed by Joseph Chamberlain, the Liberal Party could have widened its appeal and ensured its survival in office. The Whigs might have felt abandoned, but many were shortly to leave the party anyway. At least, the Liberals would have retained radical support. As it was, Gladstone's inflexibility cost the Liberals dear, and Liberalism in its traditional form had lost its way before the end of the century.

However, Parry claims that the downfall of Liberalism did not result from the split in the 1880s between aristocratic Whigs and Radicals, as has usually been assumed. Rather, he argues, it should be attributed to the personality of Gladstone. The Liberals could not live without him because of his debating abilities, yet living with him was almost equally hazardous. He had helped Peel split the Conservative Party in the 1840s, and the experience had left him a poor team-player. His sense of personal mission hardly helped; he confused an ability to manipulate the emotions of an audience with a mystical insight into the true feelings of the people. By the 1880s, even many Liberals were worried that he was becoming a demagogue, governing purely by whim. While the Liberal split was precipitated by Home Rule, the underlying cause was more a matter of personalities than policies.

Such a judgement is a harsh verdict on the man who more than anyone epitomised the spirit of late nineteenth-century Liberalism. He had forged a link between the party in Parliament and the masses, and they saw him as one of the few major parliamentary and governmental figures who sympathised with their aspirations. At Westminster, his personality inspired much respect and veneration, even among those Liberal MPs who were frustrated by his outlook and policies.

Certainly, the split over which he presided in 1886 was a major blow to the party's prospects, and his continuing presence at the helm thereafter made it difficult for the Liberals to develop new ideas and bring on new political talent, and did little to enhance his reputation. But politicians have to deal with the issues of the day, and Ireland was recognised, even by Chamberlain, as a pressing concern which needed to be tackled. Gladstone's attempt to pass the Home Rule Bill provided one of the few opportunities when a real breakthrough could have been made in resolving the Irish problem, and his efforts were heroic, if ultimately unsuccessful. He certainly made mistakes and from time to time committed tactical errors. But he was a leader whose vision went deep and at his best he was a towering force.

Arguably, his reputation would have been better served by retirement at the end of his second ministry. He would then have avoided the Home Rule crisis, and the party could have developed along the more radical lines outlined above. He was certainly lacking in empathy with the new creed of 'constructionism' which was represented by Chamberlain and others, yet this reluctance to embrace more sweeping reform would not be held against him if he had surrendered the leadership. This may be the case, but it was less apparent in the 1880s than it is in retrospect. Gladstone was still a significant political force in the middle of that decade, and there were many Liberals who were then happy to stay with the man whom they considered to be their strongest asset. Moreover, whatever damage his continuing leadership was to inflict on the party, it was not irreversible. The party went through troubled times after 1886, but it was able to resume governmental responsibilities in the new century.

Others have seen the decline of Liberalism as largely inevitable, a matter more of creed than of personality. According to this view, it was a philosophy for the nineteenth century, fitted to its needs. It flourished among the upper- and middle-class elite and never did much more than flirt with the politically emerging working classes. After 1906, it tried to clothe itself in the garb of pseudo-socialism, but underneath the old Liberal self could not for ever be concealed. According to this view, the reforms of 1906-11 were inspired by collectivist thinking, associated with socialism rather than with the ethos of traditional Liberals. Essentially Liberal causes, such as parliamentary reform, free trade and economy in government were no longer as appropriate as they had once been.

Parliamentary reform was well on the way to full accomplishment, unless the Liberals were prepared to enfranchise women, which most of its leaders seemed releuctant to do. Free trade, still the orthodoxy of Liberal politicians and a few Conservatives, was under question and in the world of the twentieth century was not destined to last much longer as other countries protected their home industries. The old Gladstonian belief in economy, the search for retrenchment, would not enable a Liberal government to finance the cost of growing social expenditure. In other words, the traditional Liberal articles of faith were no longer as applicable as they had been a generation previously.

In this interpretation, Liberalism had, almost by the end of the previous century and certainly before 1914, come to lack any homogeneity. It was argued that reform on social lines was something abhorrent to many of its supporters and political reform had gone almost as far as it could, while the views put forward by Campbell-Bannerman were really the old Gladstonian ones which saw Liberalism as freedom from state interference rather than a wider conception requiring remedial action to remedy injustice and tackle poverty.

The famous victory of 1906 had been won primarily through the failings of the Conservatives and the accidents of time; the opposing party had been in office too long. The burst of reforming measures after 1906 was not true Liberalism at all. In the words of an exponent of this view, Anthony Morris in *Parliamentary Democracy in the Nineteenth Century*,

> 1 The breath of life which Lloyd George imparted to the Liberal shade was no more than countenanced dishonesty. He performed the last rites with such splendour and such sweeping grandiloquence that people forgot the corpse. The name lived on but the
> 5 party was dead and not even Merlin, let alone the 'Welsh wizard', could have raised it.

The very passing of the Parliament Act in 1911, itself a bold and decisive response to the problem of the abuse of the powers of the second chamber, served only to symbolise the dilemma of Liberals in a new age. From now onwards, by interests and ideas, old Liberals were to find themselves on the defensive against the growing socialist challenge. In the future, any measure, however radical, could ultimately pass into law now that the Lords' permanent veto had been removed. Those conservatively-minded people who were alarmed at the threat to individual liberty posed by the new emphasis on social reform were better catered for in the Conservative Party which was a safer haven from which the propertied classes could resist the advancing democratic tide and the thrust of the left, and any 'dangerous' measures which might be produced. The Liberal Party was to find itself in the coming years in the unenviable position of being too moderate for those seeking fundamental change, and insufficiently strong for more cautious people who sought a bastion from which to resist such wholesale reform.

Many historians, with good reason, do not accept this interpretation, and several have pointed out that the policies and actions of ministers such as Lloyd George and Churchill show that far from being exhausted in 1914 the Liberals still had life and vitality. From this point of view, a more convincing analysis is that of Trevor Wilson (*The Downfall of the Liberal Party, 1914-35*). He argued that the real death-blow to the party came not from its pre-war difficulties, but rather from the circumstances of 1914 onwards. He claimed that the war presented a challenge to Liberal beliefs and behaviour far more serious than anything which had gone before.

He conceded the fact that the party had been through troubled times between 1885 and 1905, and that after 1911 it had again encountered serious problems. Religious Nonconformity had passed its peak, Ulstermen were menacing, Labour was contemplating ending its alliance with the Liberals, there was industrial unrest and by-elections looked unhealthy for the government. These were all factors which might have helped to defeat the Liberals in a forthcoming election, but they were not enough to explain the party's remarkable decline from being a party of government in 1914 to third-party status within ten years.

As for the idea that there was a 'strange' decline between 1910 and 1914, as Dangerfield alleged, Wilson found the issues of the time to be 'not a pattern of violence, rather ... an accidental convergence of unrelated events'. There was unrest, but no breakdown and certainly no anarchy. It was the war that initiated that process of disintegration in the party which by 1918 had reduced it to ruins. 'As Liberals were often the first to recognise, the onset of war jeopardised the existence of a party whose guiding principles were international conciliation, personal liberty and social reform'.

The conflict into which Liberal ministers led the country threatened the whole substance of Liberal thinking, and much of the Nonconformist element in particular found it difficult to accept that a Liberal Cabinet could have got them so involved. War calls for strong national leadership, with bellicose and inspirational statements to rally the nation in a patriotic endeavour. Flag-waving and jingoism were not natural bedfellows for men and women of conscience, committed to the idea of peace and progress. Conscription and limitations on individual freedom were not the policies for those who spoke of liberty rather than compulsion. Moreover, the personal clash between Asquith and Lloyd George was fundamentally damaging to the cause of party unity. The party which emerged from the war in 1918 was irretrievably battered and broken. But that is, as they say, another story.

People living in 1914 would have been surprised to hear that the party which was providing them for the first time with Pensions and National Insurance was never again to be elected to government. For any party with Lloyd George and other would-be reformers among its leaders was very much a living reality. In fact, there was no reason at all to assume that the party was on the verge of extinction. Asquith was firmly in control of the steering-wheel, the Cabinet was intact and seemingly united, and the party at large was in full support. There were signs of battle-fatigue and tiredness perhaps, but as yet the body bore no resemblance to a corpse.

Chronological Table

DATES	LEADER	MAIN ISSUES / EVENTS
	The Whig Era	
In Opposition		
1815-17	Ponsonby	Opposed excessive repression of post-1815 government but similarly fearful of mob
1817-21	Tierney	and popular agitation
1821-30	Leaderless in Commons	Supported reforms of 1820s, also pro-Parliamentary Reform
In Office		
1830-4	Grey	Passage of 1832 Reform Act
1834	Melbourne	Other key reforms; e.g. slavery abolition, New Poor Law
In Opposition		
1834-5	Melbourne	Melbourne dismissed by William IV
In Office		
1835-41	Melbourne	Loss of momentum and of Radical support Defeat in 1841
In Opposition		
1841-6	Russell	Support for Repeal of Corn Laws
In Office		
1846-52	Russell	Some reforms; e.g. Public Health Act, 1848 Controversial foreign policy of Palmerston, e.g. Don Pacifico incident
In Opposition		
1852	Russell	
In Office		
1852-5	Coalition led by Lord Aberdeen	Crimean War
1855-8	Lord Palmerston	
In Opposition		
1858-9	Palmerston	
In Office		
1859-65	Palmerston	Gladstone at Exchequer: 1864 speech on Parliamentary Reform Palmerston very cautious on domestic reform, less cautious on conduct of foreign policy

1865-6	Russell	Failure of attempt to carry Parliamentary Reform through House of Commons
In Opposition		
1866-8	Russell	Conservatives pass 1867 Reform Act

The Liberal Era

In Office		
1868-74	Gladstone	'Peace, Retrenchment and Reform'; many reforms 1874 electoral defeat
In Opposition		
1874-5	Gladstone	
1875-80	Hartington	1875 Gladstonian campaign on Bulgarian Atrocities
In Office		
1880-5	Gladstone	Modest reforms in general, but Third Reform Act Ministry beset by difficulties and divisions
In Opposition		
1885-6	Gladstone	
In Office		
1886	Gladstone	First Home Rule Bill defeated in 'Commons' Secession of Chamberlain and Hartington Whigs
In Opposition		
1886-92	Gladstone	
In Office		
1892-4	Gladstone	Second Home Rule Bill defeated in 'Lords'
1994-5	Rosebery	
In Opposition		
1895-6	Rosebery	Late '90s, 'faddism' in ascendant
1896-9	Harcourt	
1899-1905	Campbell-Bannerman	
In Office		
1905-8	Campbell-Bannerman	Modest reforms; opposition from House of Lords
1908-14	Asquith	Significant social improvements - legislation on pensions, national insurance, children etc. 'New Liberalism' in action. Early 'Welfare State'? People's Budget > 1911 Parliament Act Problems re unions, Suffragettes and Ulster 1914 First World War
1914		Liberalism in danger — growth of Left

Further Reading

A huge amount of literature exists on the politics of the nineteenth century, though there is a dearth of material on the development of the political parties over the whole period. Aspects of the Liberal Party, covering its personalities and policies, are described in many books, but until recently there has been no detailed history of Liberalism throughout the era. A new study by **Jonathan Parry** sets out to remedy the deficiency, but this is a one for the person involved in detailed research rather than a source of convenient reference.

The traditional works by **Woodward** and **Ensor** in the Oxford series still have their value though they are now very dated, and the volumes by **Asa Briggs** and **Donald Read** in the Longman 'A History of England' series are well-written and stimulating. More specialist study is provided in **Frank O'Gorman's** *The Emergence of the British Two-Party System, 1760-1832* and **Eric Evans'** Lancaster Pamphlet, *Political Parties in Britain, 1783-1867.* These provide useful and often contrasting insights into the growth of a recognisable party activity in Britain, and both are admirably brief and concise. **Chris Cook's** *Short History of the Liberal Party,* also succinct, offers an interesting and reliable account of its subject, but it only begins at the end of our period.

For depth of research, **John Vincent's** *The Formation of the Liberal Party 1857-68,* is unsurpassed on many key aspects, though the detail is beyond the needs of many students. **Donald Southgate's** *The Passing of the Whigs, 1832-1886* is similarly well-researched and thorough on the decline of Whiggery. **Paul Adelman's** *Victorian Radicalism* is a useful analysis of the diverse groupings and individuals within the Radical fold.

Much of the most interesting and useful material is to be found in the biographies of leading Liberal figures. Some of them are now dated and have been overtaken by recent research. Nonetheless, **Feuchtwanger's** volume on *Gladstone* is a clear and undemanding survey, and **Shannon** has completed the first of his two works of the same title; it stops at 1868. **Matthew,** who has edited the voluminous *Gladstone Diaries,* has written an excellent accompanying commentary on the years before 1874, and its insights derived from original sources are invaluable. A much shorter study of *Gladstone* is the Lancaster Pamphlet of that same name, written by **Michael Winstanley.** This provides a short and often critical account of Gladstone's life, on which it is rather selective. It also contains a useful introduction to the composition of the Liberal Party.

Another short 'Life' is that of *Joseph Chamberlain,* in the 'Personalities and Powers' series (by the author). Also relevant is the volume on *Lloyd George* which is a reliable and a stimulating read.

Roy Jenkins' *Asquith,* though not primarily aimed at the student audience, is an elegantly written account and **Kenneth Morgan's** *The Age of Lloyd George* is a useful survey of the late Victorian/Edwardian Liberal Party - as well as a clear account of its main subject.

Index